Market Mediations

Market Mediations

Semiotic Investigations on Consumers, Objects and Brands

Benoît Heilbrunn
ESCP Europe, France

palgrave
macmillan

First published 2015 by
PALGRAVE MACMILLAN

Palgrave Macmillan in the UK is an imprint of Macmillan Publishers Limited, registered in England, company number 785998, of Houndmills, Basingstoke, Hampshire RG21 6XS.

Palgrave Macmillan in the US is a division of St Martin's Press LLC, 175 Fifth Avenue, New York, NY 10010.

Palgrave Macmillan is the global academic imprint of the above companies and has companies and representatives throughout the world.

Palgrave® and Macmillan® are registered trademarks in the United States, the United Kingdom, Europe and other countries.

ISBN: 978–1–137–50996–3

This book is printed on paper suitable for recycling and made from fully managed and sustained forest sources. Logging, pulping and manufacturing processes are expected to conform to the environmental regulations of the country of origin.

A catalogue record for this book is available from the British Library.

A catalog record for this book is available from the Library of Congress.

I would like to dedicate this book to my parents Alain and Béatrice Heilbrunn as a token of gratitude for their constant support throughout all these years

Contents

List of Illustrations

Boxes

Figures

Tables

Foreword

I am pleased to write a foreword in praise of this book for the reasons I explain below. Benoît Heilbrunn complimented me by asking me to do it, and then I found his text an intriguing one. His request was also a dangerous one, because the book is so stimulating about what he thinks that I feel provoked to say what I think about these matters. However, I will not do that here but will try to finish writing my own book on related topics. There is also no point in repeating the interesting points he makes in these chapters. Therefore, I will be brief and confine myself to providing some context for this text and to encouraging readers to immerse themselves in this thoughtful and richly explained body of ideas.

This is an important book for several reasons. It is novel in undertaking to explicate a French and European semiotic perspective on consumption and branding. That means it is notable in its use of language and the phrasing of its concepts as well as the home of its examples. Rather than the common references to successful brands such as Coca-Cola, McDonald's, Starbucks, Walmart, and the Apple of Steve Jobs, it speaks of Hermès and Philippe Starck. The formulation of its ideas is both illuminating and challenging. It is illuminating because it revives interest in the semiotic approach to understanding the phenomena that Heilbrunn discusses. It is challenging because many readers will be unfamiliar with these ideas, and the English version takes on the character of a *Frenglish* that moves between plain narration and high-level abstractions. Heilbrunn's tack explicitly differs from the usual American ways of thinking and seeks to be fresh in this respect as well.

The book is also important in the way it fits several intellectual traditions. I will summarize three of them that show the developmental place of this work. They are (1) the grand tradition of research approaches and methods, (2) the semiotic tradition, and (3) the personal tradition. The grand tradition is the history of marketing study, consumer study, branding study, and their internationalization. I played a part in this history by launching the concept of brand image (Gardner and Levy, 1955) into public discourse. Branding had been going on, of course, since prehistoric times but it took on semiotic life with language about brand image, brand loyalty and switching, equity, personality, and community (Bastos and Levy, 2013).

In the 1970s, the eminence of the marketing department at Northwestern University led the French Foundation to sponsor several French students to study marketing there. (Before they came, I spent a month lecturing in Aix-en-Provence to acquaint them with an American professor, atypical as I was! I was surprised that the students shook hands every morning.) At Northwestern we were proud to graduate such scholars as Jean-Louis Chandon, Bernard DuBois, Christian Pinson, and Jean-Noel Kapferer. The community of scholars took note of the many ways of studying marketing, resulting in the publication of *Research Traditions in Marketing*, edited by Gilles Laurent, Gary Lilien, and Bernard Pras (1994). Especially relevant is the chapter by Harold H. Kassarjian, "Scholarly Traditions and European Roots of American Consumer Research" (1994). One aspect of French studies that Heilbrunn upholds is the interest in luxury goods. DuBois pursued it, as has Kapferer (Kapferer and Bastien, 2009). Recently, Bernard Pras presided and I refereed a dissertation by Anne-Flore Maman Larraufie, titled "A Journey to the Center of the World of Fashion and Luxury Counterfeiting" (2012).

The semiotic tradition was pursued in Europe by Saussure and his followers and in America by Charles Peirce and his followers. Jean Umiker-Sebeok, of the Research Center for Language and Semiotic Studies at Indiana University, and I found a community of interest and, in July 1986, held the First International Conference on Marketing and Semiotics at Northwestern University's Kellogg School of Management, with over 90 scholars from 13 countries attending (Umiker-Sebeok, 1987). I spoke as a "Semiotician *Ordinaire*" (1987). Soon afterward appeared *Marketing and Semiotics: Selected Papers from the Copenhagen Symposium*, edited by Hanne Hartvig Larsen, David G. Mick, and Christian Alsted (1991). Since then, this surge of interdisciplinary activity seems to have subsided. Perhaps Heilbrunn's book will help to revive interest in the value of semiotic thinking.

The third tradition, I might note, is a personal one. As I mentioned, Christian Pinson was a doctoral student at Northwestern University when I headed the doctoral program and then chaired the marketing department of the Kellogg School of Management. I enjoyed his participation in the seminar I taught. He wrote an outstanding dissertation, "Consumer Inferential Judgments about Products." He graduated in 1981 and went on to have a distinguished career at INSEAD in Fontainebleau, France, where Heilbrunn had the good fortune of having him as teacher and mentor and now continues to contribute insightfully to these three traditions.

Sidney J. Levy

References

Bastos, Wilson, and Sidney J. Levy (2012), "A History of the Concept of Branding: Practice and Theory," *Journal of Historical Research in Marketing*, 4, 3, 347–68.

Gardner, Burleigh B., and Sidney J. Levy (1955), "The Product and the Brand," *Harvard Business Review*, March–April, 33, 33–9.

Kapferer, Jean-Noel and V. Bastien (2009), *The Luxury Strategy*, London: Kogan Page.

Kassarjian, Harold (1994), "Scholarly Traditions and European Roots of American Consumer Research," in Gilles Laurent, Gary Lilien, and Bernard Pras (eds), *Research Traditions in Marketing*, Boston: Kluwer Academic Publishers, 265–79.

Larsen, Hanne, David G. Mick, and Christian Alsted (eds) (1991), *Marketing and Semiotics: Selected Papers from the Copenhagen Symposium*, Copenhagen: Handelshøjskolens Forlag.

Laurent, Gilles, Gary Lilien, and Bernard Pras (eds) (1994), *Research Traditions in Marketing*, Boston: Kluwer Academic Publishers.

Levy, Sidney J. (1987), "Semiotician *Ordinaire*," in Jean Umiker-Sebeok (ed.), *Marketing and Semiotics*, New York: Mouton de Gruyter, 13–20.

Maman Larraufie, Anne-Flore (2012), "A Journey to the Centre of the World of Fashion and Luxury Counterfeiting," Essec Business School: Unpublished Dissertation.

Pinson, Christian (1981), "Consumer Inferential Judgments about Products," Northwestern University: Unpublished Dissertation.

Umiker-Sebeok, Jean (ed.) (1987), *Marketing and Semiotics*, New York: Mouton de Gruyter.

List of Sources

Parts of this books have already been published as follows:

"The consamateur, or our friend bricoleur" as "Le consamateur ou l'ami bricoleur" in O. Assouly, L'amateur. *Juger, participer et consommer*, Paris, IFM-Editions du regard, 2010.

"Brandtopia and the neutralization of effect" as "Brave New Brands" in Jonathan Shroeder and Miriam Salze Mörling (eds), *Brand Culture*, London, Routledge, 2006, pp. 103–117.

"The paradoxes of a luxury brand" as "Le luxe est mort, vive le luxe!" in O. Assouly (ed.), *Le luxe. Essai sur la fabrique de l'ostentation*, IFM-Editions du Regard, Second édition, 2010.

"What is the luxury brand's philosophy of time" in *Mode/Luxe. Economie, création et marketing*, IFM/Editions du Regard, 2014.

"The blandness and delights of a daily object" in Caru A., Cova B. (eds), *Consuming Experience*, Routledge Publishers, 2006, pp. 79–91.

"In search of the lost aura: the object in the age of marketing romanticism" as "In Search of the Lost Aura: The Object in the Age of Marketing Re-illumination" in S. Brown et al. (eds), *Romancing the Market*, Routledge, 1998, pp. 187–201.

"Is design the future of marketing" as "Le marketing à l'épreuve du design" in B. Flamand (ed.), *Le design. Essai sur des théories et des pratiques*, Paris, IFM-Editions du Regard, 2006.

"Sensory misery: the difficulties of sensory marketing" as "De la misère sensible: les apories du marketing polysensoriel" in O. Assouly (ed.) *Goûts à vendre: Essais sur la captation esthétique*, Paris, IFM-Editions du Regard, 2007.

"The brand that thought with it's fingers" as "La marque qui pensait avec ses doigts", *L'artisanat, la main et l'industrialisation, Mode de recherche* n°18, IFM, 2012.

All texts have been revised for this publication.

I truly thank the publishers for giving the rights to reproduce these texts.

Introduction: Market Medi(t)ations

The economy of brands truly came into being in the mid-19th century as a way for manufacturers to transform bulk sales and commodities markets into product markets with high added value. A brand that was already established as a sign of identification and differentiation thus became a driver of social mediation to form a fictional relationship between companies and their products' end users. Initially, and in the end, the brand served to change the power relationships structuring the commodities markets, where products were sold in bulk. An unbranded market is a commodities market in which a manufacturer has difficulty creating added value because the products are largely undifferentiated. It is also a market where the manufacturer is completely dependent upon the distributor as well as on the wholesaler, who can choose his suppliers. Next come the retailers, who endorse the products they sell. A brand thus involves shifting the source of authority from the seller to the product and then on to the brand. In other words, a brand allows the enterprise to bypass the seller, as per the expression "silent salesman" that Vance Packard forged in his seminal book, *The Hidden Persuaders*, which remains the best introduction to marketing to date. A brand presupposes a means of symbolic mediation has been put in place, one through which the product can speak for itself and call out to the end customer's nose and the beard of the seller. It serves to substitute symbolic mediation for human mediation, hence the importance of the phenomena of anthropomorphization, especially through the appearance of the brand spokesmen, whose role is to give life and an identity to the brand to increase its potential to attract.

In addition to imposing their brands, manufacturers soon realized it was necessary to print a name on their products. They found it was also necessary to attract the attention of other agents to this name to ensure they would consider the brand as much as the product. It was thus necessary to turn away from the old tradition of customers who judged the quality of products based on their appearance and texture more than on their name. The rise of this ideology very clearly demonstrated the ability to lead people to accept a replacement for something by a brand name, and ensure that "the customer buys the words instead of the objects." Thus, along with the brand name and packaging, the manufacturers furnished a pragmatic response to this issue: "They tried to move the linguistic relationship between the signifier (the brand) and the signified (the product) to a third term: ... the packaging that we acquire as much for its content as for its appearance and the brand name on it. The packaging allowed the irreducible combination of the product and the brand." (Cochoy, 1999: p. 36). The packaging, through "boxes" and "cans," somehow allows the creation of a screen that conceals the old reality (that of bulk) and, above all, projects a new truth by building the brand as the only indication of origin, especially as the only possible criterion of choice. The brand certifies the origin of the products and invokes the manufacturer's liability when it guarantees a certain level of product quality. Hence, the fact that consumer society was built on the power of brands, including in the contract of reproducibility of the experience that creates the fictitious concept that the product may be identically reproduced infinitely. The brand, therefore, denotes an origin as well as identical duplication of the product and ultimately tends to label the product as much as the consumer experience associated with it.

The labeled and packaged product carries the fixation, stabilization and quality assurance upstream, that is to say, towards the industrial apparatus. It also carries the sales discussion downstream, as close as possible to the consumer. And when the packaging ensures product integrity, it also ensures the integrity of the brand discourse insofar as the customer, when he enters a store, already has some knowledge of the brands and qualities of the products to which they are attached; he may then name, ask for or require the product he wishes. The product knowledge on which the consumer relies no longer depends, in principle, upon what the merchant wants to tell him.

The deployment of brands in the 19th century was essentially linked to the manufacturers' desire to build a relationship with the end consumer and to gain control of a market exchange dominated up until now by wholesalers. The brand became a "market-mediation device" for creating a fictional relationship between a business and its product's end users. It is precisely the aim of this book to be interested in these market mediations.

To this end, we adopt a deeply thoughtful approach to semiotics and social sciences. These symbolic mediation systems are what characterize the consumer society producing and conveying the meaning. The brand is a singular semiurgic device that places the products and services exchanged in a universe of signs and meanings – signs and meanings that can greatly exceed the functional value of the products and services. The brand is therefore an essential driver of semanticization, which envelops the objects beneath the value of a name that surpasses their actual use-value (what they "do") and therefore requires some deciphering by the consumer, from the time the signs sent out by the brand do not always have full transparency. As Barthes pointed out, this branding function is so important that any object for consumption is more or less mired in meaning because the semanticization process causes it to lose its physical and functional status while also transforming it into something meaningful. Consumption, therefore, brings about the transformation of a physical substance into a meaningful substance, so the substance must necessarily be transmuted into a name or system of signs to become an object for consumption.

The brand serves to instill meaning that makes the goods for sale more desirable. Customers are first buying the names of the companies manufacturing the products or offering their services. The basic premise of semiotics (discipline focused on the creation of meaning) is that meaning exists only through signs, on one hand, and, on the other, through a principle of differentiation. In other words, the signs cannot merely signify the difference of one from the other. And as Baudrillard has clearly shown, the consumer society refers to a system of objects that comprise a vast system of signs that refer to one another.

To account for this vast system of objects and brands, we follow a path that draws heavily on the generative trajectory of meaning stemming from the structural semiotics of Greimas's obedience; it presupposes that meaning is produced by progressive enrichment from a constitutive core (core values) and gradually rises to the surface to its discursive implementation via objects and figurative elements. Hence, the three sequences articulating the production of meaning, namely:

(1) Introducing *or creating the plot* aiming to update actions and values programs;
(2) *A telling* of these values allows the construction of a narrative, and

(3) *Setting out in signs*, which is the choice of plastic elements at the figurative level.

This is how this book is organized: It contains six chapters, moving from the ideological dimension of the market to the sensitive nature of the market.

Chapter 1, "Love and the Market," highlights the different facets of the goods and relational gradients that link us with consumable items. It explores a consubstantial link between consumption and love by examining the forms of love at play in a consumer society, which mutates from logic of ownership to logic of use. By restoring the acclaim of the amateur, the chapter raises the question of amicability of a market that is often broken by addictive and pharmacological logics.

Chapter 2, "Simplexities," is based on a semiotic typology of consumption values and raises the question of the transformation of the economy of brands that must respond to paradoxical terms and often state positions that may appear contradictory. This utopian logic of brands raises the issue of neutralization and calls into question the principle of non-contradiction inherent in Western culture. This paradoxical logic is also evidenced through the paradoxical logic of luxury brands, especially their ambivalent relationship to time.

Chapter 3, "Oneself as Another," adresses the issue of brand identity considered in a logic that is based both narratively and ethically as a process by which the brand fulfills a contract with its customers.

Chapter 4, "Ethics Despite Amorality," raises the issue of brand ethics by offering a semiotic and philosophical framework that presupposes that the brand carries an ethical dimension and an aesthetic dimension. Brand identity is thus considered in a logic that is based both narratively and ethically on the idea that a brand is speaking as an author; this raises the issue of the brand's ability to speak and keep its word in a market characterized by its amorality.

Chapter 5, "Narrativities," focuses on the narrative dimension of the brand by offering an analytical framework of the brand narrative and consumer relationship arising from semiotics. Based on the model of the narrative scheme, this approach allows the understanding that the relationship to the brand may be read as a story with several recurring steps.

Chapter 6, "I/Materialities," is largely concerned with objects and the ways in which they build a relationship between the physical world and the non-physical world. In particular, the question of how design states a purpose through various possible design philosophies.

Chapter 7 "Embodiments," focuses on the strictly physical dimension of the market by looking into the solidity of teak objects as expressed at the studio of the designer Philippe Starck, in Pierre Hermé's bakery or in the way Hermé's uses the hand, both as a metonymic and metaphorical figure of artisanal know-how, and how French design has finally moved beyond objects.

1
Love and the Market

From goods to consumer experience

"Do things mean anything?" Considering that an object of consumption is inserted into a universe of signs and signifying practices, Barthes's question determines the conditions for the existence of that object and its semiotic challenges. Studies on consumption have long favored a semantic approach based on the study of networks of meaning attached to the object, regardless of its consumption environment. Hence, the importance of the phenomenon of semanticization of objects, that is to say, the possibility for objects to become signs (which to Baudrillard is the *conditio sine qua non* of an object of consumption) and to signify beyond their use-value. The main virtue of a semantics of objects is to make known, for objects of consumption (like all objects) – in addition to their denotative and functional value – a connotative function related to their propensity to signify beyond their strictly utilitarian values. However, this semantic approach, though crucial to studying the role of objects in our consumer society, is not the only possible semiotic field of study for goods. Have not the instrumental and symbolic dimensions traditionally attached to an object in Western culture usually buried other alternatives of consistency and meaning of the object – alternatives which sometimes have tended to resurface, as if by error, in everyday life?

The three dimensions of goods

What does it mean to consume? Consumption is not just using or destroying an object, but is rather a set of signifying practices by which individuals manipulate physical and non-physical objects to create meaning. Consumption, therefore, brings about the transformation of a *physical* substance into a *meaningful* substance, so to become an object for consumption the object must necessarily be transmuted into a name or a system of signs. This process of semanticization means that one attaches to the physical dimensions that constitute the object (its weight, color, volume, etc.) its recognizable dimensions (values, a symbolic universe, a lifestyle, etc.).

In orchestrating the strict semanticization project for a consumer society – which involves attaching imagined meanings to physical objects that are a priori put into use – marketing has often transformed consumer products and brands into elements of vast semiotic systems that convey meaning by telling their own literal and figurative stories to increase the perceived value of the system's objects. An object may only exist in one instrumental and functional relationship with the end user; it must necessarily be invested with values that exceed its single function. The physical object and its meaning must tell a story, tell of a project, and thus the meanings are enriched and enhanced by the marketing work. This is what the concept of positioning makes emblematic – which shows how the desirability of a product depends largely on how one presents a physical object and on signs: through the identification of a benefit, a usage environment, a projected target, and so forth. The brand is just one of the ways in which the physical substance of a product or service is organized into a meaningful substance with numerous channels of communication (product, logo, packaging, advertising, etc.).

From a semiotic point of view, this means that an object continuously articulates two levels: a level called *expression*, which refers to its various physical dimensions, and the level of *content* or *meaning* that corresponds to different meanings conveyed by this object. This in this way – as Saussure said about a sign being like a coin the two sides of which are inextricably linked – an object is (a) a set of meanings and (b) meanings attached to these meanings. If objects hold such an important place in our lives, it is because they occupy a physical space, a symbolic space, a mental space (by filling our minds with changes in direction about choosing, using, storing, rejecting) and a temporal space, as well as a tangle of feelings and emotions. Therefore, marketing is concerned with objects and places that permanently associate a sensitive dimension and an intelligible dimension. We can then understand the three dimensional levels that apply to all goods:

- A *physical* dimension that mostly refers to the consumption good's physical emanations, its tangible aspects and other aspects directly understood by the consumer through the senses (product color, effect of the material, product smell, etc.). The focus on the symbolic dimension of objects has somewhat tarnished the study of the proper physical anchoring of the consumer experience. Furthermore, most of the time the physical anchoring of consumption is considered only in its visual dimension, leaving little room for a truly multisensory approach. Yet "individuals are not satisfied with considering, contemplating, examining, desiring, and admiring objects, but must touch, taste, and feel them in constant collaboration of the five senses" (Löfgren, 1996).

- A *rhetorical* dimension that refers to the good's own ideological dimension, its ability to convey an imagined dimension and values. The economy of a brand exists in part because of its willingness to lend something to the consumer by imparting competence in terms of sensory discrimination skills, even when blind tests prove quite ruthless, since they show most people's inability to tell the difference between unidentified food products. Due to consumption's own semanticization phenomenon, food enjoyment is more on the order of textual enjoyment than the strictly sensorial. In other words, the consumer frequently feasts upon the words he is served more than on the dishes. Thus, every object is imbued with an ideology, that is to say, a way of seeing the world and, therefore, of thinking. As Jean-Marie Floch said, "a pocket knife always says something about its owner[;]...I therefore believe it legitimate to imagine that the handle of a knife in fact extends into a certain way of doing things, one that ultimately speaks to a certain way of life or way of being. Approaching the topic this way...we are trying to identify, if not a culture[,]...then at least a way of thinking and a particular mode of interaction between self and world." Thus, the Opinel is a mountain knife that offers a single solution for each function; it is a generalist that seems to say to its users: "You're on your own"; by contrast, the Swiss Army Knife works like a specialist by offering a specific solution according to type of use; it seems to say to its users: "Serve yourself." (Floch, 1995). Thus, consumer goods are not only systems of communication, but they are more generally given the function of cultural and ideological *transmission* by significantly changing a meaningful chain of structural elements of the socio-economic environment (belief systems, rules for behavior, rituals, etc.). The role of a brand is also often to strengthen or modify existing belief systems. Indeed, through its brand promise and its products, a major brand has always offers a kind of contract of trust that presupposes a way of seeing the world and manifests itself in all its communication channels: product design, packaging, advertising rhetoric, promotional schemes, choice of endorsers (the people chosen to represent the brand) and so forth. In so doing, by the power of their words major brands contribute to changing our relationship with the world, the relationship with our body, relationships with others.

- A *pragmatic* dimension that refers to the grasp and bodily practices that do the orchestrating, especially through the rituals of purchasing and the consumption of consumer goods. Overall, consumption presupposes staging, and it presents "ways of doing things" that are sometimes ritualized: People do not perfume themselves at just any time, in just any place, or in the company of just anyone, and especially they do not do so in no particular manner. The act of applying perfume can be broken down to a precise syntax of gestures – gestures that enable an appropriation, even an incorporation, of the product and the brand.

We may also deduce that all sensorial experiences are inseparable from a specific corporeal experience, hence the concept of techniques of the body, largely developed by Marcel Mauss. The creation of specific gestures (or rituals) is a main lever of attraction to a brand in unbranded markets.

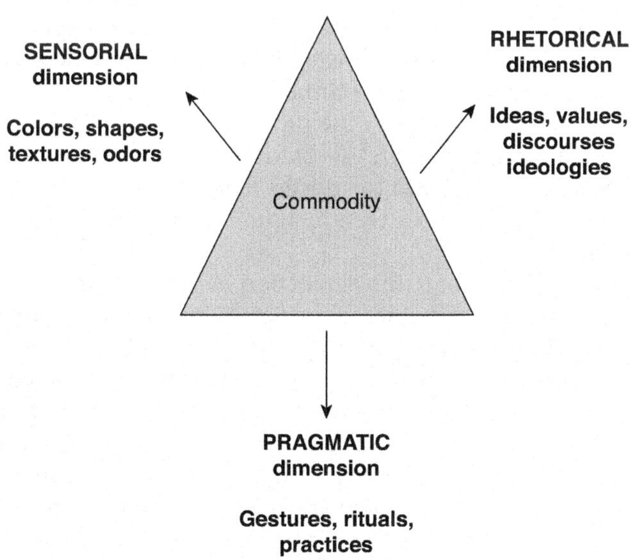

Figure 1.1 The three sides of a commodity

The song of a sign

Consumption refers to various kinds of experiences and various types of products that differ according to their degree of *materiality*, their degree of *uniqueness*, their *size*, their *frequency of purchase* or *consumption*, their *cost* (relative or absolute), their *scalability* (frequency of updating the product or packaging) and so forth.

Despite the diversity of products offered to consumers, marketing hammers on constantly about the need to de-standardize and differentiate products in increasingly competitive and increasingly commoditized markets. The object of consumption tends to weaken due to the profusion of objects in the daily lives of individuals (an individual is said to meet 20–30,000 objects in a single day), but also with "limited-edition" products, wherein the profusion of objects related to their repeated production tends to empty them of meaningful substance. Walter Benjamin noted the collapse of the unity of experience and the rupture of experience: "At every moment, the modern conscience is bombarded with data without result or consecution; automation and fragmentation of activities, prostitution of goods and people into merchandise, atomization of the masses, bursts of information". As if marketing had declared war on consciousness. At a time when technological progress has enabled almost all conceivable combinations of the forms, materials and colors that are now possible, objects scarcely provide any more the kind of initial resistance that once explained their charm, leaving consumers weary with regard to the products. A sort of infinite malleability offered by technical progress corresponds to a sort of poverty of objects, insofar as the profusion of objects has tended to empty them of their meaningful substance. The product often becomes too obvious, too familiar, and too docile. (One of the roles of marketing is to increase the degree of interest in a product by increasing consumer involvement.)

Max Weber pointed out this dereliction, which threatens an industrial object because of the object's predictability and lack of magic and surprise – a lack that characterizes the objects of industrial society due to an ongoing rationalization of production processes and consumption; this disenchantment with the world of objects harkens back to the process of mass production and to the ensuing depersonalization of contact (How can we have personal contact with an object that is replicated ad infinitum?). This process of disenchantment is one in which magic, idiosyncrasy and superstition have been erased and replaced by values such as efficiency, predictability and replicability.

Furthermore, the excessive semanticization of consumer goods has irrevocably led to a casting-off of analysis of the object as a physical entity in favor of analysis of the object as a system of meaning. One could almost say that since Baudrillard conducted his pioneering studies (1970, 1972), analyses of the object have consistently subverted the signifier over the signified, thereby removing the physical and sensory dimensions of the object. But from the moment in which we consume branded products almost exclusively, the question emerges about the role of the product and sensory and bodily experience in the selection and use of an object. Indeed, the constant staging (via packaging, a brand name, invitation to enter a magical universe) may quickly suggest that the brand introduces the sign as the principal purveyor of meaning, and, therefore, enjoyment, while reducing consumption or interaction in a semiotic experience. The fact of reducing a brand to its own communication elements often obliterates the sensorality and gestures that are necessarily imbued in any consumer experience.

In breaking away from a focus on the symbolic dimension of products and brands, the consumer experience may present an opportunity for an approach that takes greater account of the actual physical anchor in our relationship to objects. Perhaps it is time to understand the infra-ordinary mode that surrounds us, doing so in order to emerge from the saturation of the effects of meaning and a symbolic tyranny that imprison objects in a register that tends to empty them of meaning and emotion.

From meaning to multisensorial

It is important not to reduce the emotional power of objects to a system of signs if one wishes to better understand them. An object is not constantly mired in cultural and social meanings that would, a priori, inexorably determine its meaning and function: it can give rise to individual ownership by acquiring a meaning and personal value and returning to anything other than use–value or a social sign.

This emotional power of objects becomes even stronger if we consider their resolutely polysensorial nature. However, marketing is primarily a device for the audio-visual sphere and has only recently looked at polysensoriality. The rise of the so-called consumer experience justly forces marketing to delve deeper into the consumer's sphere of privacy by developing procedures related to touch, taste and smell – as evidenced, for example, by the surge in logolfs (olfactory logos) or even by the development of tactile design. In other words, the challenge for marketing is to leave the shores of typology far behind (sight, hearing) to invest in what is found nearby (touch, taste) as well as the olfactory involved an intermediate register.

Any object may be considered by following a spectrum ranging from purely instrumental values to sociability and relationships values. In doing so, the object becomes an essential mediator between the individual and his daily environment and allows for the reconfiguration of relationships between individuals: This makes the unpleasant pleasant, it eases tensions, it brings harmony. In this approach, the object is not neutral but an essential mediator of human relationships, especially in the space of the family home. In addition to the ideal–physical axis that appears crucial to understanding the mechanics of our relationship to objects, we must also consider an axis related to interpersonal relationships. Indeed, the practice of consumption is, in its essence, multi-modal: that is to say, the consumption of a product is a synesthetic experience that convenes, beyond the sensory impressions, an affective and socialized universe of consumption.

One may then consider several levels of evaluation and valuation of a product, which are, successively:

- the *substantive* level related to the valuation of materials (the feel of a fabric, the smell of a fragrance, the elements of sound design);
- the *referential* level, which refers to the various functions that occur: to have fun, to relax, to meet other people, and so forth;
- the *situational* level, which highlights the product's consumer framework and returns to different metaphors that can recover the experience of this place, be it similar to a garden where we walk, to a highway on which we travel as quickly as possible, a magical place in which one is meant to experience exotic adventures or to a playground, an art gallery, and so forth.
- the *interactional* level, which focuses on human relationships involved in the act of consumption: Are we in a purely transactional logic, a relational logic? Do we view the customer as a visitor, a friend, a passerby, someone out for a stroll?

Consumption is in the name of what form of love?

The evolution of a consumer society is often presented as a paradigm shift that illustrates the increasing importance of gifting. Participative logic would be understood as a new truism echoing the endless economic foraging logic where brands are used as a gesture characteristic

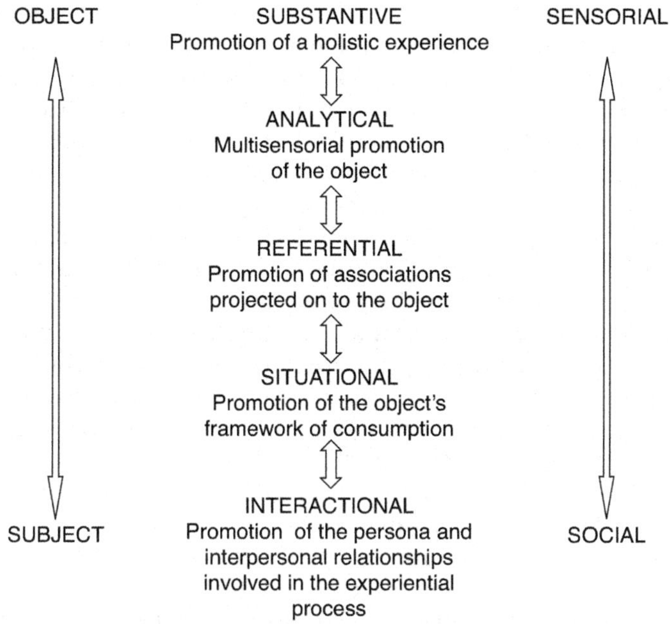

Figure 1.2 The different terms of experience with a commodity

of hypercapitalism. Will we surreptitiously go from an economy of economic and psychological harnessing to a social organization characterized by self-sacrifice and giving, so as to overturn the domination of brands? This creeping ideology asks the meaning of consumption while putting the idea of gifting back at the heart of the exchange process. The idea here is to question the sort of dogma by which we will go from harnessing to gifting. To that end, we are going to rely on the idea that consumption is always more or less a question of love. Again, we need to know what form of love.

Forget about needs

Thinking of the notion of emerging consumption, first of all carefully rethink the paradigms that underlie the analyses of consumption. Now, the clear bedrock of most theories of consumption is the idea of need and, as a result, in all works on marketing and consumer behavior we again unfortunately encounter, as a truism, Maslow's famous hierarchy of needs; this prioritization of needs is also lazily conveyed, by a number of instructors, as obvious. However, a needs approach, which for one thing is ideologically harmful, does not at all explain the complexity of the phenomenon of consumption if we at least make a point to clearly distinguish *consumation* and *consommation*. As Georges Bataille judiciously notes in a 1930 text (one which foresees in particular the analyses developed by Jean Baudrillard in *La société de consommation*), "human activity cannot be entirely reduced to production and conservation processes, and consumption must be divided into two separate parts. The first, reducible, is represented by the use of the strict minimum, for individuals of a given society, to the conservation of life and the continuation of productive activity: it thus simply has to do with the fundamental condition of the latter. The second part is represented by 'unproductive' expenses: luxury items, bereavements, war, cults, ... gambling, shows, the arts, perverse sexual activity (meaning turned away from genital activity) [which] represent many activities that, at least under primitive conditions, have their purpose in themselves" (Bataille, 1932). It was in this seminal text (published in the journal, *La Critique sociale*, which Bataille led with Marxists), that he brought up the gratuity of human activity and sketches the premises of a theory of waste that would be developed in subsequent works: "[T]he intense work of abandon, washout and storms that constitute it (human life) could be expressed by stating that it starts only with the shortfall of these systems (systems closed from the economy): at least that it allows order and reserve, doesn't it have meaning only as of the moment when ordered and reserved forces are released and lost for reasons that cannot possibly be accounted for." This notion of spending would subsequently be developed and expanded by Bataille, from 1930 to 1955, in works that we may think, as did Jean Duvignaud, to be only "minor designs around a key concern – human activity that does not accumulate to possess but to spend and waste" (Duvignaud, 1967).

For starters, it is necessary to get away from the ideas of need and usefulness when thinking of consumption. As Bataille states, "the question of usefulness distorts any discussion, knowing that there is no correct way to define what is useful to man." And, he continues, "traditional usefulness, i.e. purportedly material usefulness[,] is theoretically for pleasure – but only moderate, violent pleasure given as *pathological* – and it can be limited to shopping [practically to production] and the conservation of goods on the one hand – and the conservation of human lives on the other hand....". Bataille's thinking is attacked – beyond the purely political economy (which, basically, is set on the exchange value) – on the metaphysical principle of the economy: usefulness. Usefulness is what is targeted at its root – an apparently positive principle of capital:

accumulation, investment, redemption and so forth – in fact, the complete inability to spend, which all previous societies knew how to do; an incredible deficiency, one that cuts off the human being from any possible sovereignty. The entire economy is based on what can no longer be spent, on what can no longer become the issue of sacrifice – it is thus completely residual, a restricted social factor. And it is against the economy as a restricted social factor that Bataille makes out spending, death and sacrifice to be a social factor (Baudrillard, 1976).

Erotic harnessing

Consumer society thus functions on the capacity to capture this excess energy that Bataille recalls. This harnessing means in the literal sense gathering an energy, a fluid and, by extension, a tactic made as a conquest, basically out of self-interest; harnessing also means trying to monopolize one another, in particular the other's affection in order to elicit tolerance and earn kindness from the listener. Now, intrinsically, consumer society is wholly associated with the process of dramatization and decommodification and with semantics that transforms goods into merchandise by the projection of the imagined and by performances that increase the goods' potential for seduction. This has to do with nothing more and nothing less than capturing economic value while controlling symbolic value. That is also the role of this singular device, the brand, which ultimately seeks an esthetic, psychological and economic harnessing. This is all the more significant in that capitalism has a tendency to defunctionalize the goods of consumption by emotionalizing goods and services. Commercial seduction often is in an erotic format. The libido is still finally the main shopping engine, and the question of eroticism comes as being naturally embedded in consumption. Thus does consumer society seem absorbed in the idea of eroticism for commercial purposes, even dissipating eroticism in the mirror of consumption?

Consumer society has in fact magnified goods, then bodies, by a process of eroticization of goods in order to increase their commercial value. If we accept the idea that, in an economy of symbolic goods, the useful function of objects becomes secondary, then why do we not consider consumption as a substitute activity for the sexual act or for love relations in a joyless economy? Hence, for example, the erotic phenomenon of hyphephilia observed by the psychiatrist Gaëtan Gatian de Clérambault in the nineteenth century, presenting cases of women displaying an autoerotic passion for pieces of silk pilfered in department stores; during periods of depression, these fabrics gave them more pleasure than alcohol, drugs, erotic fantasies or even their sexual partners.

It is not an exaggeration to say that consumer society was truly created on the western side of the Atlantic, with the unveiling of women in an American society that was tainted by puritanism. At the origin of the consumer society, the American woman was breaking away from puritanism as she little by little revealed parts of her body; we can thus see as a proportioned effect a libidinal overinvestment of female attributes to sell the most ordinary products. As Stiegler (2004) stated, it was necessary to combat overproduction, meaning in reality (which Marx called "lowering the fixed rate"), developing a system of harnessing attention and channeling desire, the libido (which Sigmund Freud called "libidinal energy"), towards merchandise. Eroticization of merchandise is one of the terms for brands and advertising being substituted for human relations between the client and the seller, doing so by personifying the product.

The expansion of consumer society is in fact intimately associated with the advent of self-service and the introduction of a disintermediated economy, a harnessing of libidinal energy by a process of eroticizing tradable goods. If we consider eroticization as attributing sexual meaning to something that normally has none, it appears that eroticization based on conspicuous consumption is intrinsically associated with the development of the consumer society in the sense that the basic harnessing mechanism that marketing has established is erotic in nature. By switching from a rational economy to an emotional economy in which products will set in motion motivations even more hedonistic, emotional, imaginary and phantasmagorical, brands act as silent sellers and product must often seduce the customer to inspire shopping. As much as the object was previously magnified by its rarity and physical and symbolic distance, the product is finished, determined and can have value only within a symbolic economy. Mass production and an abundance of products result in a sort of deterioration of goods, insofar as abundance tends to drain the objects of their meaningful substance. It is thus necessary to respond to the taste of modern man for excitation and continually renew a *curiositas*, an "insatiable thirst to see to see what is lost in continually renewed possibilities" (Agamben, 1998). It is in fact this specific function that the eroticization of products will respond to and which will propel them once more in a compulsive world to fully excite individuals who are subject to an almost infinite choice of immediately accessible products. Commercial eroticization properly partakes in this logic of excitability that coincides with the development of consumer society. It aims basically to increase the level of involvement of individuals with respect to products that are primarily devoid of interest (laundry detergent, shampoo, soap, toothpaste). It is thus necessary to make the product desired, transform it into flesh and blood, through the personification of the product and the use of eroticizing attributes of the female body.

Harnessing desire and the death of the libidinal economy

Eroticization is thus a basic mechanism that transforms a society of consumption – associated with the sole destruction of goods – to a consumer society understood as a vast array of practices by which individuals market and exchange value and meaning. As Baudrillard showed perfectly in *La société de consommation*, "every little object is invested implicitly on the model of the body/object of the woman, is fetishized[,] ... hence the generalized saturation in the entire domain of 'consumption' by eroticism. This use of the body to represent objects introduces profound mechanisms of directed consumption[;] ... we see how the transition is easy, logical and necessary, from the functional appropriation of bodies to the appropriation of goods and objects in shopping. It seems that the only free compulsion is the *compulsion to shop*" (Baudrillard, 1970, p. 209). We can thus state about eroticism what Baudrillard states regarding the devil: "[A]s the most diabolical aspect of the Devil never was to exist, but to make you believe that he exists – likewise Abundance *does not exist*, but it's enough to make you believe that it exists to be an effective myth." Could we not likewise say that eroticism no longer exists but makes us believe that it exists to be an effective myth of consumer society? It must be acknowledged that consumerism has actually deflected all the consumers' desires towards the objects of consumption while becoming, as Herbert Marcuse predicted, a vast machine to destroy the libido.

The major sleight of hand in marketing is thus metonymically transforming the product to a person by eroticizing the body of the female consumer to make it desirable and to make it properly enter an infinite consumer circuit to always spend more to increase its potential for attraction in a society wherein attraction is the focus of everything. The desire for the object is thus built on desire for the person. Hence, the invention of the pin-up, for example, which revealed a complete erotic immanence, as is shown by Dany Robert Dufour (Dufour, 2008). Consumer society finally substituted eroticism of an object for eroticism of people, oversexualizing products and finally desexualizing women by what is called, the "exhibition of enjoyment." In other words, "it is constantly exhibiting what ordinarily is hidden, reserved, for example lovemaking, and to immediately invite the person to explicit enjoyment, shared with this object.... [T]he creation of communities based on the same explicit object of satisfaction" (Dufour, 2008).

But this model of eroticization of merchandise poses a problem due to a downward trend of libidinal energy and the progressive destruction of the libido that it comes from. That is why it is necessary to rethink the form of love that consumption comes from.

What is love without *eros*?

Eroticization is only a manner of applying consumption to love. But is there not another way to correlate the idea of love with consumption? To that end, let us remember that love in Western literature points to a multiple reality. The word *love* can in fact be translated by three different Greek terms that each define a specific nature of the feeling of love and confer upon it a specific moral scope. *Eros* is love as an ardent desire to be united to a specific person; it points to a hope in one's self that can be accessed only through contact with someone. *Eros is undoubtedly* the most powerful and most characteristic of human motions by its capacity to give, often suddenly, a meaning to life, to deflect, adapt and sometimes shape perceptions, thoughts and even actions. The perception of an insignificant act concerning the object of love, and out of proportion to the sweet feeling, can bring about a dramatic change in attitude and emotion in the being smitten by love. Moreover, *eros* love is often associated with exclusivity of an object, the best way being to give an account of it or an absolutely unique description. Focusing thus appeared as a characteristic of erotic love.

Philia means a relationship denoted by reciprocity and mutual esteem; this term is often translated as friendship, but the term does in fact have a larger scope, since it consists of affection for someone else and the desire to maintain a relationship with that person, a relationship that consists of a sort of moral excellence.

Aristotle, in his *Nicomachean Ethics*, introduces *philia* and develops in particular the link that friendship and reciprocity maintain. *Philia* is a term that extends from friendship of two people to the cardinal virtue of political morality, and that means sociability, a principle of all communities. It is basically an interactionist notion based on acknowledging reciprocal qualities. For friendship to take root, Aristotle recalls, the partners must have qualities – they must be in a way "worthy of being loved by one another" – which implies that friends need the same capacity to assess someone else's qualities, and thus a shared knowledge of what makes value. It is, moreover, necessary for them to interact, for each to communicate to the other the assessment that they have made of each other and that they thus have "knowledge of their feelings" (Canto-Sperber, 1996, p. 33). Friendship can pursue different purposes: the search for common usefulness, pleasure or even virtue.

An interesting element concerning the possible metaphorical extension of *philia* to the practices of collaborative consumption is the importance accorded by Aristotle to the conditions of space and time. Coexisting in the same space is, for example, considered a necessary condition for *philia,* since friendship tends to fall apart when beings are atr a distance. Moreover, Aristotle insists on the necessary reciprocal assessment of qualities, which implies not only a common measurement for assessing qualities, but also a rule of equality in mutual trade (Boltanski, 1991, p. 62). Reciprocity is subject, from each of the partners, to anticipation insofar as each expects, in return, something from the other equivalent to what each has given.

The third form of love explained by the Greeks is *agape,* love devoted to others, but others considered in their basic human quality and as one's neighbor. It is a feeling without expecting reciprocity and, in a certain manner, independent of what or whom is loved. The term agape, largely used in the New Testament (in which the term *eros* did not appear anywhere), means basically the love that Christianity exalts; unknown in Classical Greek (which uses the verb *agapân*), agape was introduced in the writings of the first Christian authors to mean the love that Jesus Christ embodied, different from other forms of tender or loving feelings, such as *eros* or *philia* (El Murr, 2015, p. 215). Agape is the term that defines God, himself; it has to do with the Creator's plan for His creation, manifested by the gift of Himself that God gave by the gift of His son. The human response to God's infinite love is also called agape, the Greek word for charity, as a duty to love one's neighbor. The ideas of reciprocity and mutual awareness of being loved, characteristics of *philia,* are described in this special and deeply unequal relationship that is God's love. Agape is different from *eros* and *philia* in that it is not associated with the desire or need for reciprocity: agape demands no reciprocity and expects nothing. Moreover, actions that inspire agape are not determined by the fact that we are loved: love is given here independent of the history that binds the loving being to his or her beloved. The need for mutual awareness, so critical for *eros* and *philia,* has no meaning here. To that end, agape implies no common life, no mutual awareness of those to which it is given and no common understanding, feelings or opinions. Thus, the idea of connection that was the basis for friendship in ancient times does not at all have the same meaning for Christian agape.

Finally, agape does not take into account the morality of the one who is loved (whereas this condition of morality is so crucial for *philia*). Agape, in fact, does not take into account the qualities of those to whom it is given. It is blind to any social, economic or political quality and especially to any moral quality. This is, also, how it most clearly differs from *philia*, which cannot exist without considering the value of the person loved. We can also consider charity to be the opposite of *philia* insofar as the act of love that involves charity creates value: loving creates the quality in the one who is loved, whereas *philia* perceives values by which the friend is loved.

From consumer *eros* to participative agape

Thinking of participative consumption as an act of giving: it is implicitly making the assumption of a transition from *eros* to agape insofar as gifting is the result of a sort of contract by which a person (donor or originator) presently and irrevocably casts off the thing given in favor of the donee who accepts it. Gifting implies the idea of a gift of one's self, a gift we submit to someone without receiving anything in return. As Jacques Derrida (1991) demonstrated, for there to be a gift, the donee *must not* render, remunerate, reimburse, pay, enter into any contract, never incur any debt (the donee even *owes it to himself* not to render; he has the *duty* to *not owe*, and the donor not to expect payback). Ultimately, he must not acknowledge the gift as a gift. If he acknowledges it as a gift, if the gift seems like a gift to him, if the present is presented to him as a present, this simple *acknowledgement* cancels out the gift. The other person needs to receive the gift, and not only receive it in the sense that, as we say in French, we receive a good, money or a reward, but receive the nature of giving in it, receive the sense or the intention, the intentional sense of the gift, so that this simple acknowledgement of the gift as a gift, as such, before even becoming an acknowledgement as gratitude, cancels out the gift as a gift. Simply identifying the gift seems to destroy it. Simply identifying the gift as such, meaning something that can be identified among several, would be nothing more than destroying the gift. Ultimately, the gift as a gift should not appear as a gift: neither to the donee, nor to the donor. Consumption considered as sacrifice is thus not a gift but makes it possible to express moral values. In this sense participative consumption does not at all express a gift of one's self without anything in return. It is a game of acknowledging that is also characteristic of our democratic societies, of which consumer society is a part.

It is in fact important to review at this time the analysis that the onset of marketing and the subsequent development of consumer society coincided with the European revolutions that came with the progressive incline of aristocratic societies towards democratic societies. Now, this explains in large part why one of the major aspects of marketing is recognition by the client. In fact, in an aristocracy individuals do not question their identity since their social value depends strictly on their birth and their social rank in a largely vertical society. Consumers thus can show their social rank in a very codified manner: for example, the development of table manners – as analyzed by the historian Norbert Elias – which developed as of the sixteenth century in Europe due to the process of curialization (development of a court society). Thus, the fork and the handkerchief were invented as objects that characterize nobility. The same does not apply in a democratic society, which has a tendency to dissolve the social order. Aristocratic societies valued heroic acts, honor and fidelity, whereas democratic societies placed performance at the center of hierarchical mechanisms, with individuals basically considered equal. Such is no longer the case, however, in democratic societies that demand that individuals demonstrate their individuality. In other words, the basic expectation of individuals in a democratic order is recognition. It is also one of the main aspects of brands and marketing. Participating in an act of collaborative consumption is thus basically attracting recognition.

Consumption and sacrifice

Recognition in this case often assumes the aspect of sacrifice. Sacrifice is what shows a collection of works from the material culture, following in particular Daniel Miller (Miller, 1998). The idea of sacrifice goes back to the tradition of giving something precious to a deity in the hope of communicating with that deity. The key elements here are self-sacrifice, communication between the profane and the sacred and the legitimation of broader social forces. Sacrifice follows the logic of *do ut des*, meaning through a commutation agreement by which we give something in the hope of receiving something. There is no sacrifice that has a contractual element, and that is why self-sacrifice is never devoid of personal interest. The art of self-sacrifice thus involves each sacrifice frequently recalling the conscience of the individual and the presence of collective forces, and ensuring that those forces continue to exist. Consumption does not reflect static social relations or a cultural system as much as dynamic relations by which individuals are capable of renegotiating their culture and social relations. Individuals transform resources (they have purchased) into expressive elements, daily routines and cosmologic ideals that allow them to signify their place and value in the broader society. The interpretative approaches to consumption that are concerned with food practices illustrate, in Daniel Miller's works, that consumption of food is not guided so much by satisfaction as by the love for members of the family. Love is not understood here in its romantic dimension, but as a duty of devotion that takes the form of the wife's or mother's concern to satisfy the desire to be loved through the various practices of consumption. Meal preparation can thus be considered an important opportunity to reinforce the identity of the family and each individual's position within it. As with any phenomenon of gifting based on reciprocity and cultural equivalence, the family's resources are allocated through *do-ut-des* systems that perpetuate love and belonging among members. Women's gifts are gifted in exchange for the husband's salary, although Miller considers this exchange uneven and not reciprocal, since wives give more than they receive: hence, the idea that this represents a modern form of sacrifice, insofar as women save a sort of exceptional value that will then be reinvested in extraordinary instances of consumption during which they celebrate the object of their devotion (children) and thereby reinforce their identity as devoted mothers. In other words consumption can be understood as activating a love considered a shared, sustainable moral idea that is superior to the sole diktat of instrumentality. In other words, love that comes from consumption is by nature normative and grants connection and even transcendence values, and as a result emblematizes a contemporary vision of religious cosmology.

Philia or consumption as reciprocity

If the path of agape turns out to be disappointing to understanding the practices of consumption, let us also look at *philia*. As Michel de Certeau subtly highlighted, the form of poaching that consumers' tactics undertake induces another form of exchange, an economy of gifting (*generosity* to return the favor), an esthetic of blows (artistic operations) and an ethic of tenacity (a thousand ways to refuse the established order's status of the law, sense or fatality). The reconfiguration that allows these tactics to develop produces a style of resistance, an esthetic of any other type. For the use of the market and its standard model in which each person tries to raise his or her personal interest, Certeau substitutes another logic: a concrete symbolic exchange characterized by gifting and by desire. It is here that the face of the amateur appears, one that is fed inevitably by *philia*. The amateur consumer unearths choice little spots far from standard guides and shares them with others. But yet again, it is a behavior of consumption that aims to be involved in commercial relations in considering that the one who offers is someone friendly to the individual whom you wish well: hence, the fact that the amateur does not hesitate to share with others his knowledge of his favorite spots, both to make his friends happy and to help the supplier develop its commercial network. Maybe it has to do with rekindling commercial relations – logically considered cold – tinging them with a specific love relationship. Cochoy also suggested the idea that the birth of marketing and related commercial intermediation devices seemed so much like a game of "hot hands" (Cochoy, 1999). In the game of desire and friendliness, the amateur attempts to rekindle the commercial link via relations based on acknowledging reciprocal qualities. For friendship to take root, the partners must first be "worthy of being loved by one another", which assumes the same capacity from the friends – to assess someone else's qualities, and thus share a common knowledge of what makes value. Now does that not rightly characterize the aspect of the amateur?

It is necessary on the other hand for amateurs to interact, to communicate with one another as to their assessments of one another, and that they have, as Aristotle stated, "knowledge of their feelings." Kindness that comes from *philia* must be "reciprocal", which thus implies not only a common measurement for assessing qualities, but also a rule of equality in mutual trade (Boltanski, 1990, p. 162). Hence, the fact that the link that is made between friendship and assessing qualities on the one hand and, on the other hand, between friendship and reciprocity, the theory of friendship relates with the theory of justice, theories which are not completely separate anyway (rendering justice to talent for example). Since, in friendship, reciprocity is not exercised blindly. It is subject to expectations from each of the partners, who expect from one another something in return equivalent to what each has given. The emphasis is on reciprocity, and the expectation of reciprocity accounts for the hierarchical classification of friendships based on pleasure, interest or virtue. Is this not ultimately what the amateur consumer teaches us – meaning the use of tactical tricks to make commercial relations less utilitarian, to instill them with pleasure and virtue?

The consamateur, or our friend the bricoleur

The consumer has alternately been described as *homo economicus making choices*, an explorer seeking to communicate and express himself, as well as a hedonist, artist, victim, rebel, activist, citizen (Gabriel and Lang, 1995) and chameleon. Never have so many different metaphors been attributed to the figure of the amateur. How can we picture amateurs in a world of consumption that exposes us to mostly manufactured products that never stop reminding us how they dictate our tastes and induce stereotypical practices? Is not the consumer ultimately a "social idiot," only good for gorging on pseudo-cultural gadgets? Such is the question posed by the concept of amateurism as applied to the world of consumption. How, indeed, to make sense of a manufactured product copied identically over and over unto infinity? How to project impact and emotion into a product if my neighbor is likely to have the same one? The issue of amateurism reminds us that the meaning of objects is not only found in their ontological or functional sense, but emerges in an interactive process, so that we, as consumers, take part in defining the social and personal meanings of objects by ourselves projecting meaning on those objects, especially through the idea of reappropriation. Moreover, speaking of an amateur implies a belief that we love consumer goods because love is a "must" in an etymological meaning. Amateurism has led to envisioning loving relationships in a market that has long been described as a purely functional or symbolic exchange of values. Questioning the role of the amateur involves rethinking the object for consumption in relation to the object, and even the nature of market relationships.

The message of reification

The message to the consumer has long been dependent on a doxa linked to the reification of the subject, which cancels out any idea of authenticity and calls for a revealing framework of rationality in the closed world of merchandise. According to the critical paradigm of the Frankfurt School, culture in the industrial age is only an instrumental manipulation of an anesthetic vocation of the people. The masses would be confined to passivity in a totally closed-off world in which they remain forever prisoners, to the extent that the alienating workplace is relayed in a never-ending circle by the equally fictitious places for recreation, culture and, thus, goods. Not only does such confinement aim to perpetuate artificiality, but it also has the true function of neutralizing any inclination to protest for, or desire, social change. Consumers could, therefore, only follow what has been programmed for them, revealing their explicit insignificance and inability to act to the extent that quasi-Pavlovian patterns prevail, the consumer's attitude being considered, *a priori*, to conform to what was preregistered in the program. It is clear that no room is left here for any form of amateurism in the sense that the amateur is someone who loves, for there cannot be loving relationships with regard to the merchandise.

Alienation is what separates the object from its manufacturing process, leading to a fetishism that overshadows relationships between individuals, mediated by objects having their own, but certainly artificial, life. Capitalist modernity has definitely accelerated the reign of artificiality, of the merchandise, each time degrading "everyday life" a little bit more from a daily life devalued for having suffered the adverse effects of modernization. With this in mind, an individual is subject to an ever-faster rate of traffic – in codes, signs and objects – and the consumption system is no longer considered a complement to the production system, marrying together its training techniques. Consumption, therefore, would lead to nothing other (to use Baudrillard's formula) than an era of "semiotic totalitarianism" (Baudrillard, 1970, p. 18). The world of consumption is one of products and not objects. Recall that the object is formed on the aspect of *resistance* to the individual (as shown by the German *Gegenstand* that sets beings apart from thought and reason) and therefore it returns to the subject. Meanwhile, marketing has transformed the object into a product, with all that the past participle indicates here in programmatic use. Moreover, a focus on the symbolic dimension of products and brands has indeed tarnished the study of physical and sensual anchoring in the consumer experience. Have they not just buried other alternatives of consistency and the meaning of consumption, which also sometimes tend to resurface by default in daily life? How can an object still surprise us and delight us, despite the wear and tear of everyday life? Perhaps the time has come to understand the infra-ordinary fashion that surrounds us and compels us to leave behind the saturation effects of meaning and symbolic tyranny that trap objects in a register that tends to empty them of meaning, of emotion and, undoubtedly, of efficiency. We need to understand how consumption takes shape and is expressed through gesture and matter, since that is what the very personage of the amateur requires.

The rise of the personage of the amateur

An individual who loves carrying out research (certain things, certain activities), one who cultivates an art or a science just for his own enjoyment (not his profession) or is an avid collector of objets d'art – this individual may be considered an amateur. The term amateur refers to the qualities of a person who loves things and knowledge. Before understanding what consumer amateurism might mean, first we must understand precisely what constitutes an amateur. The basic figure of the amateur was theorized as a model for the public during the creation of the Royal Academy of Painting and Sculpture in the eighteenth century, when the amateur became a central figure in art appreciation during the Enlightenment, when new uses of art surfaced and new public admirers came forward. An amateur is first of all an emblem for an aristocratic figure, through which he also expresses nostalgia for the Old Regime: "The amateur of beautiful things, to whom God gave the grace to understand and appreciate them[;] ... taste, love of Beauty and erudition are of aristocracies, and the crowd did not greet them." (Bonnaffé, 1873) The rise of the concept of amateur is consubstantial to the professionalization and commercialization movement that changed the arts environment of the time; amateur is related to a focus on collectors, dealers and experts who became the central players in financial exchanges in the art world. Hence, in the history of taste, amateurs are found to have been slowly given a privileged role in the definition of tastes and artistic modes appearing in the figurative arts (Haskell, 1994).

From a distanced aesthetic perspective, which naturalizes taste, and a sociological reductionism that views amateurism only as an element of distinction, the amateur emerged as a central figure in the art world when taste became an indicator of social and cultural competence. The conflict between good taste and the market is at the heart of controversy about amateurs. But, as Dominique Poulot (1997) demonstrated, in France there is a clear continuity between Old Regime amateur culture and the heritage that triumphed with the birth of the National Museum. An amateur is not a disinterested figure in French art appreciation; he is a political figure whose patriotic value is self-contradictory by being split between the ideal and the progressive utility that drive the academic system and pre-revolutionary critics who reject this model. So the figure of the amateur is defined primarily around an appreciation for art. But, in the second half of the eighteenth century the amateur was not only one who loves, he was also one who supported the arts. Cited for the first time in the French Academy dictionary in 1694, the term *amateur* was then related to the field of objects, especially scholarly, literary or artistic ones: "Who loves. It is said only to show the affection we have for things & that we don't have for people. We speak of a lover of virtue, glory, letters, arts, good books, paintings." In 1751, the *Encyclopedia* was the first generalist dictionary in which the term was specifically ascribed to painting. In Europe, the term witnessed strong growth with different meanings (dilettante in Italy in 1681, *Kunstliebhaber* in the German states in the late eighteenth century and, in England, *connoisseur* borrowed from the artistic model of *virtuoso* ("men of talent") tinged with moral philosophy and the idea of neo-Stoic virtue, while *connoisseur* and *dilettante* referred to a more practical bourgeois order. In France, pictorial specialization defined the term, amateur, summed up the concept of good taste, and became the essential attribute of an amateur. The amateur is associated with the protection of the arts and artists, as well as with the collection and publication of artists' works. Here is an individual who stands out for his or her good taste and vast knowledge in one of the fine arts without ever making it their own profession. The amateur "is defined in a relationship of predilection along with good judgment and skill" (Guichard, 2009, p. 16).

Hence the figure of the amateur stands in opposition to the figure of the professional, with the amateur falling within the sphere of *otium* and cultivated leisure. Thus, in the *Encyclopedia*, the connoisseur is defined by his knowledge ("discernment") and his skill in judging the works; the connoisseur differs from the amateur, who is defined by "taste": "It is said of all those who love this art, and who have a decided taste for paintings." Hence, a curious critique associated with a form of cumulative condemnation, Krystof Pomian proved that such definitions of the curious were built around "totality of desire." In the field of semantics, this type of arrangement gives way to "taste" – connected with the amateur – and artistic skills – connected with the connoisseur, characterized by his "knowledge" and its "lights." This one announces the triumph of a system of expertise in the worlds of art. Caylus distinguished, for example, natural good taste, an instinct, a gift that does not lend itself to elucidation, and which places amateurs with artists in the world of election and talent (Guichard, 2009). Citing their ability to find "subjects happy for painting," Caylus defined amateurs, using a vocabulary of genius for whom nature had "equally divested (between) the painter and the amateur." In parallel, "acquired taste" is the product of visual and rational learning about the beauty of painting and spending one's time admiring works. This is why an amateur's artistic practices play a vital role in such learning. As early as 1747, the reformation of the Royal Academy of Painting and Sculpture affirmed the importance of taste with a goal of establishing and making known the liberal status of arts in the artistic field, in painting and sculpture as well as through policy that aims to provide a model for exercising good judgment of taste based on an alliance between artists and amateurs and opposing the opening of criticism to the public space. Lastly, the social relationships that amateurs maintained with artists should be emphasized, as should the importance in the register of arts amateurism in the language of friendship: inspired by Montaigne, friendship between painter and sponsor achieves the humanist ideal of scholars and scientists within the Republic of Letters, which speaks of friendship as the preferred means of communication. In the fifteenth century, the vocabulary of friendship opened to a new dimension; that vocabulary was closely related to protective relationships that then grew in worldly and literary social circles. Worldly protection derives its strength and value for all parties because it borrows the language of friendship and sociability, beneficence and recognition (Guichard, 2009, p. 53).

An important step in the historical formation of the figure of the amateur is the critical salon that began in the mid-eighteenth century and remains an occasional pastime of polygraphs and publicists. This new literary genre was built without any institutional legitimacy: if the role of criticism exists, it was not a foundation of social identity before the nineteenth century. Criticism is often associated with the personage of the amateur. Until the late 1760s, critics continued to traditionally present themselves in the guise of a "*gentleman* amateur" and man of the world; the amateur thereby held a strategic position in the "critical criticism" that discussed public standards of artistic judgment. Thus, the critic did not return to scholarly status, but became a wider social figure that assumed an authoritative role. The critic was often referred to by the writers of brochures as a basis for their legitimacy to judge. The term *critic* refers to a feigned impersonality. Its function is similar to that of a literary mask. Hence, the growing importance of printing with regard to technical expertise. Thus, the foundation of *criticism* is "to clearly feel the effect of a painting," contrary to the French Royal Academy, which endorsed an academic label for the amateur – a label that was reserved for its own uses.

Here, in a brief historical sweep, we begin to see several ideas that allow us to consider the figure of the amateur consumer. It is a question of art, taste, progressive de-institutionalization and, lastly, the practices of social life and friendship. This question has precisely the ingredients that capture the issue of amateur consumer in a cultural logic of the aestheticism of everyday life. Far from the formatting imposed by the economy of brands, the amateur consumer is one who poaches from the system, paving the way to tasting novel products, to seeking out unique sensory encounters, and above all, to weaving a network of suppliers with whom the critic also enjoys a friendship.

The quest for a form of reappropriation

The figure of an amateur consumer first of all is a logic of reappropriation wherein it becomes possible to literally and figuratively place a hand on the consumerist system. But how to understand reappropriation if not in a symmetrical double meaning, in that ownership refers both to the act of taking something for oneself, making it one's property, or the act of making something one's own through its use? The discussion about ownership is essentially about consumer alienation. Marketing seems to attempt to give itself a clear conscience by endorsing the idea that the consumer may reappropriate symbolic goods through a sort of symbolic re-engagement of meanings traditionally attached to those goods. Thus, the experiential paradigm that since the mid-1980s dominated thinking about consumption clearly posits that individuals are likely to project both personal and collective meanings onto consumer goods and thus reappropriate their meaning. But this symbolic message quickly reached its limits, as evidenced by the mere fact that reappropriation refers to the domain of taking and thus doing. In other words, any reappropriation would not be limited to the re-orchestration of the meaning of objects but to a raft of singular practices that make sense to individuals and allow this process to give new meaning to consumer habits that were abandoned because they were too pragmatic. In other words, reappropriation refers to the figure of the subject–consumer capable of singular actions, tastes and preferences.

Especially from a technical point of view, appropriation also refers to the functional use of an object in the sense of instrumental mastery: to have the appropriate object would mean having the cleanest object. In other words, ownership is related to "clean" – as opposed to the market or consumption that we have "messed up" – Dufour (2008) uses that term in reference to this sentence by Antonin Artaud: "(God has) messed up living/all my life" – as well as a form of mastery through sensory and motor activity whereby an individual may reappropriate a relationship to objects by construing an imaginary relationship. Ownership therefore assumes making something one's own, such as a skill, which engenders practices that allow a subject to see himself as being able to bring meaning to his environment. Ownership is strongly linked to a form of resistance to dis-subjection by individuals who involve an ideology of alienation. Amateurism may at first refer to forms of reappropriation by which it serves to retake possession. The process of reappropriation is also "consubstantially related to the act of borrowing." There is a strong identity issue in that it aims to integrate exogenous elements of a cultural background into the individual by adjusting these new elements to the rules and values that pre-exist in his culture. In terms of food, the new element must give the triple point of view to form (culinary aspects), function and meaning. Expressions of the reappropriation process are numerous: adaptation, embezzlement, name change, adoption channel, instrumentation, reinterpretation and so forth. (Sanchez, 2005).

The importance of a decision – one that actually allows making a decision in the course of one's own existence by a process of perception, orientation and action – enables human beings to think and act upon the world and achieve self-fulfillment. Here, there is an idea of sharing a common culture as well as an idea of enjoyment that are inexorably linked to the figure of the amateur in art. One may also see a form of resistance in the form of control that the society of brands represents. The society of brands exerts control over individuals, which essentially reduces any differences by denying the desiring function of the other, since "in the relation of influence, it is always a very selective *interference with the other who is the desiring subject*, which, as such, is characterized by its uniqueness, its own specificity[;] ... the influence thus reflects a fundamental trend *to neutralize the desire of others*, that is to say, to reduce all otherness, any difference, in *the abolition of any specificity*, the target being *to bring to the other the function and status of a fully assimilable object*" (Dorey, 1981). From this fundamental opposition between "influence" and "control," the amateur is the one who resists this impulse to control characteristics of a libidinal economy that ultimately denies the very concept of otherness, difference and therefore desire. Thus, the issue of the amateur is eminently a question of taste in its standard dimension. Posing the question of the amateur first means focusing on a form of resistance that is necessarily translated by the uses and practices that inevitably reflect "the explicit desire and deliberate will" (Gauchet, 1988) that characterizes the reappropriation of consumer practices and therefore their meaning.

Amateurism as a deviation: the tactics of poaching

We owe a debt to Michel de Certeau for coming up with the most acute, yet subtle, thoughts about how individuals can rightly reclaim the system of consumption. Keeping a distance from this sort of binarity, which shows the origins of something being perverted by mass consumption, means being more interested in the modes of creativity in consumer practices that no system can reduce to silence. He proposed the idea of internal invention even within everyday life by running through a series of tricks that divert the systems of control. By focusing on the tricks, intelligence, plurality and inventiveness of each individual's modes of appropriation, Certeau examines the processes of subjugation and individuation as possible ways to enjoy and respond to wants in the interstices, the constant deviations from established standards and accepted codes. Therefore, mass consumption is no longer stigmatized as a source of inauthenticity, but is considered only in the light of each individual's authenticity. He leads to the figure of the sphinx consumer "(whose) creations are disseminated within the grid of a televised, urbanistic and commercial production."

Here is where we can understand the person of the amateur through the repertoire wherein users carry out operations that are all their own. So, the question is that of the lexicon of these practices (Giard, 1994, p. xxxvii). The issue is not that of consumption-as-reception but consumption-as-production. Hence, de Certeau's question: "The users of the supermarket, the practicants of urban space, the consumers of journalistic stories and legends, what do they create with what they have 'absorbed,' received and paid for? What are they doing?" (de Certeau, 1994). A streamlined, expansionist, centralized production, one that is dramatic and noisy, must face a completely different type of production, which is called "consumption," which is known for its tricks, its breaking down over time, its poaching, its underground character, its tireless murmur, in short, a near invisibility because it is not seen through its own products (which it would prefer) but in the art of using them, which is imposed on them. Thus, de Certeau's reappropriation refers to poaching and various possible re-uses: that is to say, a turnaround in consumption of constraints established from above against themselves and through which individuals try to appropriate time and space by changing the names, by diverting them from their purpose – in brief, through tricks. *The Practice of Everyday Life* discusses an attempt to "re-enchant the world" to the extent that de Certeau seeks to bring forth from the banality of everyday life a poetic inventiveness that reveals an inexhaustible power of creativity. A *poïesis*, an active sense of re-creation that lives inside the subjects with the most routine lives (Dosse, 2007, p. 502). Everyday life, in its poetic dimension, makes possible the tricks and tactics for changing the modes of appropriation expected by strategists. It serves to exceed the cutoff postulated between an active type of production and a type of consumption that is not passive and tends to dissolve under users' continual resistance to following the rules. To speak of an amateur is to talk about consumers who are not familiar with the producers, who become poets in their own lives, blazers of trails in the jungles of functionalist rationality. Consumers produce something that appears in the "wander lines" Deligny spoke about. They map out seemingly senseless "unspecified trajectories" inconsistent with the built environment that maps out and prefabricates where they will go. As de Certeau shows, although the prescribed routes should cover them, these crossings remain heterogeneous to systems they infiltrate and where they cross the tricks of different interests and desires. They circulate, come and go, overflowing and drifting in a forced relief, movements of a frothy sea insinuated among rocks and mazes of an established order. Thus, "to live, move, speak, read, go shopping or to cook, these activities seem to match the characteristics of the tricks and surprise tactics: ... the art of shooting in someone else's field of the other, the tricks of hunters, maneuverability and polymorphic mobility, exhilarating discoveries, poetic and warlike." Whereas, for example, the tactics of the culinary arts that organize both a network of relationships, poetic bricolage and re-use of the merchant structures. Here the amateur is a poïen figure and more concerned about tactics than strategy, according to Certeau's distinction. According to him, "a strategy calls for a place likely to be independent and to serve as a basis for managing its relationships with a distinct externalization," while a tactic provides the possibility of a set of actors escaping control through their creative abilities: "I call 'tactic' a calculation that cannot rely on its own, or on a boundary that sets it apart the other as a visible totality. The tactic cannot take place of one except for the place of the other. It insinuates it piecemeal, without entering into its entirety, without being able to hold him off." While strategy defines an independent external place, outdoors, a tactic exists only in the place of another, without externalization. But this opposition grows at the rate of the totalizing extension of productive machines that leave less room for users to brand their use of consumer goods. Tactics oppose strategies through their ability to subvert interior stabilities and agreed-upon orders. The user can always distort the imposed order and the amateur is exactly the one who opens the door to possibly running the system otherwise, according to the ways of doing, by diverting or circumventing constraints in the sense of freedom regained.

As de Certeau also found, the form of poaching at play in consumers' tactics induces another form of exchange, that of a gift economy (of dependent opposing *generosities*), an aesthetic of blows (artistic operations) and a tenacity ethic (a thousand ways to reject the order established by law, meaning or fatality). The reconfiguration that allows the deployment of these tactics leads to a style (resistance), an aesthetic of a different type that brings to mind the *potlatch* of Marcel Mauss. By using the market and its standard model in which each individual seeks to maximize his or her personal gain, de Certeau substitutes another logic, that of a concrete symbolic exchange characterized by a gift and a desire.

The economy of brands or widespread pharmacology

It is a safe bet that if Honoré de Balzac were to rewrite his *Traité des excitants modernes (Treatise on Modern Stimulants)* today, he would evoke the world of goods and brand names to the extent that we live in a capitalist society the main feature of which is a libidinal economy that aims to capture the libido of people to attract their investment in consumer goods. This is what a surge in brand names such as Dior "Addict" perfume would lead one to think, or even advertising claims like this one written on a billboard for a pair of roller skates: "The kind of antidepressant that quickly becomes a drug." The resurgence of addiction lingo in the brand's message translated this way betrays the ability of brands to generate dependency phenomena. But we must view this growth surge in addictive logic against the development of marketing based largely on strategies of consumption intensification. Indeed, the economic model generated by marketing lives in part in the creation and maintenance of mechanisms of over-consumption, which alone can ultimately sustainably support demand in saturated markets. A problem arises when the intensification of consumption dictated by economic logic leads to the establishment of a compulsive economy based on addictive logic, goods in general and certain brands, in particular. Compulsive shopping thus serves as a mainspring of consumer society. Further, when compulsive shopping is considered pathological, should we not also think about the potentially addictive effects of the economy of brands as a whole?

Addiction and compulsive shopping

The role of routine is fundamental to understanding buying behavior. Consumers appear to condition themselves by giving decisive weight to their previous habits. This is why in a consumerist society daily spending is principally, or even exclusively, habituation. Also, some do not hesitate to use the term addiction to characterize purchasing and consumption phenomena, including their repetitive nature. But what is meant by addiction? While the semantic register of addiction has long been held in the psychotropic world, the use of the term has spread widely beyond the strict domain of drug abuse. The semantics of addiction refer to the idea of "indulgence," which includes a dimension of activity and gives a different meaning from that of its French synonyms – "dependence" and "usually" or "addiction" or even "subjection" – each marked by passivity and abandonment (Le Poulichet, 2000). Since the emergence of addictive behaviors in the 1970s, North American psychiatry has referred to these behaviors as a result of psychoactive substances, and the term addiction is increasingly used to describe behaviors of addiction to substances other than psychoactive ones. The start of the 1970s hippie movement, and subsequent increase in drug abuse in the United States as a social phenomenon, jointly explain the extension of the term addiction beyond the strict world of narcotics. In his 1975 book, *Love and Addiction*, Stanton Peele (1985) became one of the first to draw a parallel between drug addiction and codependency. This idea assumes that addiction is not caused by a drug but by an experience that sustains the effect, namely relief from a conflict with reality; this thesis is fundamentally unique since it is based on the idea that some subjects become dependent upon an experience, not the chemical substance. Moreover, in describing the cycle of addiction, Peele recognizes an important role addiction plays in bringing on a feeling of personal and social incompetence. The subject, when faced with an agonizing task, finds a satisfactory, predictable and "reinforcing" immediate substitute by taking the drug or food or even engaging in a specific behavior. Thus, even if addiction allows the subject to "maintain his structures of subjectivity," he faces the problem of a vicious circle wherein addiction is reinforced by repetition and its own effects, including greater feelings of worthlessness and incompetence, which perpetuates a recurring need.

To what extent can we then discuss a shopping addiction? Sociologists do not hesitate to use the term addiction to describe certain purchasing and consumption phenomena, including its repetitive nature. The question is whether compulsive shopping can actually turn into a disease. This is what has convinced some pharmaceutical companies that, in a strictly marketing logic, are trying to create a profitable market so this disease may one day be officially accepted as a mental illness requiring appropriate treatment and justifying new opportunities for their products. The potentially pathological nature of shopping was first demonstrated through the concept of impulse buying. Impulse buying is essentially characterized by: (a) a sudden desire to act that sets it apart from other forms of behavior; (b) a psychological imbalance that pushes the consumer to temporarily uncontrolled actions; (c) a psychological conflict between obtaining immediate gratification and the will to resist what may be perceived as harmful; (d) an altered ability to evaluate the usefulness of products; and (e) an occultation of negative consequences from the act of consumption (Hirschmann and Holbrook, 1992). In the 1980s, US research on purchasing behavior was clearly focused on the compulsive impulse and has contributed to demonstrating the potentially pathological nature of shopping. Compulsive shopping refers to the logic of intensification of a usual practice. Compulsive shopping is conceptually linked to broader categories of compulsive behavior, including alcoholism, drug abuse, bulimia and gambling addiction. Generally, addiction and compulsive shopping share some characteristics, among them: (a) the presence of a strong impulse to engage in such behavior; (b) the denial of the likely consequences this behavior; and (c) repeated failure in attempts to control or change the behavior. Compulsive shoppers are characterized by their low self-esteem and by a greater phantasmagoric propensity than the rest of the population.

Attachment and dependency

Further to the question of compulsive shopping, it is reasonable to ask whether, more generally, brands, under the guise of loyalty, ultimately do not attempt to sustainably hook consumers with true addictive logic. In other words, do the brands not maintain some sort of drug dependency? At a time when the term "addiction" is becoming more widely used to refer to addictive behaviors to substances other than psychoactive ones, why not discuss dependency in terms of a very strong attachment to a brand, if we view addiction as the abuse of a natural or synthetic substance likely to affect an individual's mental behavior? A more than ten-year study carried out on consumer's logic of attachment to brands allows us to study the addictive effects of certain brands. Their most loyal consumers do not hesitate to resort to the vocabulary of addiction to describe their buying of these brands. The ultimate manifestation of brand loyalty is often a form of dependence created by repeated use of the brand. The vocabulary used to describe this dependency relationship is relatively disparate ("guilty pleasure," "little pleasure," "I'm addicted," etc.), which is reminiscent of the semantics of addiction to toxic substances. For example, a certain respondent does not hesitate to mention the fact that "If I do not have my Côte d'Or chocolate square at night, I feel like I'm missing out on something," even describing himself as "Nutella-addicted[;] ... Nutella [is] an integral part of my life and [leads to] a dependency crisis and cravings with each withdrawal." Thus, some individuals do not realize what life would be like without their addictive brand: "If you asked my friends to describe me, I'm sure they would describe my addiction to the drink Mountain

Dew.... While social influences explain why I started drinking Mountain Dew, the brand has become very important in my life.... I have a caffeine addiction and without Mountain Dew, I have a headache. The addiction is not physical, it's also mental: I need Mountain Dew when I'm bored, to study at night or in the morning just because there is no better way to start the day than with Mountain Dew. Since I live in France, I don't have my favorite drink any more[;]... my boyfriend saved my life the other week by sending me a few cans."

One of the first characteristics of addiction lies in the repetition of the consumer experience, especially when linked to a ritual daily activity, like breakfast. It is common to hear this type of testimony: "I trust all my mornings to Harry's"; or even: "Nutella is the product I have consumed the most often for the longest time. I don't think I could say when I first spread my bread with Nutella, it's been so long ago." Moreover, this form of ritual is what brands like Ricoré, the breakfast friend, strive for, or Actimel, which has launched nothing short of "the healthy morning gesture." The product's influence is often based on physiological reasons, which is why the phenomenon is widespread for chocolate products containing stimulants like caffeine. But it is clear that the addictive effect, largely developed for products of an addictive nature (chocolate, coffee, cigarettes), may also be observed with brand names, as this respondent points out: "GAP is the kind of store I wouldn't usually go in without buying something or without finding some clothes I like, which I'm sure I'll come back to buy, either for myself or as a gift."

The brand, the pharmakon

And if the brand finally played the role of what in ancient times and the Middle Ages was called a love potion? This type of magic indeed was primarily active in the composition of potions, powders and concoctions that a man or woman administers to a person who would not otherwise return their love. However, in a competitive world, what is a brand trying to do if it is not attempting to be "loved" by the consumer by turning on its charm? Does not marketing ultimately aim to put the consumer under its spell – that is to say, the alienation of individuals with less sense of belonging and who will submit to the operator's desires without resistance? The brand may be understood by analogy as a kind of pharmakon that wants a consumer to become permanently attached. The Greek word pharmakeia, "poison" (from which pharmacy was derived) was in fact the equivalent of the French term for witchcraft. In Greek, pharmakon defines any substance, regardless of whether it is beneficial or harmful. A pharmakon is both cure and poison, and by extension any act that preserves, ensures salvation, improves one's condition, as well as any act that poisons and corrupts. Like a pharmakon, one may view a brand as a drug, a potion to both cure and poison whose power of enchantment may be beneficial or evil. More broadly, a pharmakon is any magical operation, song, formula, beverage, dye, or look from an eye that leads to a change, whatever the direction. The witches of Thessaly, the first to have a fearsome reputation, were named the pharmakides. They used plants with hallucinogenic effects, such as Solanaceae, harvested during a religious ceremony to concoct potions giving victims mental confusion thus rendering themselves defenseless against an amorous scheme. In the manner of a pharmakon, one may view the brand as a drug, a potion to both cure and poison and whose power of enchantment may be beneficial or evil. This is probably one of the ambivalences of attachment that provides both emotional security and the power to instill consumer dependency with respect to the brand. As Plato rightly shows in the *Phaedra*, the power of the pharmakon comes from man wanting to somehow be stripped of his domination over himself. The theme of addiction undoubtedly betrays a desire for renunciation; as is the case when eating snacks in front of the television becomes mechanical and leads to a disconnect after 20 minutes of feeling hunger and eating food (we do not stop eating without knowing whether we are still hungry or not). It is in this sense that one may refer to consumer society in terms of a generalized drug store and the brand as an addictive substance.

Does the brand play a part in a kind of generalized drug–pharmaceutical dependence? It is in this sense that one may refer to consumer society in terms of a generalized drug store, and to a brand as an addictive substance. Indeed, if we accept the definition of addiction as any abuse of a natural or synthetic substance likely to affect an individual's mental behavior, then it is appropriate to speak of dependence with regard to a very strong attachment to a brand. In the traditional sense, addiction is medically characterized by physiological dependence and tolerance (the consumer needs to increase the doses for the product to maintain its effect); the product exerts physical control on the person, an influence that is mechanically created by the pharmacological properties of the product and that is expressed by compulsive behavior. But "our epoch doesn't have a choice, no more than those who went before. It sets out its requirement for an afterlife in its way" (Lembeye, 2000). Indeed, in the broadest terms, dependence is relatively inevitable since "to think of something, or of someone, is to lean on them, to take care. All leaning, all tropism is an addiction. It is not good to lean." (Lembeye, 2001). Any leaning is indeed able to create its own specific aches and thereby "all thought is narcotic." Similarly, Plato in the *Phaedrus* shows that the one who is literally the founder is the being not separated, the dependent. Man wants somehow to be stripped of his domination over himself. As recalled by Lembeye, "placing oneself outside oneself is an essential appropriation of a human being" (Lembeye, 2001, p. 18). One could ask whether the economy of brands does not precisely return us to this desire for renunciation.

On capitalism becoming a poisoner of programs

If one agrees with the idea that capitalism would form a "gigantic accumulation and proliferation of devices" (Stiegler, 2008, p. 290 et seq.), leading to permanent control of attention and its affects, it should be understood that the economy of brands combines to control ever more libidinal energy to organize consumption, resulting in a downward trend of this libidinal energy, which then decreases the compulsion. So this is exactly a question of the economy of the libido, that is to say, an economy of objects of desire, and a desire that must be diverted. The pharmacology from which the device arises is unthinkable outside of a compulsive economy, which can both bind and release, being at once the remedy (that is to say, the support), and the poison (that is to say the ruin). This means the poison remains forever without a cure. Hence the idea that "in a disciplinary society, the devices are designed... to create docile but free bodies who assume their identity and freedom of the subject in the very process of their subjection" (Agamben, 2006, p. 41). This issue is now crucial, in that capitalism, by exploiting the libidinal economy, eventually destroys it. This leads to the disindividuation of human beings, and thus a form of social control. But, beyond the concept of influence to the concept of the brand, it seems legitimate to ask how it is that brands do not exercise any real control on the consumer. The use of the word derives from the Latin *imprendere*, itself coming from *prehendere* (to take), referring to a moral and administrative direction; morally, it is the ascendancy a subject may assume over another, while in the sense of administrative law, a grip means an action allowing the administration to "put its hands on" private property. Morally, what concerns us here is the control, taking into account the possible influence one person or thing may have on another. A subject under control loses all or part of his freedom, his autonomy: he depends upon an outside "object."

Robert Dorey gives, for example, the role of the "drive to control" in the relational sphere (Dorey, 1981). He suggests replacing the drive to control concept with "relation of control." Thus, "control is a very singular mode of interaction between two subjects" whose specificity is marked by the three original meanings of "control": ownership through dispossession of the other (the administrative meaning of control); domination (the moral meaning); the influence of the brand (the mark on the body of appropriation: to put your hands on ...), resulting from the combination of the two previous meanings. Influence and control therefore combine when "one exercises the serious control of its brand on the other." What does this control do? According to Dorey, for the one who is the actor, this relationship of control essentially consists of giving the object a place that allows it to "hide what is missing, that is to say, to reduce any difference." And what is initially denied is the desirous function of the other, since "in a relation of control, it is always and very electively interference with the other as a subject wishing that, as such, is characterized by its uniqueness, its own specificity[;] ... the influence thus reflects a fundamental tendency to neutralize the desire of others, that is to say, to reduce all otherness, any difference, the abolition of any specificity, being referred back to the other by function and having the status of a fully assimilable object." So here it falls precisely under the seal of seduction, to brand the other (a physical and symbolic meaning that covers the term *brand*) as if to deny the otherness, the brand then functions as a sign of ownership. It would therefore be, as Dorey shows, a fundamental opposition between "control" and "mastery." This may explain in general terms the brand's power to control consumers who are inextricably attached to them. This also allows a glimpse into why attachment to a brand may result in a kind of dependence that leads to a reification of the consumers whose desire is neutralized by the brand's exclusive attempt to own them.

It is therefore understandable why the call of Bernard Stiegler, in *Taking Care of the Youth and the Generations* (Stiegler, 2008), must be taken very seriously. If the economy of brands calls for developing a "pharmacology," it is important that the psycho-power thus created does not deform new generations by reducing them to mere non-subjects, consumers or "minors" lacking desires and who are driven to satisfy needs artificially created by the market.

2
Simplexities

How values structure the market?

Five pillars of the economy of brands

The rise of brands has helped to structure the market as well as to deploy a market culture that is based on five principles:

- A logic of *semanticization* consubstantial to the consumer society, which consists of enhancing market goods with an imagined dimension for staging them to make them desirable and therefore consumable. The strength of Marlboro lies in symbolically assimilating the cowboy smoking in America's wide open prairies by endowing him with the values of adventure, freedom and virility through a story, that of the Wild West, which is both a founding myth in American culture and a metaphor for the chance offered to the consumer to surpass his own limits. It is mainly through the use of symbolic code or logic of signs that goods acquire meaning. Hence the importance of brands which, by attaching values to products beyond their functional value, represent a key feature in the development of this code through an ongoing process of attributing meaning and re-attributing meaning. Smoking to become masculine or adventuresome, smearing oneself with cosmetics to dress up the faces of womanhood or using perfume to enhance one's romantic potential – these are all myths of an essentially symbolic economy of brands. Consumer society is thus based on the perpetual questioning of the concept of needs, even if it means the difference between real and artificial needs becomes impossible to discern due to the logic of social construction of needs. By substituting signs for goods, capitalism inexorably placed consumption in relation to attributing meaning more than to use and production.

- A logic of differentiation: the brand is primarily a matter of deviation and variance – *in fine*, displacement. One may especially consider two types of displacement at work in any brand: the first refers to a type of 'transportation' relationship linking the signifier to the signified; as Peninou said (1972), the brand ensures the passage of realism of the matter (the common name) to the symbolism of the name (ownership). The second displacement is the gap that the meaning of each brand must produce compared to the discursive productions of so-called competing brands. This is what we may call the brand's style as far as we are able to define style as a deviation from a standard.
- A logic of *premiumization*: the semanticization ability of a good for sale offers brands the opportunity to create goodwill and generate a *premium*, otherwise known as a *brand premium*, that is to say, a price differential the brand is likely to add compared to competing brands. The economy of brands is therefore essentially based on logic of premiumization of selling a product at a higher price than the reference retail price by casting it in an imagined dimension. The coupling of the symbolic function and premiumization function leads directly to the brand's ultimate function: to defunctionalize a commercial product by focusing attention on dimensions other than the product's functionality, doing so in order to make people forget the price and, paradoxically, also the product itself. This is the price where we are desensitized to the cost to increase awareness of the brand. It is what we call de-commoditization. In this way, Swatch does not sell watches, but "fashion accessories that incidentally tell the time." The same goes for Nike having literally transformed the sports shoe into a must-have accessory for trendy everyday wear.
- A logic of *market segmentation and benefits*: How indeed can brands claim a "premium effect" if not via positioning based on a clear, differentiated and specific benefit? Marketing's answer to this economic issue is the segmentation of benefits, from which is derived the famous dogma of the well-known USP (unique selling proposition), consisting of a brand claiming only one type of benefit in highly competitive markets. In other words, marketing ideology has long recommended that brands specialize in just one type of benefit: oral hygiene for brands like Elmex or Fluocaryl, sold in pharmacies; an active social life for Email Diamant or Ultra Brite; good taste for children's brands or a good price for most store brands (SB). In this way, the value-creation mechanism is historically linked to a segmentation of expectations logic and, therefore, a typology of consumer values.

- A logic of *rhetoric based on the principle of non-contradiction:* the brand's ability to defend a singular position is not sustainable in a Western cultural context unless from the moment the brand claims clear choices that rely on consistent principles. The very idea of an underlying conflict or contradiction that would decrease the brand's benefit is dismissed out of hand, hence the recurring difficulty of brands simultaneously to claim enjoyment and low calories, comfort, low price, and so forth. The rhetoric of Western brands is built on a series of oppositions based on the a priori exclusion of antagonistic principles.
- A logic of *expansion* that allows brands to benefit from their reputation, expertise and image to broaden their range of products (Diet Coke, Coca Cola Zero, Coca Cola Lemon, etc.) and enter into a new world of products. Thus the Bonne Maman brand, the brand of reference for jam, very successfully expanded into categories such as cookies, chilled desserts and ice cream. Another prime example is the Bic brand that we know has successfully conquered the pen market, razors, lighters, surfboards and cell phones. This expansion strategy proved less fruitful when Bic was inspired to enter the fragrance market or underwear market. These examples show that a brand extension is likely to work if three conditions are met: (a) Customers must perceive a link (in expertise or image) between the parent brand and the product emerging from the expansion; (b) the brand must have enough legitimacy to launch in this new market; and (c) the product must make a real contribution to the market and not be an existing product on which we are content to affix a logo (badging logic). Weight Watchers, for example, is much more legitimate in the healthy options market than is Colgate; Lego has failed to make a real contribution with its range of clothing for children.

Still, the dominant paradigm that rules the economy of brands is that of brand equity (the famous *brand equity*) that means to develop and enhance by employing an essentially shareholder logic characterized by separating the people who manage the brand and those who hold it. This decoupling is often very harmful, because it gives rise to the idea that the brand is just a cash machine that only serves to reinforce and increase shareholders' return on investment. However, the brand is primarily an anthropological device that, in addition to creating economic value, produces symbolic, cultural and anthropological values, as we shall now see.

Value of the brand versus consumption values

With these principles in mind, it is possible to consider the symbolic matrix that supports the economy of brands. What is this famous segmentation of principles that allows brands to position themselves and build value? The brand is a contract of trust, but this term is basically an oxymoron to the extent that a contract is needed when there is no trust, and vice versa.

Through the brand, the consumer is looking for an "object of desire," whether it be the pleasure of sleeping in a comfortable hotel bed, the comfort of a high-speed train or the social recognition gained from showing off a luxury product. The brand is therefore involved in a kind of "frivolity of value." In the words of Goux, this "frivolity" relates to a valuation of goods on the market quite characteristic of the development of capitalism. Indeed, adoption of a valuation method that takes into account the desires and expectations (i.e., personal) of the individual means a kind of abandonment of a naturalistic metaphysics of value. This value is not rooted in a stable foundation that ensures universality and stability, but is entered more in a regime of "desiring subjectivity." To quote Goux again, "the value is not a value in itself, written in the sky of ideas, inherent in things or guaranteed by the universal rule of a fixed calibration[;]...it is first of all value-for-me as I am a sentient and desiring being. The value comes not from the object to the subject, it leaves the subject (desiring) to project itself onto things, to temporarily form a valuable object" (Goux, 200: p. 11). The valuation process of a product or service by an individual includes both objective elements (which form a common template for all stakeholders involved in the process) as well as subjective elements. Car dealers are well aware that a woman will not care about the same features as a man when evaluating an automobile; she may consider elements such as the composition of the seat upholstery (is it cotton or synthetic?) or the space allocated for a child safety seat, while he undoubtedly is looking at features related to the engine, horsepower or fuel consumption. Understanding the value of a brand requires ousting a purely substantial worldview of value. The value of a brand is not an intrinsic quality but essentially depends on how it is valued (that is to say, invested with a certain value) at a given time by an individual.

So, rather than talk about value, it seems more appropriate to consider the *valuation processes*, that is to say, the ways consumers project their expectations, and thus meaning, onto brands. For example, when a consumer buys a bottle of mineral water, he can choose it for its good value or because he finds its packaging gives a good grip; or because he associates this brand with the image of a slim and toned body or he truly appreciates its taste and equates its consumption with a moment of pleasure and relaxation, or even because the packaging is recyclable.

We can actually distinguish two major categories of consumer expectations: on the one hand, very functional expectations (quality, timeliness, etc.) and, on the other, more existential expectations (fun, discovery, etc., Box 2.1).

Box 2.1 The semiotic square

The semiotic square is a tool for viewing the various modalities of a semantic category (that is to say, two contrary terms). Constructed from a pair of opposite terms (functional values versus existential values in our example), the convening of these two contradictions allows for providing a comprehensive tool for the terms of occurrence of the so-called semantic category.
Consider the "practical values versus utopian values" semantic axis. It is easy to see that these two terms are a semantic category wherein each presupposes the other by a conflicting relationship. Since structural semiotics starts from a simple principle – that any system of meaning is primarily a system of relationships – we will then focus on the various possible methods of the "continuous/discontinuous" semantic category; these two terms are linked by a conflicting relationship. One may imagine that relationships other than just conflict organize this semantic category. So, is it possible to consider, via a system of negation, the adversarial system of each of these terms? "Non-practical values" is the contradiction of "practical values." "Non-utopian values" meanwhile opposes "utopian values." Using these four terms it then becomes possible represent a square, called a semiotic square, which links the semantic category of consumption values according to the "practical-utopian" semantic axis. This square reveals three types of relationships:

- Horizontal contrary relationships
- Diagonal contradictory relationships
- Vertical complementarity relationships

This relates to a distinction made by structural semiotics between a program of use (related to functional values) and a program of life (related to existential values). Through the opposition of utilitarian values and existential values, the conflict behind a semantic category then allows, through the development of a semiotic square (called a valuation square), the identification of four types of expectations that correspond to four major value divisions (Floch, 1990).

- The practical side refers to values such as speed, functionality, and ergonomics. The consumer expects practical product brands to be easy to use, to make life easier and to streamline his existence;

- The practical side refers to budget optimization logic. The individual here is placed in a defiance relationship towards brands and expects a form of transparency of the relationship and reinsurance through values such as safety, warranty, good deals (not to be "ripped off"), and so forth.
- The utopian side offers the individual a link – that is to say, very basically the ability to place value into a world of meaning in order to build and share. This serves to maximize the social bond in all its forms: adventure, escape, dreaming, metamorphosis, and so forth.
- A hedonistic side that exists essentially in an experience economy via an optimization of sensory, emotional and affective stimulation.

To illustrate this square, take the example of the seemingly banal product that is the egg, by placing on the square possible types of consumer expectations in this product category.

The square shows four very different approaches to the egg.

- A *logic of need* values such things as availability (the brand should be easy to find), freshness (recent laying day), etc.
- A *logic of desire,* which enhances the taste, whether the product is organic or not, part of a fair-trade scheme, etc.
- A *logic of interest* that values quality/price ratio or even the labels guaranteeing the product development process.
- A *logic of enjoyment* that values things such as size, taste, color, etc.

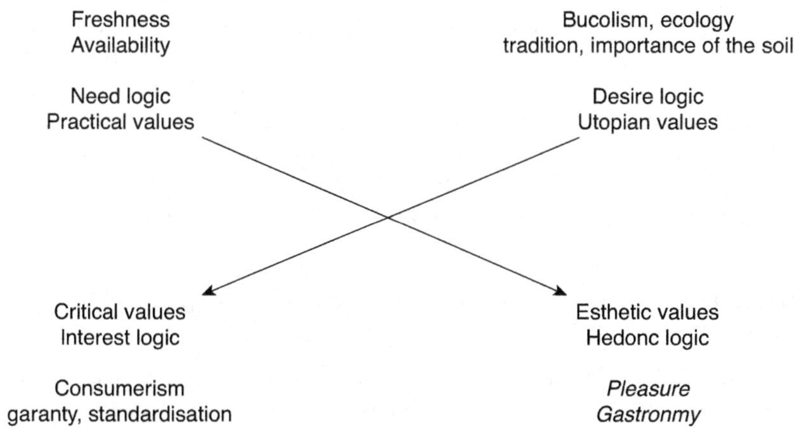

Figure 2.1 Major logics of valuing an egg
Source: Diagram designed by Jean Marie Floch.

Based on this typology, it is now possible to propose a typology of consumption values that points out the four types of contracts brands may have with their customers.

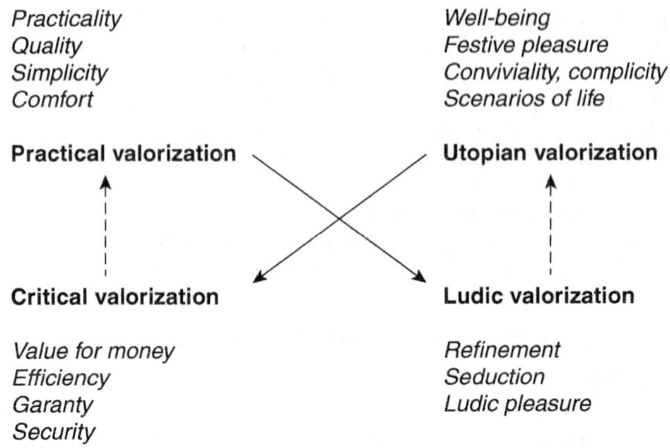

Figure 2.2 The four main areas of consumption values

The idea that a brand is a contract of trust with customers has forced brands to specify their contracts by building trusting relationships based on a clear, unique and differentiated benefit in the minds of consumers: hence, the economy of brands eventually led to a specialization of brands by area of expertise. Generally, a market is built on a functional core, so brands are not tempted to migrate to the areas of life before alternative offers can be deployed only for the critical area (low cost, the category killers, hard discount). There would be a natural evolution of brands, a kind of gentrification in which they have a natural propensity to turn utilitarian values towards life values in a clear premiumization logic in that it is actually easier to sell an expensive branded product in a utopian and hedonistic logic than in a purely practical or critical logic.

Removing symbols and the advent of the contradictory result

It is clear that premiumization reflects, as much as it reveals, a form of symbolic message, and to the extent that the brand image value is too often disconnected from the utility value of the products, the simulacrum having swallowed the symbolic power of brands to transform them into meaningless systems. But, in the environment of a perceived reduction in purchasing power, would individuals forever be willing to pay exorbitant sums to purchase branded products whose proposed benefits are as varied as joy, eternal youth or even dematerialization?

While brands have largely de-functionalized products and services to enhance value-capture in growing markets and gradually have been emptied of their substance by emphasizing the principles of image and impact, the question of legitimacy arises for these same brands in saturated markets and diminishes for most brands. No longer able to surf on purely emotional logic, and unable to simply return to a functional contract due to the complexity of expectations and delivery systems, brands must reinvent contractual arrangements with their consumers/customers. This is where a suspension of belief comes in with respect to brands that are not legitimized by differentiating expertise or actual functionality.

Some brands (well-established successful brands) offer a new approach to market value. This new approach is based on a form of de-symbolization that results by matching the brands' image value with the utility value of the products and services being sold, as well as clearly linking of principles that could be seen as contradictory.

For this reason (the logic of brand segmentation), some brands operate silently in mutation of the model structuring the economy of brands, as we shall see in the following text. Rather than thinking about means of valuation and benefits in terms of opposition, they have substituted a logic of linking in the types of contracts. In this way, we are allowed to assume that, in a post-consumer society freed from any symbolic message, the brands will have to specify four types of contracts: a *practical contract* (with products or services that are easy to use and show true technical expertise); a *critical contract* (dependable products and good value for the money); *utopian contract* (offering a vision of the world beyond the framework of its category); and a *hedonistic contract* (offering a unique consumer experience that sets in motion different sensory and affective plans). A simplicity model that emblemizes the coherent positioning logic is gradually substituted by a form of complexity wherein brands have captured the biological concept of "simplexity" covering the solutions found by living organisms in order to act in complex environments. As Berthoz, who greatly popularized this concept, recalled, these solutions are simplistic principles for dealing with situations in the light of past experience and for anticipating the future. Neither caricatures nor short cuts, they are new ways to pose problems and act on the world, sometimes at the cost of a few detours, for faster, more efficient reach and more elegant actions. This is the price that brands may pay in the complexity of the post-consumer society and become the contracts of trust that they never should have ceased to be.

'Brandtopia' and the neutralization effect

Brands have become an essential dimension of the so-called marketing democracy. They now represent economic entities but are also sources of power and legitimacy that impose modes of thinking and behaving. A brand may be viewed not solely as a sign added to products to differentiate them from competing goods, but as a semiotic engine the function of which is to constantly produce meaning and values. A brand is therefore a narrative entity that imposes itself as a natural source of ideological and biological power in the Foucauldian sense of power, which is a set of "actions on others' actions". Power does not act directly; it presupposes rather than annuls the capacity of individuals as agents; it acts upon, and through, an open set of practical and ethical possibilities (Foucault, 1997, Gordon, 1991: 5).

Furthermore, the ideology promoted both explicitly and implicitly by brands is also closely related to the main paradigm of consumption, which equals consumption with happiness. Based on these assumptions, this chapter will now attempt to show how strong brands promote ideological systems that are constantly based on utopian models. This means that branding ideologies borrow from theologico-political models developed since the book *Utopia* by Thomas More.

Utopia, you've said u-topia ...

Utopia is a word originating from both the Greek and the Latin, first used by Thomas More in his classical book, *Utopia*. Utopia literally means "nowhere", that is, a place which stands in no place, a sort of absent presence, an unreal reality, a kind of nostalgic elsewhere, an alterity with no identification. This name is therefore linked to a series of paradoxes: Amaurotus, the capital of the island is a ghost city; its river, Anhydris, has no water, its leader, Ademus, is a prince with no people to govern; its inhabitants, the Aplaopolites, are citizens without a city, and their neighbors, the Achoreans, are inhabitants with no country. Utopia is thus based on a philological transformation (a sort of prestidigitation) which aims mainly at announcing the plausibility of an upside down world and, at the same time, to cast shadow over the legitimacy of a right-side-up world.

What are the main features of this Utopia?

- *Reproductibility*: the island, which is separated from the rest of the world, comprises 54 cities, all based on the same architectural model; there is a great similarity among houses in each city; the streets and houses of the cities are built according to a geometrical pattern, with pleasant houses and gardens which are exchanged between the citizens every ten years;

- The importance of work, which is the basis of society and which creates prosperity. Stores are always full of merchandise thanks to the economy's efficiency and the rationally planed distribution system. The working system is organized in such a way that members of the commonwealth learn the craft for which they are most suited. Working hours alternate with leisure activities: six hours of the day are devoted to work, while the rest of the time is spent in healthy recreation and learning;
- The absence of possession, property and hoarding. There are no tailors or modelists so that the inhabitants focus their attention on important things. All citizens wear the same clothes of undyed wool with distinctions only for gender or marital status. The Utopians do not value gold or silver, but use them to manufacture fetters and chamber pots;
- The two fundamental dogmas on which all Utopians agree are, first, the immortality of the soul and, second, the presence in the universe of Providence. Utopians also believe in the existence of rewards and punishments after death.

Utopia as representation and fiction

These patterns serve a specific function regarding reality, history, and social relationships. This function is essentially a critical one, the aim of which is to show (through the picture drawn by the Utopian writer or designer) the *differences* between social reality and a projected model of social existence. The representation possesses this critical power without being aware of it; the critical impact of Utopia is not the model itself, but the difference between the model and reality. But this critical discourse, which is a latent characteristic of all utopias, is not separated from dominant systems of values and ideas: it expresses itself through the structures, the notions, of those systems by which individuals represent their real conditions of existence. Utopia functions as a possible intervention of reason in the social field and is nothing else than the real, iconic or textual picture of this "possibility." Utopia thus has a two-sided nature: on the one hand it expresses what is absolutely new, the "possible as such," that is, what is unthinkable in the common categories of thought used by the people at a given time; it must thus employ fiction or fable to express what it has to say; on the other hand, it appears impossible for Utopia to transcend the ordinary language of period and place – that is, it cannot totally transgress the codes by which people make reality significant to them.

So the Utopian language is a representation of an ideal mode of collective existence that at the same time must innovate to improve the existing state of affairs, and also must represent this innovation through the vocabulary used by people to interpret reality. The fictional and representative power of an utopian world must be based on the ordinary system of representation. Utopia serves as a rhetorical device. It may be conceived as a metaphor the aim of which is to convey across time some guiding principles of ideal societies though a criticism of existing political systems.

Utopia and ideology

Beyond this representational and fictional power lies a propensity for the utopian system to promote a strong ideology. We may then follow Marin's statements about the relationship between ideology and Utopia (Marin, 1973, 1977):

(1) An ideology is a system of representations of the imagined relationships individuals have with their actual living conditions.
(2) Utopia is an ideological locus: it belongs to the ideological discourse.
(3) Utopia is an ideological locus where ideology is put into play and called into question. Utopia is the stage whereon an ideology is performed and represented.
(4) A myth is a narration that fantastically "resolves" a fundamental contradiction in a given society.

The utopian system is also based on an inner contradiction that is structured by the category of the neutral.

Towards an ideology of neutrality

Utopia is a place out of place; it essentially refers to the category of the neutral (Marin, 1973). What is neutral is neither true nor false, neither masculine nor feminine, neither active nor passive, neither this, neither that.... Neutrality exists as a contradiction and, more essentially, as a differentiation of contrary terms that are maintained in a polemical movement. Neuter allows an impossible synthesis, a productive differentiation, and the reconciliation of an acting contradiction. Neutral is the name given to limits, to contradiction itself (Marin, 1977: 51).

Neutrality could define itself in a relationship to a dynamic totality the component parts of which are in opposition and in positions of marked difference. Neuter functions as a conjunction of contraries. It is placed in the center of the structure, it constitutes its organizational principle and it allows the substitution of elements in the total shape of the system. Power is what exerts itself through the potential reference of the neuter. The state, for instance, presents itself as neutral and plays arbitrator between different parties. Utopia recuperates the unbearable neutral with a logic joining together the contradictory terms. Utopia makes it possible to think of and to formulate the contradiction signified by the notion of neutral. As a fiction, Utopia transforms contradiction into a representation. Utopia, as defined by Thomas More, and as developed in many successive works of fiction or political or philosophical texts, assumes a certain number of paradoxes.

The zigzag of brands

The representational and fictional function of Utopia may in fact very well be applied to brands. A brand always more or less promotes a critical discourse on existing products and brands, that is on a given market situation. A brand always more or less implies that what it has to offer is better or different from what already exists and what competitors offer. A brand is a kind of value offer which can only be legitimized through the claim of a significant difference, be it material (a "better" or "new" product, new colors or materials, new functions, etc.) or discursive (the way the brand speaks about its products). A brand acts as a narrative program that must promote a system of material and discursive differences so as to justify and legitimize its existence among other brands and so as to create consumers' preference.

A brand cannot create a total innovation in order to avoid the risk of being rejected by the market because of an unacceptable degree of newness and strangeness; a brand must therefore communicate and build its rhetorical power on existing market codes using a psychological framework that is familiar to market actors (consumers, retailers, etc.). It means the brand should position its products using (even if it deforms them) existing market categories, existing terminologies, and so forth. Brand innovation should thus always zigzag between the two extremes, which are pure originality and banality. A brand discourse is thus always more or less utopian by nature.

Big, bing, brand: from management to government

Furthermore, it can be said that the symbolic power of brands has tremendously evolved in occidental societies. In an era of "world disenchantment" (Gauchet, 1997), new ideological sources of power emerge.

There seems to be a sort of displacement of current ideology sources from the theological and the political towards the economic. In a "desecularized" context, economic entities (and mostly brands) have taken the symbolic place left empty by the retreat of the divine. Brands now preempt symbolic spheres that used to be the privilege of either religion or the political. Among the numerous examples that could be quoted are:

- the borrowing of Judeo–Christian myths by brands: Santa Claus and its use by Coca-Cola provides a good example of this cultural and ideological borrowing;
- highly symbolic activities are now managed by economic entities: retailers now organize social events such as weddings (by taking in charge wedding lists for instance); they also sell coffins (the French retailer Leclerc has created a sub-brand that provides funerary services) and attempt to exert their power as soon as the baby is born; young mothers in the hospital are provided with sponsored baskets containing branded diapers, baby bottles and other baby products so as to create a strong emotional attachment towards these brands in a moment that is both symbolically and affectively of a high significance for parents;
- the management of urban quarters or even cities might be delegated to economic entities. Disney manages theme parks but also a whole city in the United States, with its own banks and supermarkets; Disney provides its own currencies to be used in the American parks, where it is possible to buy products with "Disney dollars," etc.

There thus seems to be a radical evolution of the role of brands from management to government. Some brands have become governing brands; we understand governmentality in the Foucauldian sense as "the conduct of conduct," that is to say, a form of activity aiming to shape, guide or affect the conduct of some person or persons. In this sense, governmentality concerns brand–consumer relationships, but also, more globally, relations within societies. Through the power of their ubiquity, their visibility and their ability to promote endless discourse, brands shape the way we see ourselves, others and the world in general. Through very prescriptive discourses, they govern part of how we think about our daily universe and most of our daily actions. We now would like to show that in order to participate in any kind of societal governmentality, brands act as utopian entities that promote a strong ideology through a series of paradoxes. This means the dialectic category of totality is unknown to Utopia. Utopia is dominated by a postulate of anti-dialectical homogeneity: it is essentially a schizophrenic universe.

"Happiness is a warm gun"

Brands have the need to promote one of contemporary society's key values: happiness. They promote an ideology based on the infusion of happiness: the better versus the best in a context of competition; differentiation creates a type of discourse not solely based on "think different" or "this is better than that", but on "this is 'The' Best," as if there were no possible alternative. Differentiation, a key branding concept, only exists through the possibility to propose joy, satisfaction, pleasure – the key values structuring the imagined universe of consumer society. A discourse on happiness is always more or less linked to a kind of theologico–political paradigm. As a narrative on the ideal society, *Utopia* is a good illustration of this necessary conjunction of economic, theological and political principles: *Utopia* is opposed to *"dystopia,"* which means negation and unhappiness.

Let us go back to the More's Utopia. Two kinds of philosophies are expressed here. In the book, two sects with opposite values coexist. There are those who believe in life after death, renounce earthly pleasures, live singly and do not eat meat (they will earn immortality). The other sect has no objection to pleasure (as long as it does not impede their work) and approve of marriage because they think that procreation is a necessary duty. There is in Utopia a sort of neutral religious philosophy which is neither humanist nor Christian and is, in fact, based (as Marin showed) on both a criticism of false pleasures (which represents, in fact, a criticism of nobility) and a criticism of honest pleasures (which represents a critical ethics of ascetism). Thus there seem to be two kinds of values expressed in the Utopian universe. On the one hand, a narrative program based on practical and critical values; and on the other hand, a narrative program based on life or existential values.

This dichotomy relates to the two main registers of values potentially conveyed by branding discourses: For one, values linked to a narrative program of usage and, second, values linked to a narrative program of life. It is now time to show that brands carry inner contradictions in the sense they always more or less articulate both sides of the semiotic square. We may even say that the power of a brand lies in its ability to articulate both practical and utopian values. Brands are paradoxical entities with a doublethink approach – see this notion of doublethink in George Orwell's novel, *Nineteen Eighty-Four* (1948). Brands have a propensity to create solliptical universes governed by their own rules. They function as small utopian models that articulate two kinds of values which, at first glance seem contradictory. This is what we previously called the "dilemma of brands" (Heilbrunn, 1998a). We will now have a look at four examples taken from different consumption universes.

McDonald's, food and fun ...

Ritzer has very well illustrated the fact that the main principles driving McDonald's philosophy of action are contradictory by nature. They are:

- efficiency (streamlining the process, simplifying the product, putting customers to work, etc.);
- calculability: emphasizing quantity rather than quality, giving the illusion of quantity, reducing processes of production and service to numbers;
- predictability: replicating the setting, scripting interaction with customers, delivering predictable products and predicting employees' behavior;
- control exerted on customers, products and processes;
- the appearance of leisure: along with the illusion of efficiency, McDonald's illustrates the propensity of restaurants to become theatrical and to become amusement parks for food. McDonald's uses for this purpose a ubiquitous clown, but also an array of cartoon characters to remind people that fun awaits them on their next visit (Ritzer, 1996: p. 125).

The reconciliation of apparently contradictory values may be seen on the semiotic square on which we tried to position all the possible material and discursive value manifestation of the McDonald's brand.

Disneyland and the destructuration of time

Disneyland is a good example of the materialization of an utopian brand's discourse through spatialization. The organization of space is a constitutive dimension of any utopia; More's Utopia represents a crisis of the historic temporalization. Historic time, as concrete and reversible, is a stranger to Utopia. The realization of any Utopia means the stopping of historical time. Utopian time is essentially de-structured, degraded. Time is suspended. In *Brave New World,* Aldous Huxley makes a remarkable suggestion: To assure the stability of human institutions and to subtract them from time ascendency, he suggests there be no interval between desire and satisfaction. This distortion of time,

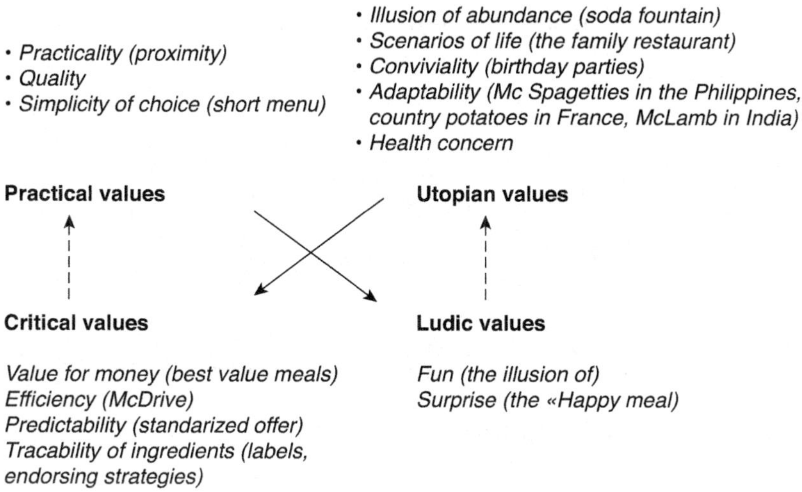

Figure 2.3 How McDonald's covers the whole spectrum of consumption values

as well as the materialization of utopian values, is highly visible in "Disneyland." Disney alienates the spectator of the park by a distorted fantasy representation of daily life, through a fascinating picture of the past and the future, of what is strange and what is familiar: comfort, luxury, consumption, scientific progress, technological innovation, superpower, morality. Marin has shown, for instance, how the material organization of Disney illustrates the inner contradictions of the utopian model. Disneyland is organized around Main Street USA, which acts as a universal operator and helps develop the narrative chosen by the park. It has three main functions: (a) a *phatic* function that allows all the possible stories to be narrated; (b) a *referential* function, through which reality becomes a fantasy and an image – an *integrative* function: this space divides Disneyland into two parts, left and right, and relates these two parts to each other. Main Street USA also has a semantic content. It is the place where the visitor may buy, in 19th-century American decor, real commodities, either with his real money or with Disney money. Main Street USA is a locus of exchange of meanings and symbols in the imaginary land of Disney, but also a real place of exchange of money and commodity. This place is also an evocation of the past, and this is an attempt to reconcile and exchange, in this very place, the past and the present – that is an ideal past and a real present. It is the symbolic center through which all the contrary poles are exchanged, in both the

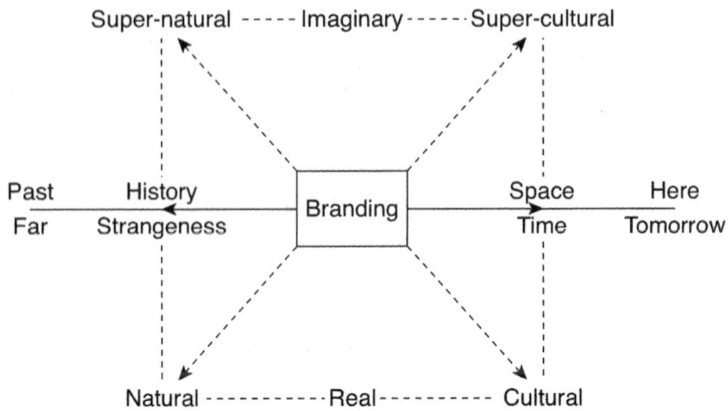

Figure 2.4 Disneyland as a degenerate utopia
Source: After Marin (1977).

economic and semantic meanings of the term. This place assures the fictional reconciliation of several opposite worlds and, by this narrative, the visitor performs, enacts, reconciliation (Marin, 1977: 58).

Brands as transformative devices

Brands are paradoxical because they promote contradictory principles, but also because they make different, and often opposite, levels coexist. They essentially act as transformative agents that allow contradictory principles to coincide. These dimensions, which necessarily coexist in any brand's discourse, are the following:

- conjunction of nature and culture: brands are technological as well as semantic devices that transform natural ingredients into products. What is a product but a cultural and marketed object that results from an industrialization process of transformation of something that is culturally consumable, that is, which fits in existing cultural categories. Be it the transformation of milk into Danone's yoghurt, the transformation of water into Evian, the transformation of leather into Hermès luggage, of cotton into a pair of Levi's jeans, or the transformation of a cow into a series of McDonald's hamburgers, branding is a magical device of transformation based on the serialization of objects, the consumability of objects. Brands make objects appear to be cultural entities (culture is seen here, according to Mary Douglas's perspective, as an entity that provides a categorization of goods and make categories visible). This transformation occurs through the conjunction of material processes (industrialization, technological know-how, etc.) and through discursive devices that help position the object in a cultural dimension though packaging, advertising discourses, and so forth. Furthermore, the process might be reversed by re-transforming this cultural object into a so-called natural object. A brand like Body Shop is a good example of this tendency to position a cultural object as a "natural" one, legitimizing it through the use of so-called natural ingredients, or by the ethical choice not to test any products on animals. A brand might therefore transform a natural object into a cultural product and this cultural product onto a naturalized object again. This naturalization of culture is a widely used strategy to meet environmental expectations (biological food products, hygiene products, etc.), but also because of a kind of nostalgia expressed by urban citizens to live closer to "nature" and their urge to consume so called "natural products."

- conjunction of super-natural and super-cultural: following the culturalization of nature and the symmetrical effect which is the naturalization of culture, there exists the possibility to "super-culturalize" products. This is especially true for technological products; the main rhetorical device of innovation is to show a technological mastering and control of the brand, which possesses the ability to find new materials, new processes, new uses of the product (the Walkman is a good illustration) or even to redefine psychological categories by which consumers view the various consumption fields. The Dockers brand is a good example of such a strategy. This sub-brand of Levi's established itself by mixing-up two existing perceptual categories in the clothing industry and by proposing the "casual-business-wear" category. In this case a brand is a super-culturalized device that establishes new cultural categories. A symmetrical device is the super-naturalization process, by which the brand transforms through a kind of magic.
- conjunction of the imaginary and the real as illustrated by Disneyland, where permanently coexist characters from imaginary universes and also visitors and staff, who definitely belong to the real world. Disneyland functions as a permanent exchange between spheres of the imaginary and spheres of reality.
- conjunction of past and present dimensions: a brand exists in a temporal dimension, and its history gives it a legitimacy and is the

main variable through which its equity is built up. Brands need to permanently reassess the customers they have acquired over a long time because this time period implies the development of a know-how, the possibility to build long-term relationships with trade partners (intermediaries) and customers. To really be instilled in the consumer's life, brands need to root their existence in an historical time. There is an implicit postulate by which a time period (at least one generation) is what gives a brand competence, which is the ability to perform; the time dimension implicitly roots a sort of performance-excellence. If one goes back to the narrative scheme that articulates the four stages of any brand–consumer relationship, it is quite obvious that the temporal dimension (in a long historical perspective) is what allows the brand to show the acquisition of competence and thus the ability to perform, thereby being able, implicitly or not, to accomplish its original mission and be credited with a positive endorsement – that is to be recognized as a hero.

- conjunction of the very-distant and the here-and-now: brands often show the power to make the distant close (that is to abolish distance) and to make the close distant (through a sort of re-enchantment power of our dull daily lives). Distance is an important paradigm, be it geographical distance (the brand brings back exotic products and ingredients into our occidental sphere) or a cultural distance (the brand borrows sources of discourses from various cultural influences). At the same time distance needs to be abolished in order to achieve a kind of proximity with consumers. Brands function as rhetorical devices whose purpose is jointly to create and to abolish distance.

Utopian brands as transformative devices

Infinitive neutralization

Strong brands are often said to impose strong ideological discourses characterized by definite positions and by strongly established differences with competitors. Paradoxically, the contrary could also be said, that is, the power of a brand lies in its ability to infuse on the market a contradictory system of values based on the category of the neutral.

Following Louis Marin's pioneering semiotic decoding of Disneyland, the decoding of brands discourses and ideologies outline the strong propensity of brands to elaborate so-called utopian models that represent in fact *a-topian* models. By a sort of magical transformation, brands help opposite values to be reconciled. By a kind of paradox, the so-called strongly established position of a brand is transformed into an out-of-time and out-of-space position, a sort of non-position, as if it were an a-position.

The brand can be called to question when it becomes demiurgic by the appropriation of a too-vast world (symbolic or physical). The brand message swells to engulf an ever-larger imaginary dimension (one that is therefore less specific) and owns the equivalent of a generic type. Hence, a kind of drifting towards infinitive thought (in the literal meaning of "endless, limitless") of the brand message which, by an amplification process, opens to an infinite and generic world. One can certainly argue that the infinitive form is important in the brand message, insofar as Fournier summoned it up (in a book with the evocative title, *Infinitive Thoughts*): "Thinking is done in the infinitive" because "all thought is in the infinitive and may only be expressed using infinitives[;]... verbs (conjugate) amongst themselves without worrying about nouns or qualifiers" (Fournier, 2000: p. 9). A brand's creation of a real language therefore imposes an ideology implicitly expressed by the infinitive form of the message. If we consider that one of the functions of metaphor, in its purely cognitive dimension, is to increase the informative value or enhance certain traits of the image, then it is perfectly legitimate to consider the relevance of using the infinitive form. But before a sort of metaphorical will snaps up the entirety of a world in a metaphorical brand signature (the world's taste, beauty, nature, etc.), a question necessarily arises about the legitimacy and relevance of said metaphor. In other words, is there not a denial of the metaphorical process when the argumentative logic has exclusive use in its imperative form? By vivacity of desire, the metaphor can graze the emptiness in that the infinitive form prevents the (implicit) relation between comparing and compared that is based precisely on the metaphorical process. This phenomenon is quite telling in the message some brands teach about the concept of life, and manifests the recovery of vital daily activities throughout the commercial sphere. For example, consider one of the shocking sentences found in Carrefour's corporate communications: "Consuming also serves to build one's life." The metaphorical effect is negated to the extent that the parallel is explicitly affirmed between the two terms ("consuming" and "build one's life"), while the metaphor requires precisely that this relationship remain implicit. This denial of metaphorical thinking accompanies the use of an infinitive form that makes the metaphor eventually lose its specific character. As you strive so hard to embrace it, the metaphor eventually hugs nothing. Even more, the infinitive form seems to get rid of any specificity, particularly the subject. As Fournier further said, thinking in the infinitive leads "to thinking without worrying about nouns or adjectives, (so that) we pass subjects. And also their substitutes and their attributes: pronouns, articles, adverbs" (Fournier, 2000: p. 9). The danger of the infinitive metaphor is then transmuted into a kind of *undefined* thought (although the metaphor must precisely specify a reality metaphorically). Fournier at once saw the power, both in the indefinite demiurgic of the infinitive form when he says "the infinitive provides us not only an ethic and aesthetic, but also an *insubstantive* metaphysic" (Fournier, 2000: p. 9). The metaphor deployed in an infinitive form refers to a fundamentally demiurgic side of "to be," which passes the comparatives and aims to abstract from a purely differential logic. The all-encompassing metaphor no longer accepts any comparative. It tends to become absolute and thereby eliminate any concept of displacement based on the substrate of the metaphor, especially from a branding perspective.

Through the infinitive, it is ultimately the indefinite that looms over the metaphor, that is to say, a kind of absence of meaning. It is in this sense that one can say that the too-large metaphorical gap is, in the end, a metonymic trick that encompasses the whole (a world of meaning) by means of the party (the brand). This question is at the heart of the issue of any major brand attempting to create a world and become the ultimate instance of speech.

The brand's two bodies

The economy of brands is based on a rapid turnover of products and ranges to attract a clientele whose shopping is largely driven by the search for variety. But, at the same time, brands derive their legitimacy from a form of historical depth that requires continuity of style and know-how. This paradox is quite telling in the world of fashion due to the scansion that imposes a whole world facing an unprecedented and permanent connection with the moment, coupled with the perseverance of every major brand's own aesthetic heritage. How to combine the need for recourse to the past with the scansion, discontinuity and thus the rupture imposed by the world of fashion? In other words, how to turn back while fashion justly requires being "rooted in the historical moment and accepting change." We believe in the new while we capitalize on the old – that is on the story that fashion brands continue to weave, often claiming to do so in the shadow of a prestigious deceased designer. Is there not an intrigue of a religious nature through which the spirit would again be present in her work?

Ghost stories

In his book, *Ghosts*, Jean-Claude Schmitt showed that in feudal society (12th to the 13th centuries), where death is not an end, there is a close link between the living and the dead, the here and the hereafter. Death is a line that is crossed in steps, it is a "passage." In the beyond, "survival of the double" remains governed by time and the memory of people, and the spaces for the dead (the cemetery, the edges of the land, etc.), without confusing them with spaces for the living, are closely associated to them. Thus the passage can move in the other direction, too: sometimes the dead visit the living. What is the nature of these apparitions? The question concerns the object of the vision (the "death," the "soul," a "spirit?") as well as the functions of the imagination that, *in fine*, return to the two sides of the same issue: the status of the person and the complex relationship of the body and soul. Now, the brand is first of all, a soul that must be incorporated into physical devices (what we can call work, object, product, etc.) in order to give substance to an essentially intangible value. The first temptation is often to return to a form of continuity of the brand's own body, which is the product. Brands have a temptation to give historical depth, to dig into their past by updating vintage products (this is the case of Adidas) or reinterpreting their past as evidenced by the nostalgia of modernizing iconic products of bygone eras (the new Beetle, the mini Cooper, etc.). This practice of self-glorification from the roots gives the brand the illusion of an archaeological base; another thing is to give a temporal thickness befitting the works. Yet, the brand cannot survive by glorifying its past ad infinitum without risking a race to the abyss. The identity dynamics of a brand cannot consist of continually repeating its past (Chanel could not survive by offering only quilted bags, shoes or the suit Coco designed), but by coherently moving away from it. Sooner or later, a brand's evolution eventually leads to breaking away from the iconic products and therefore requires forms of continuity (for lack of contiguity) to compensate for the discontinuity this world necessarily imposes by nature. Thus, Chanel lives on through an ongoing reinterpretation of its founding values (freedom and maintenance) in clothes and accessories that wisely combine classical and baroque. But beyond this maintenance of a certain ethical aim over time (free the woman) backed by an aesthetic vision, the name of the founder endures as a form of guarantee. It thus serves to add to the "know-how" that founded the brand, a necessary "make believe" that legitimizes its perseverance by often letting be heard the continuation of a work despite the death of the designer.

The story of the work

At the first level of consideration, the brand is nothing more than a device to create preference in competitive markets. It then roughly perpetuates the three anthropological features highlighted by Georges Dumézil (1968), namely (a) to provide a form of sovereignty related to the specific know-how and an original way to combine ethics and aesthetics; (b) to create one's own territory in a warlike relationship to differentiate from competing brands; and (c) ensure the reproduction of the signs and processes in the dimensions of space and time. While marketing has focused on the warlike dimensions (as evidenced by all spatial metaphors, such as linear, market share, the brand's territory, etc.) and reproduction (failing in design), the question of sovereignty in an industrial logic remains unanswered. How to give strength and power to a product in a crowded line and in a disintermediated economy?

Originally, the brand had a signature function (notably that of the artisan) that aimed to ensure a kind of link between the place of production, the artisan and the place where the product is sold. Hence, an ownership of its origins that can be traced precisely to demonstrate a source and know-how. The issue of sovereignty is not a major problem in an artisanal logic that enables a physical link between human design conditions of the object and the consumer. But how to append a name to a product (which is not implemented) in a logic of serial and industrial production? How to believe in the even-fictional presence of a pseudo-author or designer when the product comes from a standardized assembly line? Worse, how can the brand claim a designer who has died or been absent from the creative process for one reason or another? By what fictional series can the brand embody a deceased person or one who is missing from the product-development process?

In her book, *The Human Condition,* Hannah Arendt opposes *labor,* conceived as a repetitive activity that never ends, and prefers *work,* which on the contrary recognizes a beginning and an end. Artisanal production indeed knows an exact beginning and an end insofar as produce indicates the idea of creating (*poiein* in Greek), as well as to begin, to take an initiative (*archein* in Greek). However, by replacing artisanal production with manufacturing labor, the industrial revolution replaced "signed" work with an "anonymous" product. That being said, the division between labor and work is incomplete, and it is possible to consider a spectrum of cultural mediations and techniques that fall between the anonymity of the product and the signature of the work, including the degree of scarcity of the product. Artisanal work is found midway along the path. The handicraft or artisanal object is actually a series of products, but in an area in which the series is limited by the archaic state of technology and the care required to make it, which instills each one with a certain rarity. This type of product is defined by types, genres and styles that make it easily recognizable to specialists and which, in some cases, have the "signature" of the master artisan who headed production. Thus, for example, the violins of Stradivarius, the furniture of Cressent or de Boulle in the 18th century. However in the modern industrialized world, we often seek to artificially recreate the nature of "limited edition" and the scarcity of artisanal works. Next, we consider the artisanal products of contemporary luxury (from Fabergé to Hermès) as industrial stories of the artwork. Yet luxury artisanal products of the 17th and 18th centuries were a kind of artworks in series. The story of the work is possible only when assuming the kind of story that Michel Foucault speaks about (Foucault, 1994). However, as Foucault shows, in asking the question of the author, it is assumed that a certain number of productions will be considered as forming a "work," that this work can be assigned to an "author" whose proper name refers to a particular individual, with a singular biography. This should ensure the unity of the work by relating it to a single focus of expression. The paradox is that while the brand designates an assignable work, as we shall see, an individual making the product is the result of a group effort. In this sense, the brand frames individual expertise and the perseverance of a group working. So, it would be better to talk about story-author since it generally refers to an individual, whereas the development of a garment is the fruit of a collective effort, thus bringing the notion of the signing of master paintings into the logics of a workshop. It underpins a story of continuity of the act of the designer despite the death or departure of a designer (one thinks, for example, of Yves Saint-Laurent). This story is especially important in an economy of outsourcing and the designer's increasing separation from his brand (for instance, the case of Sonia Rykiel deprived of the rights of use of her brand). The signature therefore makes a charismatic legitimacy lasting in an industrial order, even when the founder is deceased or no longer active in the business.

The nominal story

The economy of brands is that of a plethora as well as a crisis of brands, so that brands face a constant problem of legitimacy in markets that are increasingly saturated and commoditized. Yet legitimacy is ultimately "the sign the product bears and that tells the consumer the product is what it appears to be." Coming from a rational kind of legitimacy related to the serialization of the product, the brand must nevertheless invoke other forms of legitimacy to create some aura with consumers. To ensure the validity of the work–brand story, it is therefore necessary to enshrine two types of legitimacy systems, such as Max Weber defined them, namely, on the one hand, "traditional legitimacy" and on the other hand, "charismatic legitimacy." Traditional legitimacy is based on a reference to the existence of *rules* and *traditional procedures* whose memory generally lies with a particular social group to whom members of society vow respect that inspires the venerable nature of the institutions (i.e., the company or brand) to be thus preserved. This type of legitimacy refers to the idea of sedimentation and temporal perpetuation of ancestral know-how (the concept of trade secret) of the brand (e.g., brands based on the mastery of a line of products like Lacoste polo shirts or Louis Vuitton trunks). Charismatic legitimacy refers, in turn, to the presence of the sacred, a presence most often embodied in a charismatic leader and evidenced by the faith that he devotes to all members of society; it is therefore based on the devotion of subjects to the leader's heroism, exceptional powers (such as the ability to perform miracles) as well as the normative order that he approves. The need to envelop manufactured products in a form of charismatic legitimacy very early led to the phenomena of personification of the brand intrinsic to the branding of the phenomenon and provides a historical transition from a production-based economy to the realism of the physical (the products have a generic name), to an economy of the brand founded on the symbolism of the person (the labeled product has a proper name that individualizes it). How, then, to conjoin these two types of legitimacy if not by the use of a patronymic brand, including the eponymous that takes the name of the founder? The first brands were historically family names because the first anthropological function of the brand is the identification function. This often takes place directly by taking on the family name of the designer (it is what we call an antonomasia). Hence a monogram's meaning more or less fills the role of a seal in ensuring the mastery of know-how, and undoubtedly brings to mind the demiurgic nature of the act of producing. We find so many family name brands in sectors where the concept of know-how is a key differentiator, namely the food sector (Lipton, Perrier, Perrier-Jouët Champagne Mercier, etc.), the automotive sector (Renault, Peugeot, Citroën, etc.) and, of course, fashion (Christian Dior, Jean-Paul Gaultier, YSL, etc.), which we will now discuss.

A signature, for example, carries a style, an aesthetic, a way to mesh materials, to imagine colors – in short a means to give an identity to a garment beyond the usual categories (dress, shirt, sweater, etc.). It is then adorned with a signature function recalling the demiurgic nature of the act of weaving. In fact, it is emblematic of a *production narrative* based primarily on the defense of know-how and special expertise.

But how to combine the idea of permanent novelty that belongs to fashion with the death or departure of the iconic figure of the founder? What relationship exists today between the multiple products associated with the Cardin brand (due to the brand's expansion through licensing) and the original designer's expertise? The eponymous raises the issue of the value of an object in an industrial society that standardizes objects and the manufacturing process. Can Poilâne bread, developed in 1932 by Pierre – hand-crafted with flour ground at the mill, using natural sourdough fermentation and baked over a wood fire, legitimately carry the same brand name as what is made today with an automated process in the Bièvres factory in Essonne?

Thus, the eponymous is not without some problems, for several reasons:

- Due to a sometimes-illegitimate and excessive use of the names of famous people to call attention to products with which they have no direct link (what link could exist between the Citroën Xsara and Picasso?);
- The fact that the creation of imaginary names could ultimately leave consumers believing in the existence of a real person. For example, the Elizabeth Arden brand was founded in 1910 by Florence Nightingale Graham by combining *Elizabeth and her German Garden,* a novel by Elizabeth von Arnim, and Tennyson's poem, *Enoch Arden*;
- Due to a possible disconnect of the manager and holder of the brand name; Chantal Thomass was fired from her own company in 1995 and prohibited from using her own brand name until she could purchase it in 1998 with help from Sara Lee;
- Due to the evolution of brand officiates and the corollary evolution of know-how; the Church brand was founded in 1873 by three brothers (Thomas, William and Alfred) through the mastery of Good Year stitching. In 1999, it was still headed by a descendant of the founders, John Church, seventh to have the name, until its sale to Prada in 1999.

Therefore, what will happen when there is no clear overlap between the person who signs the product and the one who makes it? Understandably, the brand must combine an authorial function and a body of story, in the same way as royalty and the papacy have carried on for thousands of years.

The signature, or two bodies of the brand

The signature raises the issue of the successive transfer of know-how. To the extent that it builds itself as a name uniting a community, it finally poses the same type of problem as that posed by medieval political philosophy about the representation of royalty or the republic, that is to say, the question of the identity of a group and, moreover, be invisible, in which it manifests perseverance over time and consistency in space. Ernst Kantorowitcz notably showed in *The Two Bodies of the King* how medieval jurists and theologians managed to form mental categories designed to represent the ongoing nature (or eternity) of collective entities such as the empire, the Church and the people, entities formed not as collections of individuals, but imposed on the model of the human body individually and together. It was indeed necessary that we fill the void left by the death of officeholders, by the "demise" of the king or death of a bishop, a priest and so forth. The eponymous presents the same problem in that it is a kind of story that, in particular, allows filling the void left by the replacement of the designers and employees. Now the perseverance of know-how presents the problem of the possibility of reconciling perpetuity and the continuity of individual expertise, even when the brand expands its business into the dimensions of time and space to satisfy the succession of elements that are developing their capital (people, projects, equipment devices, etc.). The perseverance of expertise involves forging the subsistence of a principle of internal consistency. This is not a problem when the company retains the same know-how or focuses its activities around a single product; similarly, the index function of the corporate brand does not change if the brand remains present in the same consumption phrase, and the consumer perceives consistency (a perceptual link) between the brand's products. Thus, the expertise of Louis Vuitton is undisputed even though it is, in fact, becoming a fashion brand and has expanded its business into pens, clothing, shoes, and so forth. The trend is the *umbrella-zation* of brands (which is not far from a sort of omnipotence), which means a very concrete diversification of the brand's activities in various sectors that are not related to their original expertise (e.g., diversification of haute-couture brands into perfume). Accepting the sustainability of the brand's expertise means that metaphorically the brand is designed on the model of a single body in which successive countless individuals replace each other and pass through from their offices, thereby a flux existing between them.

A fashion brand brings its designer into the present, making him co-present with the garments through a highly charismatic legitimatization process, like an artist with his works. This presentification works as if the garment held the brand's or designer's strength and power within it, attesting to the presence of the designer in the garment, as if the mind of the designer were continually prowling around the object. This concept of presentification is essential since it refers to a symbolic efficiency, not far from witchcraft, flowing through a magical kind of contiguity process, that is to say resemblance by contact. One of the first logos conspicuously sewn on clothing was perhaps René Lacoste's famous crocodile attesting to the resistance of the mesh by metonymically bringing to mind René Lacoste's combative spirit (nicknamed "Alligator" by the Americans) on the tennis courts. Sticking a signature on a garment at the same time induces an osmotic effect that the brand's or designer's qualities will spread through mere contact with the garment itself: Emblazoning a three-band stripe pattern on sneakers might mean that in the sports stadium the wearer can run faster than when wearing other sneakers.

Re-present or pre-sentify?

This reconnect feature is made possible through the brand's ability to "represent" (in the abstract sense) a collective being. But what is meant by represent? Re-present, as Louis Marin rightly reminds us, is to "present again (in the modality of time) or in the place of (in that of space)," that is to say, repeating a presence. "The prefix re- means in the term substitution value. Something that was there and is not any longer is now represented. Instead of representation as such, it is absent in time or space and a substitution occurs of the same of the other in its place." From this early (or original) stage in Western Christianity, the angel at the tomb on the morning of the resurrection substituted for message from the dead body and its inertia. The brand represents the expertise of know-how with a fictional double effect: it comes to the place and instead of a collective body (the company) its function is showing, intensifying and repeating a presence which is that of the deceased designer. The prefix re- is therefore also important not only for its replacement value, but in its value of intensity and exhibition. This would be the "primitive" of the representation as effect: pre-sentify the missing, as if it were coming back as the same and sometimes better, more intense, stronger than if it were the same. This is even more important if we consider the necessarily pragmatic nature of the brand.

The representational device at work in a brand redoubled the effect of presence by an effect of power.

But here lies a major distinction with what would be, for example, the photograph of the deceased on the mantle – to wit the work representation in relation to the deceased designer even though it is not figurative. Unlike choices made in other sectors such as food, fashion brands have chosen the party's monogram rather than the iconic representation of a person (he was a designer or an imaginary character). Thus, the brand does not fit into a system of strength and power that would be linked to the figurative representation of a body or a face, but into a presentational effect. This is re-giving life in another way than through a representation of the designer.

The eponymous brand therefore confronts the same type of problem as non-figurative forms of religious representation. As Augé recalled, European and Christian sensitivities were at first frightened by the enormous objects with which some African myths spoke of the bodies of the gods. Now "god" was treated as a singular presence, fully identified with an object that represented him, sometimes in his raw physicality, sometimes as a power in a relationship (his other forms taken, other gods, men in general or certain men in particular) (Augé, 1988: p. 9–10). This is exactly the same question posed for the eponymous; it can be seen as a representation of the designer on his products. We thus understand why these brands have not made use of the figurative representation as may be the case in the food industry. Indeed is not one of the hallmarks of religious symbolism not exactly as shown by Ernst Cassirer, his ambition being to open up access to a reality that these represent less than manifest, to perform, to actually insert them into the visible world. So the religious symbol implies the presence of the referent within it, posed as a power of a certain type, a power exerted in a defined area. Through the religious symbol, it is the divine power that communicates (one might almost say holds communion) with men or rather manifests in the form of power or order. Similarly, Vernant shows that "archaic Greek poetry, the rhythm, sound and semantic organization aims to produce an effect on the public, which prolongs the action of the power celebrated by singing. (Thus) the symbolic value of the procedures of archaic poetry is that of the verbal image, not the figurative representation, is working as single copy, decal or *analogue*: It is very effective, it gives listeners the feeling that through expressions that evoke a defined type of power, this particular force is mobilized effectively, [and] it unfolds through the performance of the poetic text, to make the work its own." This presentification works as if the product held the qualities of strength and power of the designer that it represents. The product retains the characteristics of a ghostly double to the appearance of a supernatural being (the designer). This concept of presentification is essential, since it refers to a symbolic effectiveness that often works by contiguity processes, that is to say, a resemblance through contact, traditionally linked to witchcraft; it is in fact governed by a particular law of similarity by which all similar calls to other similar through resemblance, as well as a law of contact or contagion where things in contact continue to act upon each other after contact ends. Thus, attaching a Christian Dior or Chanel monogram to a garment or accessory is at the same time inducing the qualities of the designer to be diffused by contact with the product itself.

The paradoxes of a luxury brand

We often consider the implicit manner of luxury according to a fairly accurate anthropo-economic logic based on a categorization of people, objects and brands. But, ultimately, what is luxury? Is it a matter of know-how, a world, brands, customers? Is so much of luxury's incessant flirting with fashion as well as meaningful changes in social demand, and so-called luxury brands' strategies raise the issue of residual specificity, or even the existence of a luxury economy. What kind of company that transforms the perennial into ephemeral can still think of luxury? Does it even think about luxury? What is it about luxury in an era of democratization and accessibility of products once reserved for the elite? What is owed to luxury in a joyless economy that promotes product rotation and pushes brands to leave the shores of the timeless to become fashion brands, or even fashionable brands?

Can a secularized society, which finds it more and more difficult to recognize charismatic legitimacy and often transmutes creation into a simple reconfiguration, still be considered luxury? Do the apathy of desire, the fragmentation of aesthetic cues and the emotional injunction that characterizes democratic society not somehow signal the death of luxury? In short, can we still talk about luxury? This is the falsely naive question that we wish to ask here, trying to find a set of indices that seem to converge to announce the impending death of luxury.

The substrate of luxury

Before discussing the possible disappearance of luxury, our task is to update the assumptions of what is commonly called luxury. The economy of luxury actually works according to a number of principles that can briefly be stated as follows:

(1) A semantic field related to what is lavish, expensive, the idea of pleasure without need, abundance in some cases. This semantic refers to a principle of scarcity that the desirability of luxury is based upon.
(2) A structure in terms of categories and products, brands or companies. Luxury is often viewed as a cross-categorical concept more than intra-categorical; thus we often speak of luxury products or luxury brands, implying that it is possible to identify an economic sector for the specific operating rules. We hear about luxury with regard to fine wines, jewelry, clothing or cars more often than with mineral water or cakes.
(3) A production narrative based essentially on the function of sovereignty (i.e., the defense of know-how and specific expertise) coupled with an expertise typically part of a legitimacy of a traditional nature (the axis of expertise) and/or charismatic (hence, the importance of names of patronymic origin in this sector). This account of production serves as an account of movement of valuables related to the values of refinement, scarcity, pleasure.
(4) A demonstration logic based on the predominance of the visual order: luxury is often ostentatious, where, for example, the fact that the "potlatch" has often been regarded as the most meaningful form of luxury. Luxury often tends to substitute the sign (logo) for the meanings (the carnal experience of interaction with a well-made object); hence, the importance of the signature, the coat of arms and all the signs allowing it to establish the voluntary nature of ostentatious luxury. The world of luxury, therefore, responds perfectly to the logic of triangulation of desire, namely the existence of a single model that raises desire through games of mimetic rivalry. It is primarily through the looks of others that my desire for luxury is formed.
(5) A link of authority that sets forth the conditions of luxury and calls for its respect. The luxury model is derived from a hierarchical model of society based on the force of authority and, thus, the implicit idea that one group has a certain form of power over another. The very idea of luxury evokes membership in a hierarchical system based on the recognition of success or status encompassing a vertical dimension of authority, as summed up in Hannah Arendt's definition: "The relationship of authority between the one who commands and the one who obeys rests neither on common reason nor on the power

of the one who commands; what they have in common is the hierarchy itself, in which each one recognizes the fairness and legitimacy, and where both have their place determined in advance." Luxury may refer either to showing an established status, or displaying a success being fulfilled: as well as "while BMW explores and signals the vocabulary of social mobility, Mercedes explores and signals the vocabulary of social success." Luxury thus induces a form of vertical and unidirectional social categorization linked to a targeted model: luxury is desirable in that it allows me to show signs of belonging to, or rising from, my class.

(6) An economic logic of margin through a selective distribution system that allows the maintaining of full control of the brand's image (and a multiplier coefficient of 2.5 in stores). The luxury product is one for which the selling price is not commensurate with the cost of manufacturing because of the play of different rates of margin and the role of price as a luxury positioning tool.

From ethics to aesthetics

How then would we identify the invariant features of everything in the sensitive world of "luxury?" Luxury is more a way of life – a way of living – than a way of doing or making do. It lies in a form of accomplishment in the work, as well as an effect of totality, in the autonomy of the object, as well as the consistency of the various sensitive forms through which it manifests itself – a consistency in its feel, weight, shape, colors... in short, in aesthetics what we call the "synaesthesia." Floch has perfectly shown that despite the multiple meanings of the term "luxury," what it actually frames is a brand's ability to conjoin ethics to aesthetics. Here we mean ethics in the sense of an ability to organize its conduct moving towards the achievement of values that we ascribe to it. We mean aesthetics like an approach to a sensitive world, that is to say, of the meanings, involving a "worldview" and self-respect in a world capable of communicating an emotion.

"Everything changes. Nothing changes."

As a Hermès advertising spot whispers to us, luxury lies in the capacity of standing firmly, both in one's time and outside of time. The Chanel example is interesting because, in addition to highlighting the sound linking of an ethical project to an aesthetic, it also illustrates the increasing porosity of the world of luxury and fashion, today called the economy of luxury. Chanel is characterized for various elements that bring instant recognition underpinning its spiritual heritage (the famous suit jacket, the quilted bag, court shoes, the multicolored brooch, etc.). Chanel's famous "total look" thus refers to a combination of the brand's timeless identifying elements with new models and accessories following an aesthetic and ethical lines. Jean-Marie Floch once again beautifully demonstrates how Chanel's identity may be understood in relation to the idea of total look, that is to say, maintaining over time a timeless silhouette. The brand presents a wardrobe message that is not reducible to a set of identifiers (the logo, the shoes, the quilted bag, the brooch, etc.), but organizes a general structure of the silhouette created by Coco Chanel.

The total look of Chanel was founded on the designer's own project, namely in 1920s and 1930s women's fashion the rejection of everything that did not correspond to a real functionality in a garment: walking, wearing, working, etc. Clothing should be practical and comfortable to serve the wearer better; thus no purely decorative buttons, no more pockets too small to slip in the hands, and so forth. The story that Coco Chanel told through her line of clothing became that of the conquest of individual freedom where modernity appears as a recurring theme. In order to serve the freedom of the body, she carefully ensures that the seams of skirts let the legs move forward freely and believes that "it is never wide enough under the arms"; likewise she shortens skirts, favors the flexibility of crepe, invents the shoulder bag, so many figurative elements that tell the brand's story. Moreover, Chanel uses meaningful elements from male fashion by correlating those denoting wealth and femininity: hence, the use of the jersey, the striped vest, beret, pants, tie and also short hair, that is, many figures representing the world of men and work.

Such a well-drawn silhouette then leaves an impression of sharpness, immediate readability and aplomb (in both meanings of the word: physical stability and psychological insurance). In this silhouette we may read, as Jean-Marie Floch did, the achievement of a coherent look related to a classical vision through lines that illustrate the braid of the suit or the shape of the little black dress. Moreover, the different treatment of the front and back of the suit, the contact of the silhouette and to the ground in a specific spot in space may be understood as an effort to clearly distinguish a number of plans in space and to prefer a frontal view of the look. The effect of closing the silhouette (by the tips of shoes, short hair as well as the ponytail) performs what is called a closed shape. The preference given to colors such as beige, black and navy, as well as the recurring choice of fabrics, such as jersey or tweed, aimed to create a kind of absolute clarity that particularly favors classical aesthetics.

However, this traditional view of the silhouette is offset by accessorizing with baroque elements like jewelry, chains, a quilted bag, and so forth. These circumscribed elements have the effect of exalting, in contrast, the fundamentally baroque vision of the silhouette.

This physical dimension of the silhouette is based on an ethical aim. Indeed, this silhouette has been repeatedly enriched, redefined and illustrated, but it nevertheless constitutes a form of consistency, perseverance – and not the preservation of an acquired good or the repetition of brand identifiers. As Floch further emphasizes, "the recognition of the invariants of this silhouette, like the review of its progressive enrichment, convinced that this silhouette is a fact of style, and it reflects a life plan, or an ethical aim, where retention is the base value. It represents, in other words, a life plan and a way of life...." This value of retention – otherwise often given for the rigidity, which it also characterizes in the 19th-century dandy ethic, helps to anchor the value of freedom and a certain invariance in the variance, insofar as the charm of dandies is that of smooth imperfection and being nothing less than human in seeming to escape the effects of time. By correlating two worlds considered antagonistic at the time, namely women's fashion and evocative practical and comfortable clothing from the world of men, Chanel launched a real snub to univocal approaches of the time by revealing a practical identity founded on freedom.

Luxury confronted by consumer romanticism

In wishing to be both of her time and timeless, Chanel illustrates a central problem of luxury today, namely the rapid turnover of products and ranges to attract a clientele whose shopping is largely driven by a search for variety. Hence, the sacredness of novelty and the unique that can increase the number of interactions between customers and the brand. Luxury undeniably fulfills the romantic quest of modern consumers, a kind of "consumptionism" in the words of Samuel Strauss, a real race running towards production and consumption that characterizes modern society. Luxury therefore fulfills a romantic ethic. But first of all, what is romance, if not as defined by Colin Campbell, "an impulse toward chaos, a way of feeling, a state of mind in which sensitivity and imagination do not take a step towards reason[,] ... a preference for the strange, curious, the unexpected?" Whereas the traditional hedonist seeks to repeat the experiences he knows to be pleasant, the modern hedonist seeks out the pleasures of daydreaming about new experiences, leading to a continual search for novelty.

The romanticism of the market requires luxury brands to know how to surprise their customers and deliver to a wide horizon of expectations. Thus the Vuitton brand dares to break its own signs of recognition by changing the famous "Monogram" canvas as evidenced by the Graffiti range, a limited edition series that allowed the brand to play with its own codes by displaying contemporary use of the tag. This serves to ensure a balance between the brand's core values and the tendency towards values of creativity and boldness that instill a bit of distance between the brand and its heritage. Moreover, this making of the brand's products short-lived in the case of limited editions allows the adoption of a scarcity strategy that greatly increases the perceived value of the products. A limited edition product becomes an identity catalyst in that it allows the brand to break away from its own codes to further develop them. Ephemeral management then depends on the subtle balance between, on the one hand, awaiting a certain reassuring repetition (which is at once the resurgence, continuity and the "sameness") through a process of reproducibility, and, on the other hand, the unexpected, a surprise through a constant process of innovation. But does one not risk a kind of luxury ephemerality by renewing products and lines?

Extension of the brand's reach

The adoption of formerly vested strategies in the order of fashion in the world of luxury raises the fundamental question of forms of deployment of so-called luxury brands. It is clear that in the logic of economic financing, luxury brands have had recourse to extension strategies to increase their capital (brand equity). This extension of luxury brands takes several forms:

(1) First, the line's expansion strategies in related product categories: Vuitton is developing new leather ranges, and even shoes from its core business, leather goods; Baccarat is developing jewelry from its crystal.
(2) Brand extensions into new product categories for the brand require new expertise and legitimacy: Hermès and perfume or tableware, Mont Blanc and leather or fragrance, Davidoff and cognac or perfume, and so forth.
(3) Vertical extension strategies often consistently widen the price range proposed by the brand within its line; thus, Mercedes and BMW, reputed to cover niche segments, have started vertical extension strategies, one after the other, allowing them to cover all market price segments.

(4) The corollary target expansion strategies of vertical extension, either by variations towards more affordable ranges (e.g., Chanel Mademoiselle) or by offering accessories that decrease the cost to access the brand.

(5) Expansion strategies in terms of distribution thus obscure the effect of distance, which formerly gave luxury products a kind of special aura. The Champs-Élysées has turned into nothing more or less than a vast hypermarket of luxury goods. A businessman will note with some amusement that the Hermès and Cartier boutiques in Terminal F at Charles de Gaulle airport are right next to a newsstand....

Democratization and subjectivation of luxury

This extension of a luxury brand's domain as a corollary of the excessive democratization of luxury brands is characteristic of their own leveling of democracy. Luxury seems unable to maintain its status except by developing increasingly affordable ranges, thus eroding the role of dreams and maintaining a distance that conveyed the same idea of luxury to the common man. The arrival of fashion in the domain of luxury calls into question the very concept of luxury, which is known to be based on the idea of distance.

The importation of the democratization of luxury model, finally part of American culture, questions the need for luxury in the social space. The transition from a society based on vertical authority to one governed more horizontally challenges the principle of vertical discrimination that supports the luxury economy. As Peter Sloterdijk recalled, "the democratization of luxury is the great idea of our time, at the same time it represents the most beautiful continuity with the progressive spirit of Europeans. It participates in the fact that, by Americanizing us, we have resigned (and) given up our own imperial ambitions and our historical pride. We have become Americans" *auf dem zweiten Bildungsweg"* through catching-up. Even poor students like us can, finally, earn our post-historical diploma by taking on the American worldview that luxury is too human to not be offered to all. At the heart of the Declaration of Human Rights, we always hear the echoes of another statement, that of the right to luxury for those who are willing to become true Americans." Luxury raises a certain number of questions, first about the ability of a society that is no longer vertically structured but is moving horizontally. Can a society that is not as clearly defined by strict and vertical categorization and is no longer governed by the principle of social trajectory still taste luxury? Nothing is less certain.

We are therefore, in the words of Peter Sloterdijk "leaving the age of symbolism in an irrevocable way (and) the new strength of the West is the power to replace any one thing by any other." So add to the horizontalization of society a form of symbolic poverty, such as Bernard Stiegler described, and our inability to share a stable symbolic order leading to a weakening of the individuation process.

In this way, the luxury is no longer what was once reserved for some but often becomes what we allow in an exceptional way, or if we allow ourselves to do more to please ourselves.

The democratization of luxury leads to a form of subjective appropriation of luxury that forces us to reconfigure the idea of luxury itself; it is not conceivable in an ontological way but depends on the logics of interactions that individuals weave with so-called luxury products. Here we touch upon a form of transubstantiation of luxury in sentiment; luxury is part of a kind of infra-ordinary bricolage by deploying a personal "ritualism" that can take various forms, including metonymic consumption (buying an accessory to have a feeling of participating in the great order of all that is the brand), the "collectionite" of brand products, and ambulation in a luxury space.

This development of portable little rites shows at what point the symbolic order will crack, upon which the luxury economy is braced. Luxury becomes more subject to subjective appropriation strategies in an evolving world that shares an order of ethical and aesthetic values. Luxury will not travel further in the macro social domain (that of class relationships and ideological and cultural confrontations) than a micro-social order (governing interactions of proximity) or autospheric (governed by the consumer's specific bodily sensations).

Luxury, drugstore, food ...

At this subjectivism of luxury goods is found a form of luxuriating of certain brands of consumer products. Parallel to the democratization of luxury products, obviously, is the deployment of logic of promoting widely consumed products such as luxury goods. We observe a "over the top" phenomenon of banalization of products so the traditional opposition between luxury and the drugstore tends to fade. The drugstore has long symbolized traditional selective distribution and all its appendages (pharmacy, specialty store, manufacturer's complete control over distribution, elitism, exceptionalism and aesthetics) while "food" represented the other extreme: mass distribution and its corollaries are the commoditization, passive loyalty marked by inertia and indifference, standardization to the bottom. But can we really still justify hesitation between prestige and mass market due to a concentric distribution of the mass marketing of luxury brands? What then are the entrenchments and what redefinition of luxury obliges us to this groundswell?

Paradoxically, through too-frequent badging strategies, luxury brands have reduced the system to the sign, mass consumer product brands have incorporated the idea of staging and have orchestrated real semiotic logic based on branding logics. In the world of today's consumer, the brand has divested its role of label to become an expressive force, a "semiotic driver" responsible for producing values and meaning. Far from being limited to a brand name, it thus becomes a real reservoir of values and meaning; what builds a brand is therefore paradoxically not its name but its genetic heritage, displayed values, its expertise, its mission, its vision of the market. It is then that we can truly consider it not (or more) merely as a simple sign of distinction and differentiation, but as a true system of meaning. This illustrates the "holistic" approach that today rules brand management in the consumer products field; the brand is truly considered a narrative system designed to give identity (in the categories of time and space) to a portfolio of offerings. Here, identity is understood in a double meaning: time, since this system is necessarily evolving due to product innovation to keep up with changing technology and customer expectations; space, as products of a brand are usually sold in several countries simultaneously. The identity model that allowed a luxury brand to show its uniqueness by articulating an ethic and an aesthetic has infused the whole economy of brands and may illustrate the semiotic-narrative structure of a brand such as Perrier.

The conflict inherent in a luxury brand

Perhaps, due to the ongoing blurring of boundaries between luxury brands and consumer brand products considered, luxury is after all a historical category deemed to disappear or at least change its content in its modes of expression.

Yet for us, luxury is consubstantial if only because it raises aspirations and proposes a discriminatory order necessary for the existence of a social order. Even if the populace hinders our idea of luxury, it is clear that unattainable luxury has not won out. But what about this intermediate luxury that touches the democratic ideal? How to think that luxury must constantly play against multiple paradoxes: appearing unattainable while knowing how to find its market; appearing to target only a few and all the while wishing to attract anyone, being in time while being outside of time... and so forth?

What then is a luxury brand? It has often been said or written that a luxury brand exemplifies an uncommon know-how. Certainly very few companies – if any – can truly compete with the expertise of Pierre Hermé when it comes to the macaroon, with Hermès working with silk, color, saddlery, and so forth. But do not forget that no company other than Bel can manufacture Babybel, and no one has been able to copy Nutella's recipe to this day. Expertise and know-how are therefore obvious characteristics of major brands, but not only of luxury brands. We have also heard or read that the power of a luxury brand lies in being able to produce codes and singular stories. But so far, it is easy to see a wide codification variance and narrative among so-called luxury brands. Also, Louis Vuitton is a far more codified brand than Hermès, and Maison Martin Margiela likely has a narrative far less rich than YSL or Chanel.

We have characterized luxury with respect to the concept of light, either relative to it or by deviation. But is the difference not the property of any dividing strategy and thus of any brand. Also it may be considered that a luxury brand is right next to our shared representations, and it questions the mental categories that allow us to think about the concept of brand.

The idea we would like to develop to conclude is that luxury challenges a certain concept of the brand coming from marketing and after assuming a form of hyper-coherence to the brand. What is the brand's marketing approach founded upon, if not the idea that a brand is necessarily based on positioning (how one wishes the brand to be perceived in the minds of customers), relayed by brand signals (logo, stylistic repertoire, iconic products for a luxury brand)? The strength of the brand then is derived from an ability to consistently repeat these brand signals, resulting in a natural drift towards *badging*, which ultimately involves selling only brand codes. This marketing approach aims to substantiate the brand by folding the question of identity ("Who am I?") into that of identification ("How am I known?"). This inertia that refers to a kind of perpetuation and invariance leads brands to maintain some consistency, both in their products and in their message (Cartier is a typical example). This consistency is rooted in the brand's ability to provide experiential reproducibility, that is, to provide consumers with a possible duplication of the consumer experience in time and in space. However, a brand cannot afford to identically and infinitely repeat products and messages or it risks boring its followers. This constraint forces it to constantly renew to surprise, engage and entertain consumers. This innovative strength thus pushes the brand to break away from its habits, while not losing any major character traits. It is precisely at the crossroads of this inertial force and the force of tearing away that one may understand the issue of identity of a luxury brand. Because, in a romantic company seeking novelty, luxury brands are also trying to be fashion brands, which drives them to change, innovate, surprise and, finally, play with their own codes. Hermès is a typical example of a brand that can upset its own codes (the saddle point, the ribbon, the color orange, the carriage, etc.) by diverting them, sometimes ironically.

A brand's identity cannot therefore be reduced to the repetition of codes (which may be understood here as luxury codes and brand codes), because even if the identity implies permanence and continuity over time, it presupposes no fixity, no rigidity. A brand's identity necessarily presupposes a divergent force against its own codes. Think of the identity of a luxury brand that needs to dispose of the concepts of substance and sameness that are traditionally associated with its concept of identity. Showing an identity means not just repeating the same defined pattern ever and ever, but knowing how to remain true to oneself while incorporating an element of otherness. To do this, it is necessary to insubstantiate our approach to the brand to return to what was originally a brand, namely a relational and dynamic process. Remember that most of the major brands (luxury) surfaced from the mid-19th century onward, companies striving to produce market intermediary devices (product, logo, advertising) to allow them to weave a relationship with the end user by short-circuiting the distributor's influence. A brand is thus a set of scripted physical devices the function of which is to ensure recognition, to attract and to generate the customer's interest. While major consumer brands were built on the hyper coherence and repetition of the brand-recognition signals – its codes – a luxury brand has its richness and specificity to support its codes by constantly energizing them. A frequently monolithic approach that characterizes the management of major consumer brands features the wealth, the contradictions and the underlying conflict of luxury brands. This is why it is impossible to codify what a luxury brand would be, from the time when such a brand must consider the procedural manner and be characterized by its ability to integrate conflicts or contradictions.

It is possible to update several regimes of conflict that characterize a luxury brand. On the plan of visibility, first of all: a luxury brand must be both visible or dramatic to induce the concept of power, doing so while remaining discreet, the *understatement* always being the basis of a contract of customer trust and esteem. On the accessibility plan next comes the measure that a luxury brand has to create desire by building various types of distance (symbolic, physical). A luxury brand maintains its desirability through the simple fact of not being accessible (compared to goods that are always available). We do not walk into the Chanel jewelry boutique at Place Vendome wearing the same clothes and with the same mental attitude as going to Starbucks, even though these two retailers are a priori accessible to everyone. However, a luxury brand cannot remain in a form of museum-like accessibility without turning into a statue itself. That is why accessibility is a possible and necessary dimension of luxury and it is, for example, possible in a Pierre Hermé boutique to be served pastries by the retailer's intermediary gesture that projects the spell of jewelry items on cake, without it being incompatible with an openly accessible space where jam, chocolate and pre-packaged macaroons are available. Thus the accessibility and availability of products are what sets a luxury product apart from a consumer product. The power of a luxury brand is creating the story of the object's accessibility, even though it has been magnified and placed under an aura upstream. Anyone who walks into a Hermès boutique has a theoretical chance of being able to touch the bags, christening cups, jewelry and other items placed within reach of the eye and the hand, but the psychological barrier created by the brand is such that these objects remain in an inaccessible system no matter what happens and require the human intermediation of the staff in contact. The paradox of the Hermès object is that it is both accessible and inaccessible, available and unavailable (most leather goods must be ordered several months in advance). The brand perfectly keeps its distance and thereby maintains spatial and temporal proximity. Similarly, one could scratch the categories of opposite words a luxury brand finds it hard to say: the dramatic versus the discreet, the invisible versus the visible, abundance versus profusion, and so forth.

So what does the luxury brand do that compels us to abandon the shores of a monolithic view of the brand that reasons in terms of stock, codes, capital, in short, repeated and valued conventions. The freedom offered by a luxury brand opens up the concepts of processes, flow, conflict and linking. In this sense luxury gives us some idea of no limits, which justly gives meaning to our limit, "unlimited to which we cannot say anything, but without which none of our limited vocables could take shape. Unlimited, is maybe... the only name we can reserve for what was previously named God." And, "perhaps luxury is like poetry, to the extent that any poetic activity is dedicated to reconcile, or at least to bring together, the limited and unlimited, the light and the dark, the breath and the form.... It may be that beauty is born when the limited and unlimited become visible at the same time, that is to say, we see the shapes while guessing that they do not tell all, [that] they are not reduced to themselves, [that] they leave the elusive its share."

What is the luxury brand's philosophy of time?

"I never like the present, the future leaves me indifferent, only the past seems beautiful." These words come from a narrative by Fernand Gregh that dates from 1886 and were put into the mouth of a character one might take to be a portrait of a 25-year-old Marcel Proust. They could also very well apply to what most emblematic luxury houses did until the end of the 20th century. Three events would appear to characterize the mutation of luxury houses into brands: (a) the industrialization of production modes and the underlying use of a rhetoric of artisanal craftsmanship; (b) the overextension into close, but often disconnected, markets such as perfumes and accessories, which has become the essential refrain of all of these brands; and finally, (c) the change in the relationship with time due to the never-ending dance that most luxury houses have with fashion culture, with the aim of increasing the frequency of interaction with the client and, as such, the average shopping trolley. As such, luxury seems to have changed its historicity regime, obliging brands to claim and conjugate the long game of luxury with the short, jerky game of fashion. The legitimacy of luxury houses comes from a sort of historic substance that demands the continuation of a style and a craftsmanship but which they must now blend with that which is up to date and in the "air du temps." So where does this leave the philosophy of time for luxury brands?

The luxury brand, or creativity continued

Most luxury houses seem to have functioned according to a vision of time that is in fact quite close to that which characterizes medieval culture. Indeed, as Georges Poulet showed in one of the 20th century's most important works of literary criticism, Western culture since the Middle Ages has built its perception of time around the idea of continuous creativity. Thus, for the Christians of the Middle Ages, "feeling that one exists, is feeling that one is, not changing, not becoming but feeling that one subsists" (Poulet, 1989, I: p. 5). In other words, the human being "could never be other than what he was." In fact, nothing distinguished him from the other beings in creation; each being had its life span, an intrinsic life span, and subsisted as things stood. But these subsisting things did not just subsist alone inasmuch as their existence remained contingent and dependent on the way they were created existences. The Christian point of view is that the human being is a precarious presence, an entity that has barely emerged from nothingness and is ready to fall back in of its own accord, unless the hand of the Creator keeps it in existence. Thus, we have the astonishing phrase by Suarez in his *Metaphysical Disputations*, according to which "creation and conservation are one indivisible action: from which there comes the absolute unity of this action and the fact that its length does not proceed from succession or from a continuation as such, but from the permanence of a same individual action."

The romanticization of consumption and the fashionization of luxury

Though far from the Middle Ages in appearance, the society of brands is based on the valorization of novelty and the obsolescence of style that enable the rapid rotation of products and ranges that can seduce a clientele for which one of the main purchasing urges is based on variety. Campbell (1987) developed a controversial thesis, according to which the Romantic Movement played a critical role in the birth of modern consumerism. In an attempt to extend Weber's thesis on the surge in modern capitalism and the inexorable movement toward rationalization, Campbell defends the idea that in the same way the puritanical ethic promoted the spirit of capitalist production, a romantic ethic promoted the complementary spirit of consumerism. As in, what is romanticism if not "an impulse toward chaos" (Campbell, 1987: p. 179) and, "a state of mind in which sensibility and imagination predominate over reason; it tends toward the new, toward individualism, revolt, escape, melancholy and fantasy" (ibid.: p. 181). Campbell adds that "other typical characteristics of this way of feeling would be: dissatisfaction with the contemporary world, anxiety in the face of life, a preference for the strange and curious, a penchant for reverie and dreaming, a leaning to mysticism, and a celebration of the irrational (ibid.)." Campbell brings romanticism and consumerism together through a distinction between traditional and modern forms of hedonism. Of course, both are "marked in contrast by a preoccupation with pleasure, envisaged as a potential quality of all expérience" (ibid.: p. 177); nevertheless, in modern hedonism, "the individual has to substitute illusory for real stimuli, and by creating and manipulating illusion and hence the emotive dimension of consciousness, construct his own pleasurable environment. This autonomous and illusory form of hedonism commonly manifests itself as day-dreaming and fantasizing" (ibid.: p. 186).

While the traditional hedonist attempts to repeat experiences that he knows to be agreeable, the modern hedonist experiments a hiatus between desire and consummation with the joys of dreaming about new experiences. Thus, Campbell concludes that modern consumerism is everything but materialistic inasmuch as the tension between the illusion and the reality creates a permanent quest in the individual and a continual search for novelty. How to conjugate the need to refer to the past with the frequency, discontinuity and thus the split imposed by the fashion universe? In other words, how can we go back when fashion demands that we be "rooted in the historical moment and accept change?

To this idea of romanticism and consumerism, we can add the idea so judiciously developed by Marine Antoni (2013) of a romantic revolution of emblematic French luxury brands, as in recent years they have operated a romantic revolution comparable to the earthquake that was Hernani, in which Victor Hugo literally broke the codes of classic tragedy; while retaining a noble and tragic subject, he radically modified the aesthetic and dramaturgical codes by dispensing with the rule of the three unities. This resulted in the fundamental distortion of the relationship of these luxury brands with time, which we will not attempt to unravel.

Fashion, erosion and waiting

By flirting with fashion, luxury brands summon us to the question of time, where, as Nicolas Grimaldi (1991) so aptly reminds us "there can be no movement or succession without some reality or thing of the past slipping into the present and compromising it with the future, or without some intestine fomenting of the future within the present, animating it, attracting it, subverting it, incessantly metamorphosing it. It is what we know as time" (Grimaldi, 1991: p. 83). "*As,* he goes on to say, *time is both this incorporation of the past and this agitation of the future in the present: continuity and change,* tradition *and* innovation, conservation *and* adventure. Inseparably" (Grimaldi, 1991: p. 86).

By "fashionizing" itself, luxury is attempting to avoid the risk of the weariness, even disenchantment, that we must remember, for Max Weber characterizes secularized industrial societies that are used to the principle of the reproducible experience and thus inexorably engender lassitude and boredom through a form of over-rationalization of procedures. It thus goes without saying that a fashion brand that repeats the same codes *ad infinitum* by proposing only tiny variations cannot create a true brand in a society that has assimilated the principle of generalized obsolescence that is part of fashion and marketing. Thus, the issue becomes how to thwart routine, the banal and the lack of the urge to surprise. As the risk is that the brand will become commonplace, that by taking root in the tedious repetition of figurative elements will result in the clients' disaffection with the brand and its products. Indeed, according to Grimaldi, we should not be surprised to have "become so indifferent to that which used to move us so, and that we just had to see every day to stop noticing it.... How is it possible that we can now read words with a disenchanted placidity that once petrified us with admiration for their depth and respiration? For having read them so much, we have in some way incorporated them so that they have become the fabric of our sensibility, its ordinary armor and tonality; to the extent that they make us expect something else from literature. By ceasing to be new, they brought to life within us a feeling of another novelty, and in preparing us for other forms of writing, they make us less sensitive to the discovery that we made with them." In short, the problem is that as they can no longer hide anything from us, can no longer promise us anything inasmuch as the habit that dissipated their newness at the same time took away the enigma, the surprise and the *wait*. "But, the *intensity* of a feeling or an emotion is entirely constituted by the tension of our conscience toward a secret of a person, a landscape or a musical phrase; and it is the anticipation that creates that tension" (Grimaldi, 1988: p. 88). No landscape, no object will move us as much as the unexpected that intrudes, along with another world on the basis of one that did not prepare us. So, living constantly in the imminence of a revelation, we felt that at every instant, something was about to begin. A feeling of never-before-seen, this vision seemed to keep the future suspended, as if time itself were going to enter into fusion with it. What was once the marveling at the unexpected will inevitably have become that banality of a now-expected ordinariness. The challenge for the luxury brand is the risk that, as we are constantly looking at it, we no longer see it, as it has become the basis on which we expect the sign of something to come. It is this "something to come" that luxury brands must conjugate with their often heritage-based dimension.

The two bodies of the luxury brand

But how to create expectation or make people believe something is new when capitalizing on the old? This is the fiction that heritage-based brands have created by laying claim to the prestigious figure of the now-dead designer. Does this not seem like a religious intrigue through which a revenant is again present in his work?

The heritage-based brand is faced with the question of the succession of the craftsmanship. Inasmuch as it builds itself up as a name that unites federates a community, it faces the same problem as that faced by medieval political philosophy about the representation of royalty or of the republic, that is to say the question of the identity of a collective and invisible entity whose longevity in time and consistence in space must be manifested. Ernst Kantorowicz showed us in *The King's Two Bodies* how medieval legal experts and theologians came to form mental categories aimed at representing the permanence (or Eternity) of collective beings such as the Empire, the Church, the people – beings formed not as collections of individuals but instituted on the model of the human body, a Body natural and a Body politic. In fact something was needed to fill the voids left by the deaths of those in office, by the demise of a king or the death of a bishop, an abbot and so forth. The eponymous pose the same problem, and a sort of a fiction enables the void to be filled by the replacement of the designer and the employees. But the survival of a skill brings up the problem of the possibility to reconcile perpetuity and the continuity of individual expertise when the brand spreads its activities into dimensions of time and space according to the succession of elements that make up its capital (individuals, projects, material setups, etc.). The survival of expertise implies forging the subsistence of a principle of internal coherence. This problem does not arise when the company retains the same skills or does all its activities around the same product. Thus no one is contesting the expertise of the Louis Vuitton brand, even though as it became a fashion brand, it extended its activities into pens, clothes, shoes and so forth. Accepting the permanence of the brand's expertise signifies that metaphorically the brand is designed on the model of one and the same body in which innumerable individuals succeed one another, replacing one another and passing on the baton of their work, thus creating a flow between them. The fiction of the brand's immortal body that enables one to intuit the link of continuity between the founder and the successors in a certain way means the specter of the hidden god that continues to work for the brand can be left to one side if we were to carry on with our medieval metaphor of continued creation. But, we must admit that luxury houses have lived for a long time on the implicit idea of a hidden god, the designer in this case, whose founding principles had to be respected. So how is it possible to conjugate this vision of eternity with the necessary deployment of these brands over time? When Vuitton has different designers reinterpret its monogram, the idea is to ensure a balance between the brand's founding values and the projection of the values of creativity and daring that create a distance between the brand and its heritage. Even more, this ephemeralization of the brand's products with the use of limited editions enables it to create organized rarity that increases the perceived value of its products considerably. The ephemeral product thus becomes an identity catalyst inasmuch as it enables the brand to free itself from its own codes in order to make them evolve. Managing a brand thus depends on the subtle balance between expectation and a certain reassuring repetition (that aims for resurgence, continuity and sameness all at the same time) through a process of reproducibility, and on the other hand the unexpected, the surprise that comes from a constant process of novation. So how is this paradox to be solved, that is to say to "change" while remaining the same? How to conjugate the form of continuity that is specific to luxury and the dimension of tearing away that is specific to fashion?

Narrative identity as the fiction of continuity

The only credible answer to this question of longevity that must blend with the perspective of tearing away is that of the narrative identity. It is located at the crossroads of the strength of inertia and the strength of tearing away and can be understood as the tension that enables a brand to remain itself while at the same time becoming something else. As Paul Ricœur showed us in his seminal work, *Oneself as Another*, it is not possible to reduce identity to an ontological stable core through time and space, as identity is an evolving process. Manifesting an identity is not simply repeating a predefined scheme once and for all, it instead is remaining faithful to oneself while integrating a certain amount of change and, as such, tearing away. Of course, there are certain brand-identity references that form its *raison d'être* (original profession, skill base, craftsmanship, iconic products, etc.), but these identity-based references are not stable over time. Far from reducing it to a static combination of permanence and difference, identity implies a dynamic tension that combines the strength of inertia and the strength of innovation in constant search for the point at which they balance out. In order to better approach the problem of the *maintenance* of personal identity over time, Ricœur came to distinguish two meanings for the term *identity* that refer to two models of permanence over time: *character* and *keeping one's word*. Character means the collection of distinctive marks that enable one to recognize a brand, that is to say the brand's "ownables." The identity of character corresponds to a form of permanence over time that excludes any idea of change and confers a sort of immutability on the identity. Here, the identity is dyed with the color of permanence.

But we must also consider identity in the sense of a journey that takes continuity into account or, on the contrary, accidents that happen along the brand's journey. This means essentially the maintenance of oneself over time that often imposes splits and discontinuities. The main point Paul Ricœur makes is finally to take the notion of identity out of the rut of repetition by opposing the notion of keeping one's word to character and by clearly marking the gap between the two modalities of permanence over time, which says clearly the term of self-maintenance by the opposition of the perpetuation of the same. The identity must thus be conceived of as a space-interval of coming and going, or more exactly, the permanent oscillation between "character" and "keeping one's word." It is the correct control of this oscillation that enables a fashion brand to go through time while also being in time. As Paul Ricœur reminds us, "this way of opposing the sameness of character with the maintenance of oneself in promise opens an *interval of meaning* that needs to be filled. This interval is open through the polarity, in temporal terms, between two models of permanence in time, the perseverance of character and the maintenance of self in a promise. So the mediation must be found in the order of time. But it is this 'middle' that is occupied by... the notion of narrative identity."

Luxury and time: luxury's historicity regimes

The use of a brand's signature is interesting in light of the narrative of luxury brands. Thus the recent choice by Hermès of the signature, *Artisan contemporain depuis 1837* (Contemporary artisan since 1837), that illustrates to what extent the combination of a form of non-temporality linked to the maintenance of self and the taking into account of a form of "presentism." It is, in fact what Hermès projected for a long time with its watch products, with the line *Tout change, rien ne change* (Everything changes, nothing changes). In the same way, it is interesting to note the gap that separates the Chanel signature from three decades ago: *La vraie beauté c'est la simplicité* (Real beauty is simplicity), and that of today: *Là commence la beauté* (Where beauty begins). What are we to understand from this inflection, this exclamation? As Georges Poulet reminds us, the exclamation is a word without articulation, rhythm and almost without syntax. It attaches itself to nothing behind it; as it bears witness to a feeling that did not yet exist in the past, but on the contrary emerges, so to speak, against and beyond the past, as a contrast. The exclamation expresses the moment better than any other form of syntax by echoing it instantly. By marking the bubbling up of a life that is exclusively in the now.

What better way to highlight a veritable regime of sensibility and a new paradigm of creation? What a reversal of the medieval vision of time in which matter is in fact that which grafts itself on to the actualization of power. Accepting Aristotle's definition of time – time is a number of change – change consisting of passing from the power to the act. Time was thus so, by virtue of the Christian dogma of the all-powerful, because there was a reason that opposed that divine action which made the being go from power to action without transition. And this reason that demanded that there was time in change was nothing but a certain fault in the matter. As Saint Thomas pointed out, "the succession in the formation of things is due to the fault in the material that is not properly disposed to receive the form: but when it is so disposed, it receives the form instantaneously."

However, what seems to emerge with "Where beauty begins," is that creation is discontinuity, which enables the revalorization of matter and thus sensibility. It means to consider that creation is made of isolated instants and elements and without any perceptible or conceivable link. As though, to take up what Paul Valéry said, it was "everything at once – attached to its own production – all effect and dependence, all translation, intermediary; but singularity, origin, and even absolute origin." This leads to a new temporal paradigm that is from elsewhere and, if we are to believe Georges Poulet, part of the work of many 20th-century writers. Whether in the work of Claudel, Valéry or Gide, the present moment does not proceed from the past; it is the creative force itself that, inherent to the present moment, pulls itself out of nothingness and makes it into a new entity each time. Escaping the yoke of the past and opening the field of the future, that is the virtue of novelty. Thus, as Georges Poulet reminds us, "regardless of which way we turn, for modern man, there is no possible passage of an abstract, objective and antecedent length to a concrete, subjective and experimental now. Living is above all touching the now. Human time does not precede that of man, it is, on the contrary, the very consequence of the way of living and of *living oneself*. The result is that everything begins with an experience and by the consciousness of this experience; as everything continues, crowns itself and ends by a transformation of this experience that corresponds exactly to the transformation of isolated moments into a coherent length." So the idea emerges, as Georges Poulet so precisely analyzed, that any moment can be lived as a new moment, and that time can always be freely created from the present moment. In other words, duration is something different from history, it is free creation. Of the type "each instant can appear like that of a choice, that is to say an act, and at the root of that act is a creative decision." Even more, "in every instant that we act, we create our action and, with it we create ourselves and the world." This means "do, and in doing, make oneself," which seems to sum up the issues facing luxury houses today.

But if the mind wants to seize itself as creator, it needs to seize an act of annihilation in its act of creation, meaning that it has to "make its own nothingness to give itself a being". The being can thus only create itself by abolishing time, by creating itself *ex nihilo*. Which brings the idea of a creation that, because of its constant novelty, proceeds by jerks or as Gabriel Marcel says, by periods of time made up of heterogeneous series. The human act through which the mind is present to a few groups of local and temporal images often appears to be an incomplete, incongruous creation, like those things that, as Supervielle says "are not meant to go together." Is this not an ethic of time and creation that is perfectly compatible with the dominant precept today of the financialization, omnipotence and overextension of luxury brands?

A brand with no idea ... or the non-thought of marketing

The economy of brands runs on the perseverance of a certain number of precepts that are unique to Western managerial thinking. But it is clear that the evolution of the brand's role, function and means challenges these precepts together and perhaps forces us to think about the brand otherwise. By leaving the cramped space of traditional media, brands have significantly expanded their sphere of action to all the physical and symbolic spaces of Western societies; they have enabled consumers to become full participants in the brand and to actively join in its co-construction. Today, we can no longer consider the brand the agent company's only point of view since the brand is within a social space of communication and transmission of beliefs and practices; it is co-constructed by a group of actors, among which the consumer holds a special place. Understanding this trend calls for updating this non-thought that restrains marketing and is not thought because it has become too obvious, too hidden in brands' practices. The objective of this chapter is first of all, to update the common fund of ideas that shape our means of thinking about brand management and secondly to try to dig ourselves out of this bias – by passing through China.

The tri-functional ideology of brands

We credit anthropologist Georges Dumézil (1968) with an analytical framework that is quite interesting to a brand via a tri-functional model that postulates that Indo-European societies were historically structured on the basis of three functions corresponding to the symbolic figures of priest, warrior and farmer. In this context, we can consider the three structural features of a brand, namely: *sovereignty*, which is a brand's ability to claim a territory of expertise and legitimacy through know-how and a particular vision it offers through its range of products; a *warrior role* to protect and defend this territory; and a *reproductive role* that distributes the brand's products in the market and ensures its survival through development strategies (line extension, brand, target, etc.).

In doing so, the brand is often seen as the driver of a situation with the power to take action and to assume an actual configuration. This worldview is linked, especially in business circles, to a proactive vision and to often-Promethean action emanating from conscious and voluntary actors. We often eliminate the concepts of chance or even of the scheme of things by attributing an action's results to an agent or group of agents – as evidenced by the mythologizing (or the placing *au pilori*) of some businessmen. This sovereignty of the brand also largely explains the use of personification and anthropomorphism mechanisms, by which we project on brands concepts such as personality, identity, charisma, and so forth.

This valuation of the agent doubles as a glorification of the strategy at the expense of the tactics. Michel de Certeau sheds light on this binary: "I call 'strategy' the calculation of power relationships that become possible from the moment a subject of will and power may be isolated in an 'environment.'" de Certeau postulates a place likely to be circumscribed as owned and serving as a basis for managing its relationships with a distinct externalization. The various modes of managerial rationality have built on this strategic model – one that divides the spaces and refers to an order structure that allows marking the market; this order structure implicitly leads to a hypertrophy of sovereignty and warlike functions; we speak of "product manager," "brand territory," competition, and so forth, mainly through the use of essentially metaphors of spatiality and of conquering the market. The brand's economic foundation thus lies in its ability, by imposing a differential position in the minds of its current and potential consumers, to create preference (at the expense of other brands), market share and mind share. This is what marketers call positioning, which aims precisely to define and defend such a position by sedimenting a group of elements that will build the mental representation of the brand. This positioning is relayed by elements of recognition, the famous brand ownables.

Efficiency and staging the narrative of power

The logic of brand efficiency is often based on a rewarding design and relatively dramatic effect. The economy of brands has clearly taken the part of flavor as opposed to blandness, including the logics of effect saturation. "Go faster, get your laundry whiter" – these are the watchwords of the consumer society straight out of rhetorical emphasis and, therefore, excess. So it is no exaggeration to say "marketing aims "to grant objects an altogether duplicable and standard coefficient of difference that imposes them to attention and seems to condemn them in advance to public favor" (Rosset, 1979, p. 44). The Western concept of a brand is essentially Promethean, to the extent that the brand may be seen as a kind of magical object likely to create transformation (of a natural object into a cultural object, a distant object into a nearby object, a past object into a present object, etc.) and granting of power (speed, omniscience, security, comfort, etc.) to consumers. Hence the inherent logic of hyper-visibility to the effect it aims to create a kind of excess area defined not as reality but as a supplement to the real, participating in both "not like the others" and the "and-more". Often from a will, "too often causal and too purely explanatory, both too-produced and too-finished to be able to account for the effectiveness that is at work," the effect is often considered in its resultant dimension, visible and dramatic. This logic of overestimating is deployed largely in a Western narrative model that irrigates all advertising philosophy that is firmly based on the recurrence of narrative stages, which are as follows:

- The detection of a *problem* met by a consumer (made visible by a task) subject to a phenomenon of exaggeration; here we circumscribe an effect;
- The demonstration of power and effect in its causal, resultant and dramatic configuration;
- The *glorification* of the brand that appears as an agent with a power to act on the world, that is to say, metaphorically a *hero* able to win the heart (or, to be specific, the wallet and wardrobe) of the consumer.

This narrative structure characteristic of a Promethean and visible logic also made an emblem of a teleological vision stating terminal values (expected effects) and instrumental values (supposed means).

Thus Western managerial thinking seems to express itself as a metaphorical language whose watchwords are agent, causation, visibility, efficiency and finality. Let us now turn away from this terminology to take a look, in relation to this concept of management, at a shift offered by Chinese thought.

From efficiency to *effect*: Chinese expression of the brand

In contrast to the strategy, the tactic provides the possibility of a set of actors escaping control through their creative abilities: de Certeau tells us:"I call a 'tactic' a calculation that cannot rely on independence, or a boundary that sets it apart from the other like the visible totality". The tactic does not have any other place than the place of the other. It insinuates it piecemeal, without entering in its entirety, without being able to hold him off. While the strategy defines an independent external place, outdoors, the tactic exists only in the place of another, without externalization. The Chinese vision of brands supposes leaving the exclusive order of strategy to consider it the most deceptive tactic. Considering that the brand has no independent space or specific location, the consumer has the possibility to deploy ways to do it; these operational performances derive from very ancient knowledge that the Greeks designated as "metis." A thought propensity opens to the possibility of tactics that justly oppose strategies by their ability to subvert from within the stabilities and agreed orders. De Certeau offers a postulate creative activity to the practitioners of the ordinary, highlighting and formalizing ways of doing things, traces of creativity that no system can silence. He proposes the idea of invention even within everyday life by running through a series of tricks that divert the systems of control. The user can always distort the imposed order. Here, a double trick is at play: from one part brands enter, casually, in daily and intimate space for individuals and the other, that of consumers reclaimé the meaning of consumer goods through bricolage and diversion strategies. It follows that the brand has to take into account a certain plan of propensity, to let themselves be carried by a certain device on the market, considering that the market can truly be the carrier, that is to say, it has promised some development, on which it will be possible to build. Instead of doing everything depending upon the company's initiative, it serves to recognize that a certain potential forms part of the market situation, which is to identify, and it is then possible to leave "carried" by it. Hence the need to identify a certain configuration (*provision*) seen as an operating system and not to view the market as an object one could hold in his hands and force.

To a psychology of will and purpose, Chinese thought offers *effect* and also propensity, this ability to slip, slip into the scheme of things. Unlike the effect that is the target of the action in a means–end relationship, this effect is not "to search" directly and voluntarily; this effect is called to arise "naturally" from the process engaged. Any strategy will, in turn, involve the process upstream; hence, the effect will then be to drive himself "to come." From there, it becomes easy to show how Chinese thought leads to another view of efficiency, and even of "time." Not projecting, time passes, not by a means–end relationship, but by the condition of consequence: the effect must arise naturally (immanently) from previously arranged conditions. What would such an approach mean for brands? The ability to abandon a regime of mainly dramatization for an advertising message to enter in the course of the brands' existence in the most natural way possible. By granting a gift of ubiquity, brands are able to interfere in the private lives of citizens through mechanisms that we term infiltration. Marketers of a brand like Coca-Cola aim to maximize opportunities to consume by following the individual all throughout the day and throughout his life, hence the presence of soda machines in the brand's colors in places as disparate as schools, train stations, companies, sports clubs, and so forth. Candy brands like M&M's or Milka have recently developed spin-off products (alarm clocks, pencil pouches, book bags, plush toys) that allow them to become a real partner of a child consumer. Beyond the search for dramatic effect, it is necessary to spin a web around the individual to imprison him in the mesh of the brand. In this sense, to borrow a metaphor from Jean Baudrillard, a brand is "a parasite or intestinal flora, which allows us to metabolize what we eat, to make the world and the world's violence a consumable substance." Indeed, most major brands have gradually turned away from traditional advertising media to capture consumers in their daily lives, whether through operations of proximity (point-of-sale promotions, renovation of urban monuments, etc.) or by creating spin-off products and mascots that ensure strong brand visibility and enter into consumers' everyday worlds and emotions. This de-dramatization of marketing – brands turning away from traditional advertising channels to invite themselves into our homes, our bodies, our minds and our lives – broadly takes place in the willingness of brands to appear casually in cultural products, whether in films (through product placement strategies), in literary works (through name dropping) or even in cultural codes (Coca Cola and Santa Claus, for example). This ability to transform the dramatic into an effect is well illustrated by the "Mr. Clean" brand detergents. The brand's communication strategy has evolved over several years, from a demonstration of its power and effectiveness via television spots, to a sneaky strategy designed to enter into consumers' privacy (T-shirts with the brand image, alarm clocks, etc.)

and communication activities related to rituals (e.g., very heavy promotional brand support for Mother's Day).

The plant versus the war: Failure of the brand manager

Chinese thought leads to a particular approach to the action that opposes two logics: one, that of activism, of spending and endless accumulation, in the "never-enough" mode, according to which we never learn and always want to go further; and the other, on the contrary, in which it continues to entrench its interference, to reduce its busyness. In Chinese thought, the worldview of efficiency is to learn to let the effect happen: to not target the effect directly, but to involve it as a consequence; that is to say, not to seek the effect out but to collect it – to let it happen. Thus, the Chinese worldview of "effectiveness" implies that it cannot be directly pursued as a goal, meeting a set schedule or following a model, but it proceeds indirectly, as result. There is no term relayed in advance that would direct the process and guide in the journey. It serves to move from a worldview of *application* (in which a preconceived theory would cover the actual, then to be modeled upon it) to a worldview of *exploitation*, each time taking advantage of the potential involved in a given situation. Accepting this primacy of exploitation requires discarding the theory of the agent, the theory of action and an underlying theory of efficiency. Accepting a principle that immanence rules the flow of things requires abandoning the concept of *agent* in the meaning of "individual self," conceived as an independent agent whose initiative and faculties significantly influence the course of things. It no longer serves to assign an agent to this or that course, but to truly give up the category to the subject, to find recourse a process where the source of the immanence of things is found. The concept of immanence does not accept what does exist (it is disinterested); rather, it is an act that is neither dependent nor deserving ("without support"), it is/leaves a flourish – but, without exercising authority, makes obsolete the subject/object distinction that organizes the managerial worldview. It is less our personal investment that counts, but more the objective conditioning stemming from the situation, and the mechanics consider, for example, the potential energy of a situation. Thus, brands have indeed long been governed by the trifunctional ideology assigning management to a warrior; it does seem to reflect an efficiency model with which a number of Western brands are imbued. Could we not imagine an efficiency model where the brand is no longer this body, given powers, and producers of a force modeling the real, but rather a more discrete force, a kind of catalyst for starting up inexorable processes wherein most are natural and organic phenomena?

The model favored by Chinese thought is also taken from the growth of plants. Pulling on a plant will not make it grow faster (image of direct action) and neither will pulling weeds from around its roots (by favorable conditioning). We cannot force a plant to grow, we must not forsake it; but by removing what could hinder its development, we will let it grow. This logic of procession also applies to fruit, which by imperceptibly transforming, comes to ripen, without any heroic gesture that claims to having accomplished it. Then we can legitimately transfer this plant metaphor to the world of organizations by stating that a brand is like a plant, on which we cannot and should not act directly. Moreover, the Anglo-Americans do not hesitate to talk about brand extension, to use the rubber metaphor of "brand stretching," as if the brand were given a power of elasticity (not infinite). However, in wanting to pull on a brand too much, especially for financial reasons, we risk breaking it, and that is what happened when the Tati brand expanded too rapidly in different directions, such as eyeglasses, bridal shops, candy stores, travel agencies and even jewelry.

In the context of wanting to act on the market, it would be absurd to not follow the trend objectively involved and govern its development. It would be equally futile to try to interfere in the course of reality instead of complying with the logic of the propensity that results from the given situation. This approach does not, however, imply an escape from action and does not advocate inaction, but aims specifically to eliminate any naïve "activism," to ignore one's own desire for initiative, for power, along the lines of phenomena, to enjoy their dynamism and have them cooperate. This is nothing less than to bring out the principle of internal consistency that reflects the processes of reality.

That is what we could say to parody a Chinese sage rather than a great manager, if there is not much to praise. This action without acting is also part of a brand's biological vision that is allowed to happen and flourish rather than acting by imposing, by force. Management would no longer represent the practical application of a preconceived theory or the implementation of deliberate actions aiming to act on reality, but on the contrary, it would carry out an act that is neither dependent nor deserving and let it flourish without exercising authority.

Flavor versus blandness

A manager's failure to act raises again the issue of a brand's effect, in the sense that it is explanatory, produced, complete (it breaks down reality) and often dramatic. Thus, brand communication very often tends to substantiate forms (graphic, verbal, auditory, etc.) as illustrated by the repetition of advertising codes or the stricter brand identifiers through brand charters that allow recognizing the impact of the brand. However, how to account for this principle of vital energy that may be characterized by the brand and that can truly reach us, quietly, discreetly and without an enormous gap, while its use is to provoke, push and shake up the surrounding world? The Chinese expression of a brand may mean the ability to speak elliptically and enigmatically, drawing effectiveness in discretion and not "seeking" an effect – doing so in the manner of a Chinese strategist. It serves to focus on transformation which, unlike local and momentary action, is always comprehensive, progressive – so it does not stand out. So it goes unnoticed. We do not see it at work; we see only the effects. Instead of valuing the dramatic, praising effort and risk, Chinese thought focuses on what is discreet, recommends efficiency that does not confront or force, both without exerting energy and without resistance. Hence this *gray efficiency,* flowing into the course of events and, by not standing out, the less it is noticed, the better it works....

Moreover, in markets saturated with products and messages, is it not best stand apart, just remaining silent while others are doing, and to make one's silence heard in the great uproar? A logic of *effect,* therefore, needs to leave behind the saturation of the effect that rules advertising culture. To paraphrase François Jullien in *In Praise of Blandness*, we understand how the burst of flavor runs out in the news and the short term, while blandness remains open to all possibilities, the propensity of things to be, without even being visible and sensitive. It acts to let meanings "steep," rather than expose them and cast them to the winds. Blandness comes from an individual's experience of the world based on inner detachment; as much as flavor attracts us, blandness detaches us. The first draws us in, obsesses us, while the second frees us from outside pressures, feelings, artificial intensity. This praise of blandness, which is a fundamental characteristic of Chinese thought, may be seen as an antidote to Western civilization's ideology of over-differentiation and over-semanticizing independent objects. Thus, the efficiency of Hermès lies mainly in its discretion: Hermès never indulges the dramatic; the brand suggests much more than it reveals. While the sophistication of leather and designing shapes and seams are the product of exclusively artisanal work, mythical bags like the Kelly or Birkin go almost unnoticed, hiding under false airs of simplicity or naïveté (sleek design and solid colors) and finally asserting themselves as real luxury because they are of incomparable rarity (in number and value). This goes along with the brand's low-key distribution and infrequent advertising campaigns.

Hermès is a brand whose communication, on the surface, seems dull: offering soft colors, almost washed out, on nearly empty visuals, and where no Hermès object actually speaks out, in a game of transparency between the air and the water and in a logic that ultimately returns to the productive categories of Chinese pictorial art – the wave, the indistinct, recollection, transformation, and so forth. Thinking about the blandness of the brand means leaving behind the saturation of sensations and symbolic tyranny that imprison the images in a register that tends to empty them of meaning, emotion and, undoubtedly, of efficiency.

Towards brands without ideas ...

Thus a brand's reassuring hum on largely commoditized markets brings us to propose the paradoxical idea of a brand without an idea. What is meant by this? Not so much marketing's breathlessness that an idea according to which the brand's ownership would be precisely the wisest idea, to be without. We will conclude (provisionally) that a brand should be without an idea. "No idea" does not mean running out of ideas, but being careful not to put one idea ahead of the rest at the expense of the others; "no idea" is to say, knowing to throw out an idea posited in principle and that serves as a foundation from which to deploy thought. "No idea" would mean not being in possession of any, or rather being possessed by none. "No idea" is to say, without building an action plan from an initial idea freezing the actual, without leaving anything aside or dropping it. "No idea" is to say, without favoring a particular angle, without being dependent on an initial train of thought, without trying constantly to return to this train by wanting to crinkle it up, to cancel it out. "No idea" is to say, lacking a train of thought....

3 Oneself as Another

A brand immediately raises a paradox because of the often-contradictory expectations customers develop with regard to it. Indeed, the primary function of a brand is to enable clients to find it – in an uncertain world saturated with news and information – by providing guarantees and reassurance. This inertia pushes brands to maintain some longevity, both in its products and in its actions. However, a brand cannot afford to continue making the same products and sending the same messages infinitely, at the risk of boring its customers. Paradoxically, this constraint leads brands to continuously renew themselves in order to surprise, engage and entertain their customers. A necessary innovative strength thus obliges any brand to break away from its old habits while not losing any major character traits. It is precisely at the crossroads of this inertial force and the force of tearing away that one may understand the issue of identity. Managing identity requires any brand to guarantee consistency over time, while always knowing how to surprise its customers to maintain their curiosity and desire in keeping the right pace between repetition and surprise, reassurance and the unexpected. This consideration of two principles that may appear antagonistic raises the question of brand identity. How can a brand meet these two contradictory constraints imposed by marketing ideology? The answer: stay up to date to be recognizable, while incorporating the necessary scansions and breaks to stimulate consumer interest.

Discard the identification message

The implicit vision that developed west of the brand is based on stable geometric shapes (triangle, square, prism) and a static view of the brand.

Written with the friendly help of Jean-Paul Petitimbert.

However, one cannot reduce brand identity to a stable ontological core through time and space because it is much better to consider identity as the end of an evolutionary process.... Indeed, far from being reduced to a series of identifying features, the identity of a brand must essentially be viewed as a differential process (one acquires an identity in the difference), dialogue (one negotiates facets of identity with other social stakeholders rather than having just one identity) and temporal (identity results from a temporal process rather than a state).

Certainly one may consider existing brand identity referents that substantiate its reason-for-being (its core business, competencies, know-how, etc.), but we must recognize that these identity referents are not stable over time. What convinces some brands to diversify and what leads them to resize the scope of their business, acquire new know-how and broaden their range of competencies? Identity is not a stable state to be defined once and for all; it refers to an evolving and dynamic process by which a subject (whether an individual, a country, or a brand) persists through time and space. As noted by Michel Foucault, "identities are defined by trajectories." There is therefore no question of reducing brand identity to an immutable substrate that would make the brand a being unaffected by change. Otherwise, how could we understand the strategic intention of "wanting to stay ourselves while innovating," as we can see outlined in number of strategic branding programs? The identity necessarily presupposes a dimension of innovation that integrates the difference. As we shall see, this dimension, which is essential to the perpetuation of an identity, allows for the consideration of an identity that "change does not burst," in the words of the philosopher Paul Ricoeur.

Identity as process and dialogue

In one of his fundamental works, *Oneself as Another*, Ricoeur rightly shows that the identity of a subject (individual or brand) can be identified only within a speech setting, namely the verbal and non-verbal speech of a brand. Based on the simple principle that one of a brand's main activities is to "tell" stories, whether through its advertising (speech *about* products) or through its product concepts (speech of the products themselves), we speak *of narrative identity* in this capacity. The narrative assumes that the identity of a brand is based on a formal staging that will guide the positioning and development of the brand contract. But what to say if it is not "saying who did what, why and how, by spreading in time the connection between these views?" The narrative identity must be understood as a concept seen "throughout an entire life." "In many narratives, the self seeks its identity throughout one's entire life," Ricoeur affirms. If we can recognize what forms our identity or that of others, let alone what constitutes a brand's identity, it is because we consider its course, which must be far enough advanced or achieved to reveal traces of an identity. Lastly, if Ricoeur directly ties identity and narrative together, it is partly because any narrative, by its conclusion and fullness, allows for what he calls a "heterogeneous synthesis" and, on the other hand, partly because he argues that no narrative is ethically neutral. However, ethics for him is one of the constitutive dimensions of identity, as we shall see further on.

Yet the *doxa* of marketing only envisages identity statically in time and space, through a relatively behaviorist view of communication (that is to say, based on the stimulus–response model). In this perspective, the brand is designed according to a traditional model of communication linking a transmitter to a receiver. This representation, which haunts numerous advertising and brand managers, led to a philosophy of action giving predominance to studies (taking the pulse of customers at every change of the message) and putting emphasis on the brand's message-reception process (and the famous message of the image of the brand). The main idea of this approach is to consider that brand identity is reinforced (to be communicable), while identity should not be considered as a state acquired once and for all through dialogue.

The dialectical balance between permanence and rupture

Brand identity raises the issue of maintaining a certain continuity while remaining attentive to constantly changing social demands. Such is the main challenge of fashion (in this, fashion and marketing are synonymous), that is, the variation of a particular temporality that is between the discovery of a pre-existing need and anticipation of trends; it means to constantly manage a balance between what "is" and what is "to come" and that will manifest itself through new products. Any brand, let alone any fashion brand, has to know how to remain itself while proposing changes that both circumscribe and go beyond customer expectations. How, then, to resolve this paradox, that is to say "change" while remaining ourselves?

Paul Ricoeur put forward a model and definition of identity that seems to answer that nagging question of brand marketing. If for him, as for many, a subject's identity is necessarily linked to the size of the difference (having an identity that is different from others) and permanence (keeping an identity presupposes continuity in time and space), it is largely on the second that he insists. He developed the idea that the "permanence" slope of identity must be understood as a dialectic between two drivers, between two forces: first an inertial force of acquired values, postures and habits that grow to reproduce signs that ensure recognition by others and enter the topic in the social code; and the other, a force that pulls towards the full realization of itself, a life project – this ethical, constant force, consisting of the assumed choice of certain values until switching over existence because, sooner or later, it leads to breaking with what previously allowed the subject to be recognized. In other words, the "permanence" identity Ricoeur conceived of opposes and dialecticizes, on one hand, the repetition, preservation, continuation and, *in fine*, the sedimentation, and on the other hand, constancy, loyalty to oneself, to one's values, one's ethics, and in time, the healthy reaction and the innovation that comes to break the habit that had sedimented. Each of these two forces is rooted in the two great principles of permanence: the *idem*, otherwise put, the same, dependent by definition on the passage of time and the *ipse*, which is to say, the self that does not depend on the passage of time but refers to the ethical foundation of the subject. If, after coinciding with each other, the *idem* begins to cover the *ipse*, this is how the force of habit, the inertia of acquired values and the automations, settles in that we have recognized one time, countless times. Ricoeur calls the resulting driver of this relationship between *idem* and *ipse*, the "character":

> By character, I mean all the hallmarks that allow the re-identification of a human individual as being the same.... The temporal dimensions of these brands is of interest in that it simulates the expected stability of a structure; the character, in this sense, refers to all the sustainable provisions by which a person is recognized. (Ricoeur, 1990)

This "character" is fully related to repetition over time, and above all, leads to sedimentation, to the extent that it "tends to cover and, ultimately, to abolish innovation." However, as the *ipse* suddenly releases the *idem*, which the subject puts to an end (temporarily) to the repetition of the same, what he abolished resurfaces in the self, and here appears this innovative strength that Ricoeur calls "keeping one's word." Keeping one's word is obviously not dependent upon the passage of time, as character may be, because it refers to the concept of a life project, that is to say, the assumed values, promoted and sought after by the subject (the individual or the brand), what could be called its ethical aim. This resultant driver of the inversion of the relationship between the *idem* and the *ipse* therefore defines strength opposed to character. It is a strength of self-constancy, loyalty to oneself and keeping one's word (hence its name), but it is mostly a strength for innovation because it emerges from an ethical requirement that may lead to breakage, denial and abandonment of provisions that only seemed to persist indefinitely. Furthermore, if Ricoeur calls it "keeping one's word," it is by keeping one's word that the subject demonstrates an ability to stay true to his commitments despite changes that could affect them; This is what Ricoeur calls self-constancy, which corresponds to a higher form of identity that makes the subject someone others can count on and vice versa.

Ricoeur's narrative identity sees a space-interval that comes and goes, or rather a constant oscillation between "character" and "keeping one's word," between the repetition of the same and an emergence of self that comes to abolish the former.

Thus, identity viewed as self-constancy over time requires a series of breaks and discontinuities that emerge from the ethical foundation of the subject. We are quite far, as we have seen, from a reduction of identity into a stable ontological core through time and space because, to Ricoeur, identity is viewed as the result of an evolutionary process that realizes creating any intrigue or narrative. Manifesting an identity is not, once again, merely being content to continually repeat the same pattern once and for all, but that is part of integrating otherness to be true to yourself. Far from being a static combination of permanence and difference, identity implies a dynamic and conflicted view linking these two forces: the force of inertia (the character) and the force of innovation (keeping one's word) in an ongoing search for equilibrium. As Ricoeur recalls again: "This new manner... of opposing the sameness of character to the constancy of the self by promising opens an *interval of meaning* which remains to be filled in. This interval is opened by a polarity, in temporal terms, between two models of permanence, perseverance of character and the constancy of the self in promising. It is into this scheme of temporality that mediation is sought. However, that is what this 'milieu' comes to occupy... the concept of narrative identity." Only the mastery of this oscillation actually allows a brand to know how to endure through time all while being of its time.

Brand identity and promise

If we accept the idea that the brand always involves an implicit or explicit contract between the company and its current and potential

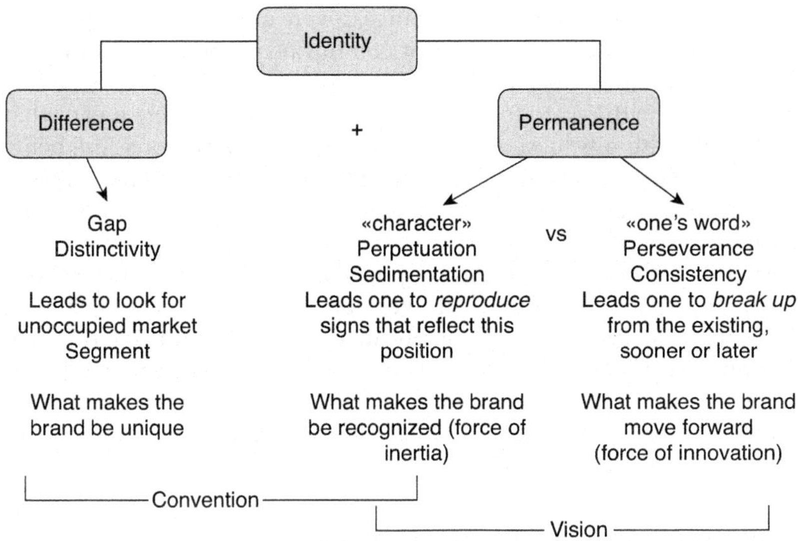

Figure 3.1 Brand identity in a Ricoeurian perspective
Source: Adapted from Ricoeur (1990) and Floch (1995).

customers, the identity process must be a constant strengthening of the terms of this contract. Thus, the Mugler brand's various collections highlight some invariants in the vision that the brand develops for women. The Mugler woman is defined in relation to a power she has over herself and men (dominatrix seduction logic) and an underlying capacity to go "too far," or even "to the end of her fantasies." The body here is contrived to better enslave men, as illustrated by the specific shape of the Mugler silhouette, highly structured, hypertrophied attributes (wasp waist, swimmer's shoulders, rounded hips, bulging breasts, long legs etc.) This vision of women, which translates into specific codes, has not prevented the brand from innovating precisely in order to renew the contract of trust between itself and its customers. Through innovation, a brand capitalizes on a contract of trust, which allows it to move forward and offer customers a different – that is to say, not necessarily new, even extraordinary or dramatic, but another – way of looking at the world and the objects that haunt our daily lives. Innovation is thus strengthening the brand's vision, in that the contract at work in any innovation worthy of the name enjoins a promise to customers, insofar as promise etymologically (from the Latin *promittere*) literally means "to go forward" and figuratively "to guarantee, insure or predict." The promise that covers innovation is a kind of commitment and sometimes even an annunciation in that it shows a strong anticipation of the public's expectations with regard to a given object. The promise here means that the brand "naturally" responds to its customers' expectations and, being boosted by the strong relationship of trust created over time, it is able to meet expectations, to anticipate them by reconfiguring the view held by a user of a given object.

After this detour into Ricoeurean philosophy, which we believe essential for understanding of the problem of identity, the relationship of the path to identity over time clearly appears. Thus, as Jean-Marie Floch explains, "Loyalty from one brand to itself, respect for its life project[,] ... is not the problem of a reproduction of signs, but that of invariance of a particular message realized according to various and changing modes of manifestation" (Floch, 1994: p. 7).

Semiotics to the rescue of marketing

Marketing doxa considers that the management of brand identity consists of developing and then repeating, in time and in space, a set of brand-recognition signals. These brand signals, the famous *brand ownables*, are figurative or graphic elements that allow brand recognition. They may be a logo, visual identity colors, a form of a product, a sound signature, and so forth – in short, any of the elements that a brand may own and imprint upon the minds of the public.

This same marketing doxa further claims that a brand's strength depends on its ability to define a position (the way we want the brand to be perceived in the minds of target customers) and to manifest this position through its own signs, therefore considered codes of the brand. The world of luxury, with its attendant signatures, initials or monograms, is by far the domain that best illustrates this logic of repetition in brand codes. This approach has the merit of stabilizing the problematic figurative and graphic elements of a brand in that it risks turning them into stone and immobilizing them even as our romantic society expects the unexpected and surprises. Here, particularly, semiotics may help a company to control the identity of a brand to the extent that it allows us to understand and make operational the idea that the proper management of a brand's identity involves more than simply repeating the identification elements, the "brand codes," whether in time and in space. This reduction of identity to one dimension of "brand signifiers" is likely to lead to a phenomenon of scaling of the brand, to the extent the brand codes eventually take over the brand project and suffocate it under an invasion of sedimented identification signs that nearly paralyze it. From this point of view, if managing brand identity is limited to the mere repetition of identification signs in the hope of ensuring the brand will remain strictly identical to itself, then this management will not guarantee its identity, but rather dissolve it.

Thus conceived, identity necessarily presupposes an element of innovation that incorporates an element of otherness (in the meaning of becoming other), and therefore cannot be reduced to a fixity, because even if it implies a certain continuity over time, it does not imply any sort of rigidity.

What this take on semiotics brings is that brand continuity discusses the means of perseverance and brand loyalty and not, as one might think at first, the means of simple repetition of identifiers. So when Vuitton had different designers reinterpret his monogram, it was done to ensure a balance between the brand's founding values and the range of values of creativity and boldness that create a distance between the brand and its heritage. Furthermore, the ephemeral nature of the brand's products through the use of limited editions allows for putting a scarcity strategy in place, which significantly increases the perceived value of the products. A limited edition product becomes an identity catalyst when it lets the brand break away from its own codes to better develop them. Brand identity management thus depends on a subtle balance between, firstly, waiting for reassuring repetition (which at once targets resurgence, continuity and sameness) through a process of reproducibility and, secondly, the unexpected, a surprise through a constant process of innovation. It is precisely the ability of brands to include a dimension of otherness, temporality and imbalance that allows them to go beyond their simple labeling function and increase the emotional and hedonistic nature of the consumer experience by building a sustainable relationship with their customers.

Identity levels of the brand

For the semiotician, all phenomena, from the time they are considered to have meaning and are taken as objects for analysis, may be described in two aspects: that of the system and that of the process. The *system* means the relationships of difference that define the object, or its components, relative to other objects or likely components that together form a world in which the object takes on meaning. The *process* is the arrangement of the components that have been chosen and combined to form the object at hand. When we consider the object analyzed like a semiotic object, that is, an object that functions as a language produces meaning, an analysis of its *system* refers to the paradigmatic axis, which is traditionally visually represented by a vertical, and the analysis of its *process* refers to a syntactical axis, represented by a horizontal. Each of these axes is characterized by the type of relationship between its various constituent elements. On the paradigmatic axis, relationships are of the "or ... or ..." type. This is an axis of potentialities and choices: for example, to form a sentence, we will tap into the virtuality of vocabulary and choose some words instead of others. In terms of the relationships that characterize the syntactical axis, they are relationships of the "and ... and ..." type. This is the axis of sequences, consecutives or series, along with fixtures, associations or co-presences: the analyzed object may be considered in terms of its temporal development, as our phrase composed of chosen words and then placed one *after* the other, or even under that of its spatial organization, such as a house composed of walls and windows and a roof and a fireplace, all present *at the same time* to form a meaningful object that we call a house. Thus, to further simplify without going into detail, the semiotic definition of another object with everyday meaning, such as a chair, will be paradigmatic insofar as in the world (the system) of "seats," a chair differs from an armchair, a stool, a bench, a love seat, a couch, a recliner, a lounge chair or a folding chair. But this definition is also syntactical insofar as the chair is the result of a process: it consists of an arrangement of four feet and bars and a seat and a backrest, this arrangement is considered from the temporal angle of its development, that is to say, the sequence in which a woodworker assembles it, or in terms of its final spatial configuration, that is to say, the order or hierarchy of the different parts of a co-presence constitute it like a chair: its front part and its back part, its horizontal and vertical components, the over and the underside, the top and the base, and so forth.

Considering that a brand is, above all, an "object" of meaning and that one of its key functions is to "semanticize" its system of offerings, then it can then be analyzed according to our two axes. Marketing is haunted by vertigo of differentiation because the strategic thinking of a brand first follows this paradigmatic type logic: it is primarily concerned with partition, segmentation, singularity, originality and uniqueness (think about, to convince us, the ancient and famous USP, "Unique Selling Proposition"). But marketing thought also follows another logic, complementary to the first, which is syntactical, because it is also concerned with the consistency of the brand message over time, the homogeneity of its offer, along with the relevance and accuracy of its responses to the request. The strategist seeks to attract new customers, here he/she is – unwittingly – engaged in a paradigmatic type of thinking whereby it will hail its target by promoting its brand as opposed to others, and it will try, implicitly or explicitly, to devalue. It seeks instead to retain current customers, and it is a syntactical step in that it will no longer be calling new clients and affirming the (superior) values of its brand, and instead will remind those customers of the same values and the satisfaction they have experienced. If, as we have seen, identity is a combination of difference and permanence, while its difference in identity is, first, of a paradigmatic nature and, second, by its permanence, also of a syntactical nature. This semiotic model applies to every feature of the brand, which is first defined by its difference from all the other brands, particularly those that compete in the same markets or market segments. And it is also defined by its syntactical nature, as per the two points of view that we have defined: first, that of the co-presence of the various units that compose it and, second, its history. Any brand, far from being a given crude monolithic good, consists of a set of components both physical (its products, shops, etc.) and intangible (its values, its imagined dimension, etc.), which when placed end-to-end constitute a brand. But any brand is also part of a story, in a temporal sequence where, over the course of launches, advertising campaigns, brand extensions, diversification and so forth, its managers have undoubtedly tried, worked and striven to send a message of consistency. The identity of a brand is found at the confluence of the two axes that structure any language: it is both the paradigmatic difference and syntactical permanence.

This first approximation established, it remains to consider in a greater level of detail the dual nature of the changeable permanence of brand identity according to Ricoeur. We have seen it focuses primarily on the permanent side of its model by distinguishing, on the one hand, the "character" permanence, wherein the same coincides with itself to very quickly meet and cover strengths through repetition and, on the other hand, the "keeping one's word" permanence, where it is the self's turn to take over and overcome the monotony of itself by moving ahead in the form of innovation. Here it seems important to remember that if the role of a brand is to "semanticize" its products, it is essentially through speech that it succeeds. To give meaning to what it offers, a brand speaks to its consumer: according to Jean-Marie Floch's expression, a brand is essentially a "being of discourse" (an enunciator) that sends its speech (through its statements) to its consumers (its enunciatees). This speech cannot be restricted only to verbal language used by the brand in its advertising or communication in the widest sense (hook, slogan, signature, claim, etc.). A brand "speaks" at least as much – if not more – through its other channels. Its designs, concepts, products, displays, points of sale, stores or corners, if it has any, are also defined as objects with meaning. These words are truly "mute" channels; semiotics calls them non-verbal or non-linguistic paths because they are expressed in languages other than our spoken language but, nevertheless, not only do they significantly contribute to give meaning to the brand, but undoubtedly this "silent" meaning is also understood by those to whom the brand addresses itself: to customers and consumers. Moreover, the whole point of semiotics is to set a goal to study and describe the conditions in which meaning can be produced and seized upon no matter what languages are at work – in other words, whatever the nature of the signs used, whether verbal or non-verbal. "The semiotics of the brand must be accounted for in the speech *of* the products, not only speech *about* the products," writes Jean-Marie Floch. Pushing away his thoughts, in a dazzling shortcut, he tells us that a brand is primarily a word. Floch sees brands not only as "*speaking,*" calling out to the consumer for his attention, but also "*giving one's word*" to the customer to attract or persuade (what marketing calls a "promise") and, even beyond that, influenced by Ricoeur, a brand is also "*keeping one's word*" to satisfy this customer and earn his loyalty, and ultimately create a form of attachment with him. In summary, a brand speaks, gives its word and keeps its word: it challenges, it promises and delivers.

Assuming of the primacy of the word being given, it is now time to explain the deep collusion between managing a brand's identity (the Ricoeur model) and semiotics methodology. Recall that in our mapping of the identity model developed by the philosopher, the "permanence" side of identity, located on the horizontal syntactical axis, splits off like a tree branch between "character" and "keeping one's word". This visual representation is not unlike the one he adopted in semiotics to account for the distinction and prioritization that one of the founding fathers of semiotics, the Danish linguist Louis Hjelmslev, formed between different planes and levels that he defined as constituting any language and that could describe any use of language (any "word"), regardless of the signs that this language borrows. If a language, any language at all, verbal or non-verbal, works well on two axes (the paradigmatic and syntactical), it also works on two levels, which we call the level of expression and the level of content, which we will briefly describe now. The level of expression is the perceived side of a language, and it organizes qualities of its own: the sound qualities for a vocal language; the pictorial or chromatic qualities for a visual language like painting or photography; the kinesthetic qualities for a body language like dance; and the quality of taste for a "culinary" language, and so forth. In terms of content, it is that which corresponds to the intelligible side of language and organizes the concepts to which the term refers – that is to say, what is meant, what is "said." Its expression calls upon our five senses to perceive it and on our intellect to understand its content. Hjelmslev then places each of these planes on two levels: the level of form and that of substance. The forms are the levels where the units of each plane are located, but above all, the invariant relationships they have with each other. This formal invariance is why language is seen as a system like no other. For their part, the substances are somehow the equivalent of the changing raw materials of each level, in how these units are built "before" being cut up by forms and structures between them, by invariant relationships. If the forms have an invariant nature, they are therefore opposed to substances that are inherently variable. Thus the same concept (form of content) may be expressed in different substances of expression: by the voice (sound substance), by writing (graphic substance), by drawing (iconic substance), by mime (kinetic substance), and so forth.

Continuing with the work of Greimas and Floch (1995), we may consider a brand not as a sign that can be reduced to the linking of a signifier and a signified but, indeed, it does link a plane of content and a plane of expression. Semiotics recognizes a distinction and a hierarchy of different planes and levels that can be recognized in any language (verbal or non-verbal). As per Hjelmslev, first we distinguish a plane of expression that is the sensible and visible side of a language; it organizes the sound, the visual and other specific qualities; secondly, a plane of content, which is the intelligible and organized side of language and speaks to the world – that is, in its way of "telling the world." On the other hand, Hjelmslev distinguishes two levels in each plane, namely:

- A level of form where *invariant relationships* are found that make such a language a system unlike any other;
- A level of substance wherein variable sensitive or conceptual materials are found, which, subject to these relationships, allow them to operate.

As the figure reveals, the two levels of the form (form of expression and form of content) are linked (by a double arrow), because the brand's invariants of speech are found precisely at these levels; these two levels

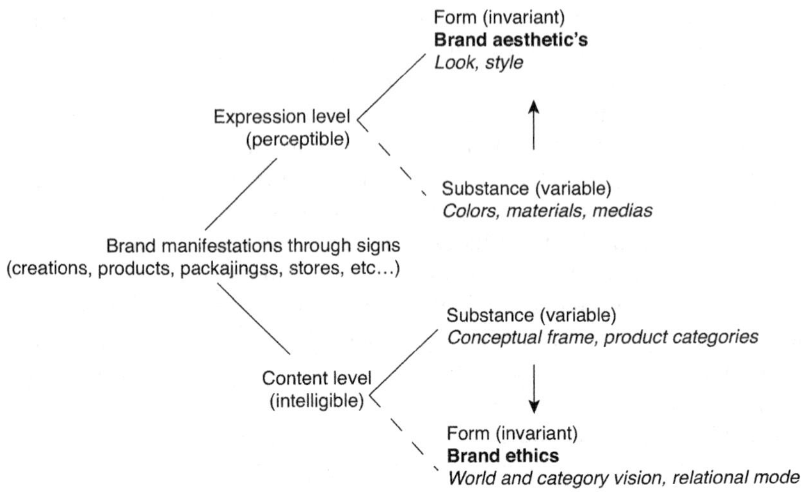

Figure 3.2 The planes of language of a brand

have solidarity. Thus a change in one of these levels necessarily leads to a concomitant change in the other level. This solidarity at both levels permits understanding the variation in the invariance that was at issue in Ricoeur's theory of narrative identity. This is where the heart of the argument takes place as the linking of these two levels helps us understand how a brand can evolve while still remaining itself.

On the plane of expression, we can match the sensitive characteristics of manifestations of the brand: all that it gives to perceive itself and that gives it a concrete physicality: palpable, as it were. Symmetrically, on the plane of content, it matches the intelligible dimension of the brand, which organizes all that our mind can grasp, what we can understand and, ultimately, say. True to Hjelmslev, levels of the substance and form can be distinguished on each of these planes. Floch defines the substance of a brand's content as consisting of a conceptual world that it invests and uses. In other words, and in simplifying a bit, this substance content covers the activity sectors, product categories and markets or market segments in which the brand operates. Substance roughly includes, for example, the world of perfume for the Guerlain brand, tableware for Christofle and haute couture for Thierry Mugler. As for the substance of the expression of a brand: substance returns to it the techniques, media, materials or raw materials processed and worked by the brand in question to achieve its goals. Returning term-by-term to one the above examples, Guerlain will have for substance the expression of all fragrances comprising the palette of a nose (perfume organ); Christofle works with porcelain, silver and crystal; and Mugler uses textiles, materials and fabrics. The forms of expression and content are invariant levels that precisely result from information operations – cutting and organization – specifically performed by a brand on substances it invests in, both physical and conceptual. In the form of the content of the brand, it matches the way it sees itself or the conceptual world in which it operates and that it brings to itself, its way of considering and structuring the environment in which it operates, to position itself. At this level is found its business philosophy, or "credo," its worldview or its relationship to others, competitors as well as customers. Floch defines this layer of the brand as *"what it works on,"* that is to say a sort of "engine": a certain vision of women's haute couture for Mugler, an individual philosophy of Guerlain perfume, an original artistic tableware design for Christofle and so forth. This credo eventually qualifies as the "ethics of the brand," where the term "ethics" should remind us of Ricoeur's *ipse*, this ethical foundation of self, whose philosophy is based on the permanent slope of its model, the main driver of the resulting identity Ricoeur calls "keeping one's word."

As to the form of expression, Floch states it is at the perceptible level where sensitive attributes specific to statements of the brand are found, the invariant features of style that characterize them. According to the languages the brand borrows to "speak," these characteristics are either plastic in nature, rhythmic, melodic or prosodic, gustatory, tactile or olfactory; they apply to substances of expression, the "raw materials" with which the brand works; they "brand" its productions; they leave a footprint, a stamp and make it specific, or – especially if the brand is well managed – unique and inimitable: the famous Guerlinade, this "family resemblance" seen in Guerlain perfumes, the silhouette of the Mugler woman, the "Louis XV contemporary" design by Christofle. Floch described this layer as the "brand aesthetic," defined according to him as *"what we recognize"* in the brand. Ricoeurean accents of such a name have undoubtedly not escaped anyone. Speaking of recognition, this is obviously alluding to the "character" aspect of Ricoeur's permanence-identity, this force of inertia, dominated by an *idem* that covers the *ipse*, and leads to cultivating the continuation and perpetuation of the same.

So, here, reconciliation is shown between the identity philosophy and semiotic methodology. In this philosophical-semiotic view, both formal semiotic levels (ethical and brand aesthetic) and the two philosophical dimensions (character and keeping one's word) are counterparts. But beyond this simple approval, the relationships between the two terms of each structure are similar in respect to solidarity: as well as a brand aesthetic that only conceives it from the founding ethic, and that a brand ethic does not make noticeable, or "reflected" in its aesthetics. The same applies if the character reflects keeping one's word: it "motivates" the character. In other words, these solidarity relationships are generative in nature. On the other hand, even in Ricoeur the narrative identity of a subject, throughout the course of his life, is built in a dialectical relationship between the sedimentation of his character and periodic upsurges of keeping one's word that, in a battle towards full self-realization, also coming to say "removing the tartar," in the words of Floch, and free from this debilitating cangue of monotonous repetition; likewise, and symmetrically, good management (semiotic) of the brand's identity over time consists of identifying and maintaining the balance between the aesthetics and ethics of the brand, between "what you recognize it by" (form of expression) and "what it works on" (form of content), given that, as is the case for the Ricoeurean object, the brand also tends to settle under the weight of habit: the trouble is indeed that many brand managers are happy with an appearance of coherence and are more worried about ensuring visibility of the "brand ownables" and superficial brand recognition than willing to understand and master the logic of production. This good question therefore assumes the following paradox: ensuring the brand identity for which we are responsible necessarily means refusing to rely solely on the continuation and repetition of established brand signals, and even going beyond that, promoting, encouraging, putting forward or provoking regular questioning, periodic breaks and discontinuities in the brand's history. In other words, good management involves beneficial and steady dropping of the existing, "cultural revolution" innovations, aiming in appearance only to free the brand, identified it. It is neither more nor less than to constantly remember that, like small children, who are believed to assert their self-awareness from the moment they first say the word "no", by a brand's refusal it asserts its identity above all. For example, many brands have started off on the wrong foot, or by putting their foot in their mouth, that is, and puns aside, many brands have grown through opposition: by refusing to fit the mold of ready-to-think of their time, by striving to promote values contrary to those of their competitors, practicing the strategy of Jean-Marie Dru (1997), who theorized and consecrated under the name of "disruption" or, more simply, because of the spirit of contradiction that drove their founders. This good management follows then, and it is equally important to periodically break away from the signs or "brand signifiers" that have long identified it so obviously that they end up suffocating it, or, because it is believed that their presence alone on any manifestation (product, service, etc.) is enough to justify anything, and they end up contributing to diluting the brand. If, of course, the "good" brand manager cannot be concerned with "what does this sign do" (that is to say, superficial communication manifestation units), this concern must always remain secondary to the fundamental question of "what makes sense" for a brand. By leaning precisely on the "engine" of the brand, the workings of the "brand machine" (the *machine*, it will be recalled, is intended to produce a meaning of its own), which is found well below or far beyond the only signs emitted at the surface, the identity can be controlled more closely. It is in this sense that regarding the management of brand identity, we can declare with certainty the superiority of semiotics over semiotics. Indeed, semiotics has a goal of studying the signs (their classification, their types, etc.), so its intervention may be only very limited. The identity of a brand, once again, is not a matter of signs, not a question that deals with the superficial level of the manifestation, but at the immanent level of production of meaning, that is to say, on the planes below the signs where the brand's own invariant relationships that generate the specificity of its message are etched. In other words, we cannot reduce a brand to a collection of signs. Rather, it is better to see it as a production logic of these signs. A semiology of signs could possibly be useful to reflect the nature of a brand, the "brand signifiers" of "that by which it is recognized," but in no case when it comes to understanding "keeping one's word," where only semiotics of the production of meaning is able to account for its generative dimension, to allow defining "what it works on."

Which identity strategy for the brand?

Such an approach may be helpful in order to understand and manage brand diversification strategies. Diversification downstream implies the brand's ability to engage in new ways initiated upstream and poses the dual question of its legitimacy to do so and, thereby, the possible dilution of its identity that such a decision would entail. In terms of diversification, the problem is to ensure optimum compliance conditions for innovation, so that this novelty, in passing from production to seizure by consumers is perceived as both legitimate and consistent with brand identity.

It should be noted at the outset what we mean by brand diversification. In terms of diversification, it is common to confuse what are called *range extension* and *brand extension*. Range extension is a case of a small sidestep in a product category in which the brand is already established or in an immediately adjacent category, whereas brand extension of brand stretching is a wide step that involves the brand investing in a completely unfamiliar product category. Obviously the latter scenario begs the question of legitimacy and possible dissolution of brand identity, the first ("flankering") seems self-evident. However, how many new product launches, which at first seemed so simple and easy to carry out, were disappointing or ended in failure and the withdrawal of products from distribution channels? And how many wild bets with the odds stacked against them have proven hugely successful? From the point of view of good brand identity management, there are no small or large launches, there is no hierarchy. Any diversification, any extension, regardless of the line or the brand requires the greatest care, not just the "what makes a sign," again but "what makes sense." Any manifestation of the brand must both carry its identity and nourish it. In other words, any innovation, from conception to execution and to being placed on the market, must build invariant relationships that characterize the brand's ethics and aesthetics, its own forms of content and expression, since according to this approach, developed and defended by Floch, "the play of these relationships has a generative nature, that is to say that they are a small engine to create meaning and value, an ability to produce new signs (or to make one's own) and new products that will be different from those that exist or have existed, of course, but that still carry the same 'spirit,' the same approach to the market."

In the first place, consider the supposed diversification the most difficult, that of an extension of the brand, the "brand stretch." To illustrate this, we will use a case in point, that of Hermès. A brand extension is, as we have seen, taking a big step away from the brand, not by innovating in a world of products where it is already situated, legitimate and established, but rather in a distant world, which is foreign to it and where a priori it has little or no legitimacy. In this world of products, markets or market segments, we might be tempted to believe that such a move involves only one single layer of the substance of content in Floch's model. But that would mean forgetting that there is only an adaptation to the world of marketing in the Hjelmslev model, and that it is only an abstract semiotic sham of how the brand operates. Maybe here we reach the limit of collusion, as are often so numerous in the field of linguistics, where it is certainly fair to not pay attention to some substances, and the commercial area, where it plays a meaningful role: we must recognize that a brand does not sell or buy in layers of abstract concepts floating in ether, much less by weight as for primary raw materials, but rather in the form of finished branded products we could not concretely obtain other than in exchange for cold hard cash. Indeed, in "real life" these substances of content are industries that are everything but abstractions. They consist of things, objects, products, all tangible, all having an irreducible physicality, all coming from a certain substance of expression. In "real life," the substances of content and substance of expression are integral to each other, and together form the so-called markets. Thus, when the Hermès brand, founded in 1837 as a maker of saddles and harnesses for horses, in 1878 launched into leather goods and glove-making, and in 1914 added luggage and bags, there was still congruence between these substances of content (saddlery, leather goods, gloves and luggage) and substances of expression (leather) so it was able to extend the surface of the substance of its content (diversifying into a different world of products) without fundamentally changing its substance of expression without changing the "raw material". But in 1920, when it began to throws, scarves, coats and jackets to adapt to a new means of locomotion, which was the automobile, it not only invested in a new substance of content (clothing), but it also had to invest in a new substance of expression (textiles). Similarly, in the 1930s, when it added watchmaking and jewelry to these substances of content, it also needed to invest in a new substance of expression, which was precious metals. And so on, in the 1950s creating the perfume house (substance of content) and fragrant essences (substance of expression), or in the 1980s with tableware (substance of content) and porcelain, silver and crystal (substances of expression). Today, all the categories that the Hermès brand covers are most likely one of the largest "territories" for a single brand, and neither its legitimacy nor identity are challenged by such variety. Hermès's "territory" encompasses an extremely disparate set of product worlds, each of which is irreducibly related in know-how and skilled trades and, in turn, the materials and specific processing and treatment techniques. Through this example, we can therefore understand, on the one hand, the variability of substances, and on the other hand, their solidarity. The changing of one substance of content to another (from one conceptual world to another) generally leads to a corresponding change from one substance of expression to another. This presupposes, in most cases, a doubling of the complexity associated with product development. The brand must not only understand this new world, by incorporating the rules of operation, capturing the dynamics or stakes involved, which ultimately is just an exercise of the mind, but it must also incorporate the new related materials and, above all, the techniques and know-how. This is frequently the challenge brand managers claim to be the most difficult to overcome. There is yet another equally important challenge, if not more important, which is paying attention to the brand's loyalty to itself in this process of change. The arduous task of diversification involves applying these new invariant forms of substances that are unique to the brand. In other words, how to apply "brand ethics" to a new content of substance, a new conceptual world? Where will the aesthetic translations of new materials and this application of "brand ethics" finally lead? What brings unity to the disparate worlds in which Hermès has diversified? It is primarily the translation of the same aesthetic to each category and, therefore, the same brand ethics. The House of Hermès invested in each of these disparate worlds following the same and singular logic of the brand, based on the rejection of ostentatious luxury combined with the cultivation of a certain imaginative craftsmanship characterized by Levi-Strauss's concept of dilated time, "the pleasure of doing" (Floch, 1995).

> All the art of Hermès consists of giving articles from everyday life (neck ties, watches, belts, bags ...) a quality, an aesthetic and a pleasure in use. We are not a fashion house. We are not trying to be fashionable.... Refined discretion will ultimately prevail over the culture of the logo.... Our job is that of artisans looking to make beautiful objects with a high creative content.... We do everything by hand. We do not work in an assembly line. For a single bag, an artisan has to work fifteen to twenty hours, for a saddle, twenty-five hours.... At Hermès, I discovered that the financial could be based on a poetic project. (Patrick Thomas)

That is what "keeping one's word" means to Hermès. It is also the same brand ethic that not only allowed it to manage and unify all its diversifications, all these jumps from one substance to another, and that is not the least of its generated virtues. Because, I repeat, like Hermès, any brand's well-managed identity brings about "forsaking the self for self-constancy." If Hermès had resisted the power of innovation and the ethical aim of "keeping one's word" that tends towards the full realization of the subject-brand, if it were left "tartaring up" the repetition of the same, there is a good chance that this great company would still, as on the day it was founded, be nothing more than a small accessories shop for riders and carriages.

What we have just seen about brand extensions is equally true for line extensions, the "flankers", that is to say, new products launched on the brand's market of reference (on its substance of "historical" content), such as a new car model in the case of a brand like Renault or Peugeot.

Thus we can understand how a brand can support a project by ensuring consistency while developing the identifiers of the brand. This is expressed very well by a brand like Louis Vuitton, which reconciles three dimensions in a project to bring it to life:

(1) A dimension linked to tradition and know-how that the brand claims embodies the values of quality, durability and timelessness and is transmitted by institutional communications (designed to set out the values of boldness and modernity while using its know-how) and by axes such as patronage and sponsorship.
(2) A dimension related to the soul of the journey that goes back to the roots of the brand in reconciling the values of innovation, functionality and robustness in brand communications, whose main role is re-injecting the dream through real and dream-travel themes.
(3) A dimension related to the unique balance between fashion and timeless luxury strictly based on product communications reaffirming the values of audacity, simplicity and wealth, and whose objective is to create desire (to visit the shops, to buy).

Which ethic for brand identity?

Let us try to conclude by embracing a more general framework, showing that the relationship with time is actually a critical variable in any brand dynamics. What should a brand do with its past and how should it take it into account when evaluating a project for likely risks of several kinds, especially the logic of mergers and acquisitions and inherent phenomena of transferring power that often raise the issue of the persistence of stylistic codes? To move ahead, a brand, like a person, must have a more or less coordinated past from where it can set about building a present and a future. A little "like a lady walking with a long train; when she changes direction abruptly, a little kick, and she puts the train back behind her." (Vernant, 1996: p. 31)

We can then distinguish between what make a style and what makes a fashion. A brand ranked as having made a fashion differs essentially from what it is recognized for, that is to say, its aesthetic invariants are identifiable and readable at a given moment. This is to show its codes of recognition. In contrast, a stylish brand translates signing on for the long-term by the values and ethics guiding its creations, and whose long-term projection of identifiable notable units are only the consequence.

A brand thus has many ways to manage the handling of its past. We can distinguish four routes for identity:

- An ethic of *tradition* that involves registering the brand in a filiation logic by reproducing the brand's codes to sustain it and sign it on for the long-term. This starts from researching the roots of the brand by exploring (and benefiting from) its roots; For example, Hermès strategy following the arrival of Martin Margiela, which has been to continue the brand's strong values related to craftsmanship, know-how, research and timelessness.
- An ethic of *transmission* that involves establishing the brand's codes and then moving into the competitive landscape. It somehow helps to blow on the ashes of a forgotten past and hope to rekindle the flame. An agricultural metaphor that refers to the plant seems important to us to illustrate the main idea of this strategy, which involves planting the seeds of brand identity and caring for them until they germinate.
- An ethic of *novation* that involves breaking the existing codes by creating a breaking-off effect with the original territory of the brand. This logic is often used by brands with an unpleasant or complicated past that might appear out of step with the times. A type of strategy deliberately designed not to exploit a rich heritage may also be the result of a new leader wishing to put his stamp on the brand or a creative director wanting to leave a personal mark overflowing with identifying attributes of the brand. Gucci's collaboration with Tom Ford is a good example of this type of strategy, where the style of the designer pre-empts the identity of the brand.
- An ethic of *mutation* that involves staging a regeneration of the brand, a real change of skin "by advancing the brand's codes without denying them." Both Burberry and Louis Vuitton have demonstrated such strategies (Figure 3.3).

The syntax of brands

We now understand how this dynamic theory of brand identity can materialize through figurative elements of the brand. The syntax approach will enable us to resolve this issue. Structural analysis has indeed updated the fact that many cultural practices such as fashion,

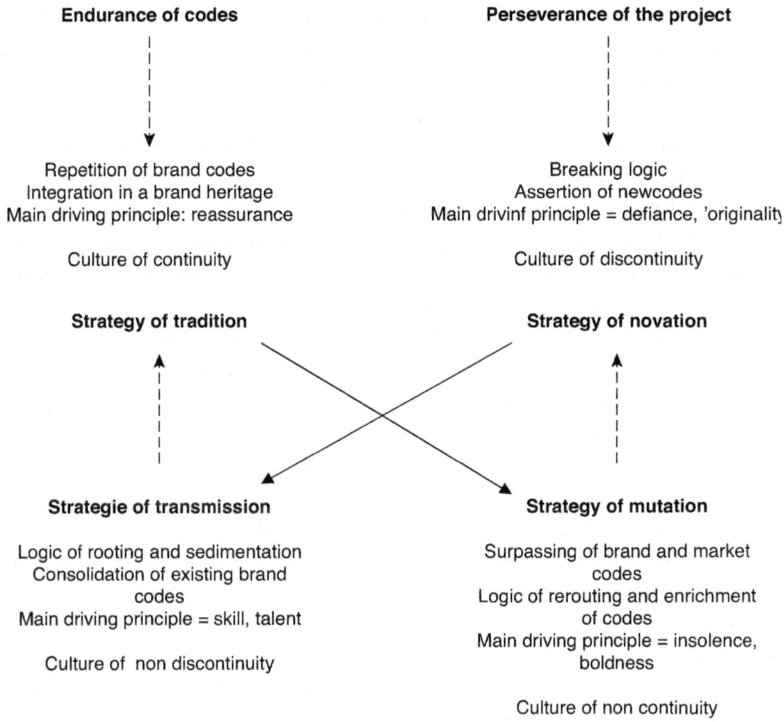

Figure 3.3 The four-identity strategy of brands

food and consumption actually are similar to real systems of meaning stated by rules specific to language systems; hence the underlying possibility of reading or decoding these systems of meaning using syntax rules governing linguistic systems. There are many examples of work demonstrating the fact that an object is an integral part of a more complex system of meanings, itself governed by its own relationship to language systems. Kehret Ward (1987, 1988), for example, has well illustrated the fact that a system of products is governed by opposing and complementary relationships as it would in a linguistic system. Our approach to maque syntax follows the line of the famous (though maligned) Barthes study (1967) on the fashion system that leads him to describe the syntax organization of the clothing system; one, starting from a stack of fashion magazines, updates the minimum units of the system, which he calls *vestèmes,* and shows that the organization of a clothing system refers to the opposing and complementary relationships between these various elements. If, as we have assumed, the brand is similar to a system and not only a single brand element (a sign), a structural analysis of the brand should refer to the description of this particular system of meaning, that is, updating its organizational rules. First we must show how the functioning of this particular system that is the brand is largely comparable to the functioning of a linguistic system. A key concept for understanding the syntax dimension of the brand is once again the concept of bricolage, beautifully developed in the first chapter through the well-known writings of Lévi-Strauss: *The Savage Mind*. As Levi-Strauss reminds us, in its original meaning, the term bricoleur implies a notion of difference, namely that the bricoleur is essentially one who, in ways like a skilled artist, uses means diverted from other uses. Bricolage is also, according to Levi-Strauss, the essence of mythical thought, in that it induces an ability to speak with a limited repertoire whose composition is disparate. There is therefore an essentially "mythopoetical" character to bricolage; Bricolage is primarily *Muthos*, that is to say, a practice that refers to a narrative trajectory (it takes place over a span of time), but it also implies a poïen, "*do*," by which the individual produces an object using disparate elements. Unlike an engineer, a bricoleur is one who makes things "on a shoestring," that is to say, plans his project with the aid of a finite set of materials and disparate tools he is constrained to use: He works within a "closed instrumental world" and subjects his project to items at hand, unlike the engineer, whose tools and materials are newly designed according to each of his projects. Thus, the bricoleur is using what is already "semi-customized," that is to say, elements that are by nature reserved for "a specific and determined task"; all of the bricoleur's play involves only using this half-constraint as a freedom, by reorganizing the functional value of each element via the definition of new relationships between the system components he has available. One could almost say that the work of a bricoleur is quasi-structuralist obedience, since it focuses on the relationship, not the elements. Bricolage is somehow creating a sense of purpose by the meaningful reorganization of relationships between pre-constrained elements. How to think about the relationship between an object and a brand? At first glance, the object represents the first level of linking of this system that is the brand. Is this first link the only option? As Barthes stated, an object is not comparable to a word, but is more like a sentence (Barthes, 1964, 1985). Thus, one can understand a product as the basic semantic unit of the language that is the brand. The object serves to illustrate a second possible linking because it is possible to break it down into several semantic units that we suggest naming, in homage to Barthes, the *marquèmes*. Thus, the system of brands is subject to the principle of double linking. In this sense it brings together various product lines (first link) and each product is broken down in turn into several basic semantic units. The originality of this holistic approach to the brand is to involve a structural homology between this complex system of objects that is a brand and linguistic systems. What we apply to the brand is none other than the effect the painter Arcimboldo applied to his pictorial system, by representing heads made from objects (Barthes, 1982). We remember a well-known writing by Barthes about Arcimboldo's effect (Barthes, 1982), where he illustrates the creation of a pictorial system that follows the linguistic principle of double linking. As Barthes pointed out, "we wish to remember, once again, the structure of human language: it is linked two times: what follows a speech may be split into words, and the words, in turn, may be cut into sounds (or letters). However, there is a big difference between these two links: each of the first produced units already has a meaning (these are the words) the second produces meaningless units (phonemes are: a phoneme in itself means nothing). This structure is known, does not apply to the visual arts; ... painting knows only one link. From there, we can understand the structural paradox of Arcimboldo's compositions. Arcimboldo makes his paintings in a true language, he gives them a double linking (Barthes 1982, 126). Is that not exactly the mechanism at work in this particular system, which is the brand? Conceived in the holistic sense, the brand covers, in fact, a range of units that are subject to a first link (products), themselves composed of base units that, as per Barthes, we propose to call *marquèmes* (!) Thus the products cannot be conceived as part of a family or a constellation brought together by a brand. Conversely, due to belonging to an identity system, the product can be broken down into marquèmes, which

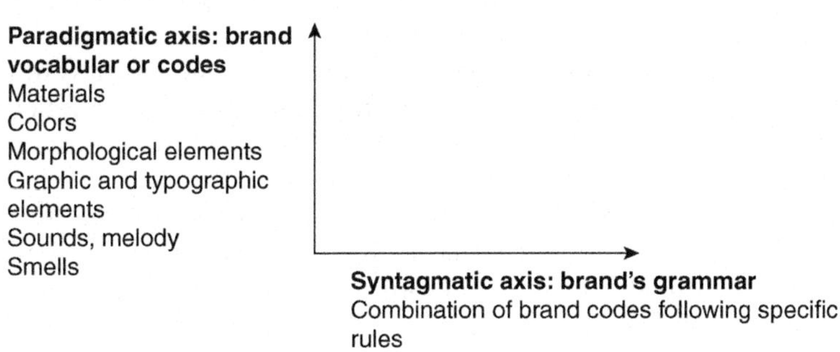

Figure 3.4 The brand as a system

form the minimum semantic units in a brand system. This view of the product as an arrangeable and modular system of elements refers to a new way of looking at the brand and the object.

The brand, as a language, allows the constitution (and nesting) of narratives, that is, the possibility of syntactically linking a number of semantic elements to achieve a certain narrative program. The value of each element of the system is not related to its substantial presence, but to its functional presence in a particular phrase. So we must necessarily consider the brand, not as a singular and undivided entity, but an orchestration of several levels of language. This practice of bricolage is all the more interesting in that some studies point to the development of bricolage in Western societies leading up to an individual and symbolic re-appropriation of the object in consumer practices. So there is every reason to link the idea of the brand as a symbolic bricolage and the idea of consumption becoming *consonnation*, as developed by Francesco Morace (1990) to illustrate the fact that in modern society an object is invested with a hidden meaning allowing its acquirer not so much to consume than "resonate" with the object, that is, to establish a close resonating relationship."

From the physical imprint to the mental imprint: leaving a trace

The sole purpose of a visual identity is to leave a trace in the consumer's mind. A trace allows you to note the presence of something in its absence. A brand is a physical, written or drawn trace, whose purpose is to create a psychic trace and a memory trace to use the trichotomy of traces suggested by Paul Ricoeur. The pervasiveness of identifiers and the desire to create mental traces have led most brands towards a substantialization of their formal expressions (graphic, verbal, acoustic, etc.) as shown by the repetitions of brand codes and the rigid use of brand identifiers set out in brand guidelines and which make the brand clearly recognizable. This is also where the link between visual identity and the very idea of representation comes in, following on more or less in the wake of the search for objectivity, which is characteristic of a reflex of Western thought whereby an "object" has to be circumscribed to make it visible and recognizable.

Visual identity is therefore characterized by condensation and repetition over time and in different plastic media which identify the brand. It is precisely this stability which enables a visual identity to trigger the consumer's instantaneous cognitive and affective response.

Visual identity is a fundamentally symbolic system insofar as it makes a conventional (but not arbitrary) link between two parts, one of which is the brand itself and the other its identifiers (a symbol, a color code, a brand personality, etc.). It therefore plays a role in the free association of the two parts for which it must constantly justify the sociation. Is it not the case, however, that this purely symbolic construction of visual identities has drowned out other options for coherence, which have nonetheless sometimes resurfaced, almost as if by stealth, in painting and modern poetry?

This is why many brands are tempted to turn to indicative signs or hints rather than engaging directly in wars about sovereign symbols. So the visual identity of Pathé, for example, articulates elements such as a yellow/gray color code, an exclamation point, a typeface, a bubble and a cockerel, which are brought into play depending on the context of the communication. What we are talking about here is the index, which is a sign governed by the natural relationship between expression and content. The index is incontrovertible, as it carries the trace of a body and like a fingerprint or a bloodstain it demonstrates a presence. So, perhaps the only way for a brand to co-exist with its array of signs is to use a proper system of indices which can settle any questions about legitimacy.

From sign to system: the Arcimboldo effect

The idea is to create a plastic language that can break down into minimal indicative units whose function is to ensure brand recognition, in whatever context it is applied (products, posters, etc.) For brands today the challenge is to create systems of visual identity that allow them to differentiate themselves, while at the same time being capable of evolving in harmony with the way the brand itself develops and diversifies into other sectors of activity. (For instance, Virgin markets music products, soft drinks, insurance and airline services, etc.). Furthermore, in the context of market globalization, brand recognition codes must be capable of crossing borders and cultures seamlessly and with no risk of creating confusion. This model of visual identity is designed not so much as a repetition of visual identifiers, but formed as a collection made up like a human body, which is both whole and articulated. The idea is to create order over a system of internal subordinates which operates through the articulation of plastic invariants.

How best then to explain the organization of a brand as a syncretic system? We can find a response in painting and, in particular, in the work of Arcimboldo and through what Barthes judiciously called the Arcimboldo effect. "Let us recall, once again, the structure of our human language: it is doubly articulated: the sequence of discourse can be divided into words, and the words divided in their turn into sounds (or into letters). Yet there is a great difference between these two articulations: the first produces units each of which already has a meaning (the words); the second produces non-signifying units (the phonemes: a phoneme, in itself, signifies nothing). This structure, we know, is not valid for the visual arts;... painting knows only one articulation. Hence, we can readily understand the structural paradox of the Arcimboldesque compositions. Arcimboldo makes painting into a veritable language, he gives it a double articulation: the head of *Calvin* first decomposes into forms which are *already* namable objects – in other words, *words*; a chicken carcass, a drumstick, a fishtail, scribbled pages: these objects in their turn decompose into forms which in themselves signify nothing: here we return to the double scale of words and sounds" (Barthes, 1985: p. 136).

In the same way that Barthes remarked that an object cannot be assimilated to a word but rather to a phrase, we can consider a visual identity not so much as a repetition of patterns, but rather as the articulation of different basic plastic or visual units all of which are elements of brand recognition that, following on from Barthes, we might call "brandemes"; they can include indices for colors, shapes, sounds, smells and so forth. Brand identity would therefore display the articulation of these various elements according to the brand's own syntagmatic rules of complementarity and juxtaposition.

We need to disinter our symbolic and strictly visual tradition of identity to envisage a system of imprints which will not be cramped into the confines of form, but can be transformed by breathing in and out of emptiness and fullness and show the incentive which supports life in the polarities of the indicative signs. Paradoxically, this is a process of de-representation. Indeed, a logo is essentially a signature denoting the representation and appearance of a being, whereas indicative identities are more concerned with transitions and modifications, a passage from one thing to another. Here, we are touching on the principles of Chinese pictorial art (Jullien, 2003). Unlike Western representation, which always plays disjunctively on the presence/absence coupling (representation ultimately aims at making an absence present), Chinese painters or poets do not paint with distinctive strokes, even less so with disjunctive ones. They do not paint such things to put them on display or bring out their presence. Rather they paint them as both being and not-being: present-absent, half-light half-dark, both light and dark. Consequently, Chinese pictorial art offers other fertile categories in which images can be thought about: vagueness, indistinction, quiet reflection, transformation, and so forth. It seems to provide a perfect opportunity to leave behind the over-saturation of meaning and the tyranny of symbols which imprison images in a register that tends to empty them of meaning, emotion and, probably, efficacy. This is, therefore, de-representation, as the index now only indicates itself and does not represent anything else. The index is self-referential, which perhaps prefigures a potential for brands to leave behind the symbolic order and enter into some kind of an a-symbolic or mute order corresponding to the de-substantialization of their discourse.

4
Ethics Despite Amorality

Capitalism is not the natural result of market activities. As Karl Polyani has shown, market activities are embedded in a large set of inextricably political, religious and cultural conditions which organize their meanings and limits. Historically, the capitalist system only appeared once it was capable of assuming its own presuppositions (for example, the widespread dissolution of man's links to the earth and to his tools), and thereby to obtain the opportunity of developing according to its own laws. The question remains what combination of circumstances made possible the emergence of a world dominated, as it is today, by the conceptualization of economic growth. Going further, if "a human being's supreme wealth and the key to his happiness has always been *the agreement with himself*" as postulated by Michéa (2008) how does this fit into the "broken world of victorious liberalism"?

Market amorality

Stripped back to its essential principles, liberalism can be seen as the construct of a minimal society in which Law defines the form and Economy defines the content, or more precisely freedom and growth. A duality underpins philosophical liberalism's proposal of the utopian rational society whose peaceful existence is founded solely on the impersonal structures of the market and the law. Thus, the historical reality which profoundly transforms modern societies must essentially be understood as the logical outcome of the liberal philosophical construct, as it has been formulated since the 17th century, and more particularly since the philosophy of the Enlightenment.

Although some partial attempts to experiment with liberalism in government took place under the monarchy in France, philosophical liberalism must, above all, be understood as a *post-revolutionary project* which only became possible when the foundations of the *Ancien Régime* had been definitively destroyed, when it could become the active principle for the transformation of civilization in the West and around the planet. Liberalism is therefore the emblem *par excellence* of modern ideology, which is by definition without previous philosophical parentage unlike, for instance, the republican ideal, imbued as it is with classical virtues, or original socialism, rooted in ideas of morality and community. The logic of liberalism implies the destitution of all the normative constructs that explicitly refer to a symbolic law, in favor only of the "axiologically neutral" mechanisms of the market and the law. It assumes that a human community can function coherently without the least reliance on shared moral values, whence a kind of inward-looking doctrine which postulates the spirit of tolerance and the refusal to reject the Other as a sort of substitute ethics. But what might a concept as ambiguous as tolerance actually mean? Does it mean, for example, generalizing to all human beings these attitudes of respect, benevolence and indeed empathy that each community usually reserves for its closest members, so that tolerance can be understood as the highest degree of any moral perfection? The question is to understand how liberalism has been able to conjugate selfish interests with the work that humans must unceasingly perform on themselves in order to maintain and develop the conditions of their own humanity. The author maintains that the universalization of fundamental human values is essentially linked to the mechanisms that effectively pacified modern Europe and which really got under way in the 16th century through the actions of the intellectuals and men of power known as the "Politicals." Unlike the classical Humanists, the Politicals were convinced that the end of the wars of religion and a new equilibrium between the European powers could only be obtained and sustainably guaranteed on the condition that the strict rules of "political realism" were respected. This implied that the parties involved agreed to put aside their personal convictions as to the meaning of the good life. Liberalism, therefore, took root in a strategy of lesser evil given the miserable condition of humanity (who, according to Pascal, was "incapable of truth and goodness") and the destructive nature of its passions. As Michéa has shown, we then see the appearance of a kind of disillusioned anthropology which explains the constant recourse, from the 16th century onward, to the metaphysical idea of "necessity" which was rapidly to become the philosophical keystone of all political constructs, including in their now-dominant form, the ideas of growth and progress.

Once human survival can no longer depend on human free will or on appeals to moral or religious conscience, the only problem left to solve is how to neutralize the action of the various moral philosophies and religions from which people had previously drawn their different reasons for living. Liberalism could only claim to be the accomplished form of political wisdom once it had dissolved into a purely technical management of "necessity". The rhetoric of good and evil was therefore replaced by a technical metaphor which also had the corollary of transforming ancient political philosophy (which pondered the nature of the best government or the "Ideal City") into the art of managing all problems encountered in a purely instrumental way.

Michéa considers that one of the fundamental mechanisms of this contingent historical configuration is the ideal of Science, whence the particular role that ideology has played since the 16th century in Western policies of modernization. Liberalism is rooted in the determination to organize humanity scientifically with a claim to state the truth about good governance by mimicking the methodology of the natural sciences and the modalities of technical action it validates. Referring to numerous, original works on the history of ideas, techniques and science, Michéa shows that liberalism is a result of the invention of experimental natural science, the *Scienza nuova*, which forged the ideal of science as capable of making man "master and owner of nature" by providing a model of symbolic authority that could challenge the Church. The goal was to discover the mechanisms (i.e., the systems of weights and counter-weights on the model of physical theories of balance) which could generate the necessary order and harmony without the need for subjects to be virtuous or not. This ideal of science resulting from Galilean physics not only provided a metaphysical foundation for the notion of progress, but also helped to legitimize the belief in the potential construction of a "social physics" the ultimate goal of which, by applying Galilean method to the study of human nature, was to enable a scientific and impartial treatment of political problems.

Added to these scientific premises was the crystallization in the 17th century of other civilizational factors favorable to the emergence of such an ideology, namely the fear of violent death (due to the development of new weapons and infantry), the rejection of all ideological fanaticism (arising from the massacres caused by the wars of religion) and the desire for a quiet, peaceful life offering a new way of being, which was to become the purview of modernity. The only war still possible was that between mankind and nature, which would be waged with the weapons of science and technology. It was no more and no less a war of substitution, which would progressively turn most of the energy hitherto expended in wars pitting man against man, towards work and industry. However, this modern compromise has never been founded on a politics of reciprocal recognition. The Other is no longer a being of interest on his own account. It is just a question of accommodating the Other's existence as a purely technical practicality of the *modus vivendi*, which is established by suspending ideological differences. Tolerance as formulated by liberal thought therefore only designates a minimal manner of coexisting with one's contemporaries "after the bands of affection are broken" (to use the words of Adam Ferguson). The liberal project is built on the conviction that it is possible to avoid the war of all against all by creating a free, peaceful, prosperous society, even if individuals only operate according to their own particular interest. The idea is that it is sufficient for this purpose to channel the energy of private vices to the benefit of the community, by delegating the harmonization of individual behavior to the neutral, impersonal mechanisms of the Law and the Market, hence, the need to banish from public space the moral values from which various past civilizations had drawn part of their reason for being. Leave is thus taken of the outdated morality of the philosophers (to use the words of Hobbes) in order to usher in a coherent capitalist ethic which "proudly promotes and supports rational egoism." The conceptual formation of modern societies stems from a deep-seated distrust of the moral capacities of human beings and, therefore, of their ability to live together without harming one another. The resulting philosophical ambitions are therefore limited to the search for the *least bad society possible*.

What are the practical effects of liberalism once the belief that gave it structure had been formulated with such abundant clarity in the 18th century by Bernard Mandeville in his famous *Fable of the Bees*? As Hobbes well understood, "the Origin of all great, and lasting Societies, consisted not in the mutual good will men had towards each other, but in the mutual fear they had of each other." So it would seem that there was a kind of original *anti-humanism* underpinning the various political, economic and cultural arrangements that ordered the actual reality of the contemporary world. We must, therefore, suppose that man is "incapable of truth and goodness" and is in fact more harmful by his illusory claims to virtue than by the exercise of his vices. Is it not the case that what shocked Enlightenment Europe in 1704 – that is, the idea that "private vices make for public virtue" – is in fact the perverse morality that governs our planet today under the imprint of liberalism?

The necessary distinction between ethics and morals

How then should we think of brands and ethics if we assume the market's fundamental amorality in a liberal context? Ultimately, two presuppositions stop us from thinking of the possibility of brand ethics. The first is to consider that ethics and morals overlap, and that a brand cannot be moral in the sense that capitalism and morality function on registers of values that are not proportional. The second rests on a positive approach of the community (such as of something shared) that ultimately dismisses the notion of a duty (specifically of the brand vis-a-vis its consumer). If we accept the idea of the community from the perspective of debt and duty, we must now show how this notion of debt ultimately readjusts to that of ethics. To do this, we shall follow the provisions of Paul Ricoeur, specifically according to his work, *Soi-même comme un autre* (*Oneself as Another*), which will allow us to bestow a clear notion of ethics. Essentially, Ricoeur tells us (1990: p. 200 et seq.), what is in the distinction between ethics and morals when nothing in the etymology or the history of the use of these terms dictates it? One comes from Greek, the other from Latin; and both refer to the intuitive idea of morals, with the double connotation of that which is *deemed good*, on the one hand, and that which is *imposed as obligatory*, on the other. Also, Ricoeur proposes to reserve the term ethics for the objective of a fulfilled life and that of morals to articulate this objective in the bounds characterized by the claims of universality and by the effect of restraint.

The question of the overlapping ideas of ethics and morals brings us back to a classic philosophical distinction between the ethics of a good life, derived from Aristotle, and the moral norm clearly formulated by Kant. It is, in fact, about the difference between teleological ethics that underscores the role of the basis of good action in the entirety of the concrete habits and practices that constitute a good life, and the insistence of the moral law outside of any consideration of its material insertion. Also, ethics may be characterized by its teleological perspective (the objective of a good life), whereas morals fall more within in a deontological perspective. In addition, what we can trace in the lineage of the ethical line is the idea of an objective (linked to a certain concept of a good life) as well as the idea of an engagement, and thus duties, to which we shall return later.

From management to government

In a secular society, a society which is no longer structured by a system of religious beliefs, and largely depoliticized, the big brands largely contribute to constructing meaning and to shaping citizens' modes of thinking and action. One can truly talk about a government being exercised by some big brands, which, surreptitiously being slid into our intimate daily lives, succeed at shaping our attitudes and our behaviors. Here, one will understand governmentality, in the Foucauldian sense, specifically the capacity to shape the sphere of others' thoughts and actions. Such brands have become governing bodies because they have largely preempted the physical, symbolic and ideological space of Western societies and have succeeded at governing our ways of thinking, speaking and acting. To play this role of governance over body and soul, brands have become powerful ideological driving forces, a sort of storytelling machine to stage the products of consumption and to make them omnipresent in social space. A brand like Nike is, for example, a gigantic stage-setter of products allowing the individual to live certain experiences (pushing oneself to the limit, achievements in sports, etc.). This ideological power of international brands is specifically possible because of the size of their operating budgets (which, it should not be forgotten, are often comparable to the budget of entire governments), which allow them the gift of ubiquity and a constant presence in the media. But what is governing? In the French tradition, the government essentially gives the capacity to carry out the common good to the state. Stemming from Christian tradition and philosophical reason, made secular by the state, the common good is the basis for the entirety of the perception of the state and the fundamental purpose of all government. Thus, it is what unites us, and without which, power has no justification.

Brands and the ethics of the common good

What exactly is the capability (and the need) for brands to want to govern the common good? That is the question posed by the very notion of ethical brands. For Quessada (2002), publicity (but what we will call here the brand) ultimately seeks the finalization of the philosophical project elaborated in Plato's *The Republic*, namely the organization of a harmonious and happy city through the auspices of rational speech. The brand, moving little by little away from its strictly commercial function, has literally engulfed the entirety of social, political and cultural life and engulfed each practice aimed at the public. In so doing, through publicity the brand surreptitiously claimed the status of discourse of discussion, the exact status boasted by philosophy. However, philosophy, by denying the seductive power of sophism (this art of spectacle-making with words, as Quessada exactly recalls) has also disqualified public opinion. In this way, the brand would be an actualization of what philosophy would potentially contain. The brand has, in some way, by reusing sophism, reclaimed the ideals of platonic philosophy to make them incarnate in the reality of contemporary republics. Also, advertising contributes to the definition of an order by establishing the place and the functions of *good objects*, which is to say, those designated by enjoyment. The sophisticated techniques of marketing essentially allow advertisers to hold a general knowledge of desires and of society; they become like custodians of a knowledge of the order, which allows them to define (as philosophy did in the past) the proper way to achieve happiness, an attitude that continues in the discourse of brands as it does in philosophy by adhering to a discursive rationality. Consequently, the brand is both to promote the ideal elaborated by Plato and to finally bring into being the philosophic project in the city-world. In this way, by ultimately representing the principle themes of antique philosophy, the brand often raises itself up as a eudemonic or universalist principle.

Ancient ethics is essentially centered on the theme of eudemonia, the achievement of the individual life, which everyone wants but most often without knowing what it consists of. Ancient ethics is a doctrine of the art of living and, moreover, is often a eudemonic ethic that seeks to establish an interest in the principle of the well-being of others, and beyond that, to give responsibility not only *to oneself*, but also *regarding oneself*. In this case, the ethics (called universalist) of duty is to elucidate an interest that leads the individual to desire for himself that which he perceives good and that which everyone desires. Included here is the auctorial and scriptural principle of the brand that we will now question, namely, that "to write consists (with Kant) to be absorbed by others, to flow in their veins, to occupy their thoughts. Simply put, the actor would like to no longer be himself, in order to become this universal other that he already carries within himself" (Edelman, 2004: pp. 312–3).

The problematization of governing the ethics of the brand

From the moment in which the brand becomes no longer only an apparatus of management but an instance of governmentality, is it perceivable to expect a brand to have any sort of ethical principal? Moreover, is it possible to apply the same code of ethical reflexion to brands that we apply to individuals?

A first approach consists of wondering whether these ethics are not, in the end, contradictory to the very principles of management. Essentially, one can think that the growing confusion between the spheres of governmentality and management cause problems since the directing values and principles that they represent are not homothetic. Of course, "to manage" etymologically relates to the management of households and private affairs. Nevertheless, to manage is above all to steer an organization with the objective of creating value that is financial, but also human, technological, societal and, therefore, ideological. However, the brand is often no longer only steered by business, and it is situated at an intersection of a network of actors (the famous stakeholders); it is, thus, often the site of tension between, on the one hand, the shareholders who demand that it create the most profit (financial logic) and the consumers who expect an element of identification.

It seems exactly to be at the crossroads of these two paths regarding the debate over the ethical character of the brand, a site of tension between a strictly financial approach and a utopic approach. Thus, the issue is the disjunction of the orders that specifically constitute the principal argument of Comte-Sponville (2004) regarding the amorality of capitalism. He distinguishes four orders, namely:

- the *technical–scientific order*, internally structured by the opposing forces of what is possible and what is impossible, but incapable of limiting itself and thus limited by a second order,
- the *legal-political order*, which is internally structured by the opposing forces of what is legal and what is illegal, itself limited by a third order,
- the *moral order*, founded on the principle of a duty and what is forbidden, which is begun by and ruled from above by a fourth order,
- the *ethical order* or the order of love.

The differences in the respective types and internal structures of these orders render them incompatible and foreign to each other. In the first order (the economic–technical–scientific order) nothing is moral. At the same time, strictly speaking, nothing is ever immoral (Comte-Sponville, 2003: p. 76). The same argument is found in the article "Applied Ethics" in the *Dictionnaire d'éthique et de philosophie morale* (*The Dictionary of Ethics and Moral Philosophy*) (Canto-Sperber, 1996, 2004). Additionally, "our societies are acted upon by three normative forces that converge or are opposed: firstly[,] the economy which supplies values (efficiency, returns, competition) as well as a rationality by which everything is evaluated in terms of costs/benefits; secondly[,] the technical-scientific which, by using an operational rationality, provides procedures and means to the economy; thirdly, the law, which, by regulating social situations, establishes norms and interdictions," (Parizeau, 1996: p. 536). This approach leads to a form of desperation regarding the ethics of capitalism and the brand. "There is no reason to suppose the existence of a systematic harmony between that which ethics recommend and that which requires the maximization of profit," (Van Parijs, 1996: p. 464).

The question of ascription

To accept the idea and the necessity of an ethics of the brand ultimately poses the question of an agent, and thus ascription – in other words, the responses we give to the question of "Who?" and likewise, to which are attributed psychic and physical predicates which become a "someone" in response to the question "Who?". However, it must be noted that a brand never says "I". We must then abandon a substantial, ontological and identificatory approach regarding the brand to attempt to query the susceptible assimilation or distance existing between ascription and moral and legal imputation. Because, if we separate corporate brands, who is ultimately involved behind the brand? In other words, who is the actor behind the brand? Foucault showed that the actor is essentially an initiator of discursivity; and the actor has only one, single objective: to show, to demonstrate, to prove that it is *he*, in his own name, who speaks; sovereignty is reduced to *voicing* in its name (Edelman, 2004: p. 319). The question of the actor and ascription leads us to a path on the way to ethics. An actor, in the sense of the Luminaries, "is essentially a teller of truth, an issuer of reason, a circulator of norms" and spreads the good news of a "possible and feasible emancipation of humanity. To fully accomplish its mission, to be fully efficient, it must be absorbed in its function, to be itself which it instructs[;] ... in other words, it must initiate, between its own self, the same connection it has with another" (Edelman, 2004: p. 311–12). This correction is fundamental, since it gives us a minimal definition of ethics as an operatory means of behaviors. Also, a minimum definition of ethics should conform with the commitments of the brand, with its actions and behavior; in other words, ethics would allow for the capacity of the brand to keep its promises, as much to itself as to different publics.

From identification to character of the brand

Thinking of the ethics of the brand to reevaluate the question of identification, one too often reduces the brand. Ricoeur reminds us of the quasi homonym that exists in Greek between êthos (character) and ethos (habits, customs) by which we move to hexis (acquired disposition) (Ricoeur, 1990: p. 146). Character is a combination of dispositions that allow one to be recognized by the other. But how to think of the character outside of that? We must go from character to the character considering, moreover, the "force of character in order to highlight that it is not about the force of *the* character, but of its *takeover of itself.* However, even though it should be dependent on a given character ("I am what I am"), this force of character escapes... any moral judgment, any condemnation and any excuse" (Audi, 1999: p. 203). Through what filter is this character manifested? "If the force of character is not that of the character, it is surely straightforward, because the person who declares to the world: I am who I am, hardly decides what he is, nor what he should do. He neither seeks to justify, in one way or another this 'how he is;' but he chooses and affirms the way in which he intends to conduct his being, that is to say, that he opts for a certain way of holding himself" (Audi, 1999: p. 203). It is rather the issue of the force of character than putting oneself entirely in the service of something external. "To have character is to respond, given one's unique character, to this supreme demand: 'know that no matter where you find yourself, acknowledge your axis. Next you reflect'" (Audi, 1999: p. 204). "Thus character is this axis upon which each of us, as long as we are alive, we are supposed to *rest* – this axis which holds us upright, that trains us, retrains us and allows us, the case being, to freely address the world without staggering forward or faltering in our 'position'. That is *character*" (Audi, 1999: p. 204).

Character, thus, makes us come out of the rule of moral values and judgments that sanctify and allows the reflection of weak thoughts within which we can strengthen the question of morals. We leave the shore of virtues to board that of ethics, and the assumptions that characterize them. Character is, thus, about holding, retaining or, more precisely, retaking of the self "that does not extend in time, but measures itself only in terms of force or strength of the soul" (Audi, 1999: p. 205). Character is this immediate way of not wanting to cede the smallest bit of reality to the law of the world, this form of insurrection of self that is always like "a challenge held in its glow by the refusal to combine with all the forces that perpetually tend to reduce us to that which is simply not us" (Audi, 1999: p. 207). Here, we are further approaching the distinction between ethics and morals as identified by Robert Musil. What characterizes morals is, above all, an insistence of uniformity, regularity and repeatability, while ethics provides the experiences that are, by their unique essence, happening in real time and impossible to reproduce exactly (Bouveresse, 2004: p. 155).

The ethical brand, thus, commits to an ethic of itself founded on a promise, the word given and the word held. If one accepts the idea that the brand always involves an implicit or explicit contract between the business and its current and potential clients, the identifying process must be a constant reinforcement of the terms of that contract. The contract that is the work of all brands worthy of the name, thus, naturally enjoins a promise made to the consumers in that, etymologically, to promise (from the Latin *promittere*) signifies in a literal sense "to move forward," and in a figurative sense "to guarantee, to ensure," even "to predict." Thus, the promise is a sort of commitment, and sometimes even an annunciation: It signifies that the brand responds to the expectations of its clients, but also that, despite the relationship of confidence created at the time, it is incapable of reaching these expectations, anticipating them, reconfiguring the concept that the user of a given object may have. Also, as Floch explains, "the loyalty of a brand to itself, the respect of its project of life[,] ... is not the problem of a reproduction of signs, but that of the invariance of a particular discourse being carried out according to the diverse and changing modes of presentation" (Floch, 1994: p. 7).

From the symbol to duty

It is specifically in revisiting the idea of duty that the brand can play the community role that it exercises quite often. Do we not, moreover, find in the etymology a clear response to the question of the ethics of the brand? So, the brand is a symbol, knowing that we find among the acceptances of the word *sumbollon*, the idea of convention, contract or even dues (in the sense of paying one's dues). Now, is it not specifically of obligation that the notion of community attests? In fact, the first meaning attested by dictionaries of the substantive *communitas* defines community by its opposition to the word itself. As Esposito (2000) put forth, common in all Latin-derived languages is the expression "what is not specific to," which starts where the specific ends. That which is common belongs to more than one, to several or to all, and consequently is public, as opposed to private, or even general (but also shared) in contradiction with individual. But to this first meaning we add another meaning, that *munus* promotes the idea of "duty" (obligation, burden, chore, function). Once we accept *munus*, we have the obligation to give something in return, either in terms of a good, or in terms of service. *Munus* is, after all, the gift that we give because we must give and what we cannot not give. But paradoxically, although it is born of the previously received benefit, *munus* means only the gift that we give, not what we receive. It is entirely oriented in the transitive act that consists of giving. It in no way implies the stability of a possession and even less the dynamics of acquiring a gain, but a loss, a deletion, a transfer. It is a "pledge" or "tribute" that we have to pay. Is it not specifically this tribute that allows us to better understand the ethical dimension of the brand?

5
Narrativities

When Snow White dates Mister Clean

The brand is a device whose basic function is to tell its customers stories (in the literal and sometimes figurative sense!). Now, what is a story if not the confrontation of different characters through a certain number of stages? Speaking of tales concerning the brand is to assimilate it to other types of stories such as fairy tales, detective stories and more generally, any process based on the resolution of an initial intrigue.

The narrative dimension of identity

As Ricoeur showed, identity exists only within something put to discourse, regardless of the mode of expressing this discourse: the identity of a brand exists only within (in particular) verbal and plastic discourses that highlight the consistency of the brand. To that effect, we speak of *narrative identity*. The brand is based on a tale that is supposed to form an intelligible whole with a beginning, middle and end. This tale in particular introduces a plot that will guide the positioning and development of the brand contract. Now, what is it to tell a story if not the act of "saying who did what, why and how, by spreading over time the connection between these points of view." (Ricoeur, 1990: p. 174). "It is not only the action, but specially the character itself and more specifically its identity that are the subject of a plot. So we can't bring up characters like Antigone, Cinderella or Oedipus without bring up the stories they are featured in, thus their identity is built and transformed as the tale progresses. This congruence between the story told and the character, affirmed for the first time by Aristotle in *Poétique*, means that it's in the story told, united and complete, that gives it a plot, that the character maintains throughout the story the identity correlating to the story's identity." (Ricoeur, 1988: p. 290). In other words, the brand (as a character in a tale) cannot be disassociated from the plot and actions that it recounts through its brand tale. The identity of the brand can thus only be proven through a process of narration.

What is a tale?

From a semiotic viewpoint, consumption refers to mini tales, meaning processes seeking value through objects of desire. Now what is a tale but the quest for an object of desire by a subject? Through the brand, the consumer is searching for an "object of desire," whether it is the pleasure of sleeping in a comfortable hotel bed, the comfort of a high-speed train, the social recognition that comes from showing off a luxury product.

In 1928, Vladimir Propp attempted a morphological description of tales in the popular Russian tradition: as a botanist studies the components of plants, their mutual relations and relations of the parts of the plant to the whole plant, the morphological approach categorizes the different elements of a tale. In attempting to understand the main organizers of any narrative form, Propp highlights the existence of variable elements on the one hand, and invariable elements on the other hand, in each tale studied. The variable parts of a tale refer to the names and qualities of the *dramatis personae*, while the characters' actions represent the invariable parts. Through this approach Propp defines 31 functions, constant elements totally independent in how they are accomplished and in the person accomplishing them. An intrigue consists in this acceptance of resulting functions (absence, restriction, etc.) following one another in an order largely determined by aesthetic motives (Box 5.1).

Box 5.1 The actantial model

The actantial model developed by the semiotic is a fertile tool to visualize the relations at work in the tale. It is based on the principle that all tales are the quest for an object of value by a subject. In other terms, the tale is a temporal process that changes a state of initial separation ("disjunction") into a state of the subject meeting the object ("conjunction"). This transition from the initial disjunction (of the subject and object) to the conjunction occurs by various interactions of characters that will either encourage or prevent the subject from meeting its object of desire. Now, generally, desire is the essential engine of consumption; the desire that the brand whose "primary characteristic is to simplify the relationship between the product and the consumer, to smooth away difficulties, to bring them closer, meaning making the conjunction from an initial disjunctive state. So, three axes exist in a tale: (a) an *axis of desire*: the quest for the object of value by a subject; (b) an *axis of transfer*: the object is transferred from a sender to a recipient; and (c) an *axis of power*: helpers assist the subject in the quest for the object of desire, whereas opponents hamper the quest process.

Based on Propp's analyses, it is thus possible, as Greimas and Courtès in particular highlighted, to summarize these functions boil down to three types of movements that reveal the existence of a canonical narrative structure:

- a qualifying test: the character must acquire skills through tests, struggles or initiation rites;
- a decisive test: the character must accomplish a program of actions by completing a certain number of tests that assess the character's skills;
- a glorifying test: the character is recognized based on behavior and accomplishments.

These three movements then sketch the face of the narrative analysis, one of the main contributions of structural semiotics, which is broken down into four steps:

- a contract: inside a system of values, a program of actions is proposed to the character;
- a skills-acquisition phase: the character must acquire the skills necessary to accomplish the performance generated by the contract;
- a performance phase that represents executing the program;
- a sanction that represents comparing the program of actions and the initial mission. This evaluation can result from a negative sanction (the character is dishonored) or a positive one (the character is glorified and becomes a sort of *hero*).

From fairy tale to spot remover

We shall demonstrate that the story structure at work in a fairy tale can also be found in the world of laundry detergent advertising. To convince ourselves of this, let us look at two examples, seemingly quite different from each other but nonetheless demonstrating a very close narrative similarity: Snow White, on the one hand, and Mr. Clean, on the other. What strikes us most about the story of Snow White, if not the fact that it is a tale about a young princess who, having lost her own mother, becomes the object of her stepmother's jealousy? The story plays out as the quest for a valuable prize (beauty) with an accompanying division of the characters into the opposing camps of good and evil, a polarization which is found at work in almost all fairy tales of Western tradition. The story develops from a tension between these two characters, which will lead to attempted poisoning by the stepmother. The course of the narrative process will therefore be to bring the inanimate Snow White back to life. This pseudo-resurrection comes about because certain characters (the Seven Dwarfs and, especially, Prince Charming) will aid in the process; the primary mission is accomplished by the young prince, endowed with certain powers, who brings Snow White back to life, for which he will be acclaimed. By achieving his mission, the Prince becomes the *hero* of the story and is rewarded by winning the hand of Snow White (after which they marry and have many children).

The story can be summarized up in four major steps:

- the start of a *mission* to bring the heroine back to life;
- the entrance of characters who, armed with special *skills*, will play a role in solving the primary problem (the dwarfs and, above all, the Prince);
- the *solution* of the problem: Snow White is reborn to life thanks to the Prince's kiss;
- the *glorification* of the Prince, who becomes a *hero* and gets his reward.

Now, let us change our frame of reference to consider another type of story, namely an advertisement for a household cleaner such as Mister Clean. Although it employs different storytelling elements, this brand (as with almost all products of this sort) tells the same story, that is:

- the story of a spot (an on-the-spot *problem* needing to be solved) which will drive the narrative: we are shown a bathroom or kitchen riddled with stains, often using exaggeration as a means to involve the viewer in a rather commonplace situation;
- highlighting of the brand's *special properties*, whether by listing its active ingredients, or by recourse to a close source (the neighbor, mother), or by use of a scientific endorsement (the scientist certifies that this brand has the special properties required) and so forth;
- the *demonstration*: someone shows the brand at work (which in this case involves removing the stains without any effort on the consumer's part) meaning this brand is able to get rid of stains that competing brands could never touch;
- the *glorification* of the brand which becomes "THE" brand, after the manner of the Prince in the story of Snow White. By gaining implicit

approval as the best product, the brand becomes the hero capable of winning the heart (that is to say, the wallet and cabinet space) of the consumer.

A simultaneous reading of these two stories reveals the close similarity between their narrative structures, which are summarized in the following table. Each story shows four major milestones that form the underlying foundation of the narrative.

My brand, the hero

The success of the concept of consumer – brand relationship means that the way we look on both the consumer and the brand has evolved considerably over the past two decades. The analysis of consumer practices has grown greatly, mainly because of an increasing awareness of consumers' emotional, hedonistic and reactive response factors. Thus, consumption is no longer reduced to the act of a single purchase but

Table 5.1 Narrative similarities between Snow White and Mister Clean

	Mission	Special Abilities	Demonstration	Glorification
General structure	Proposal of a program of actions to be completed	Acquisition of the special skills needed to accomplish the mission	Implementation	Evaluation of the completed agenda
Means	The to-do list	The know-how	The doing	The being
Snow White	A cast was spelled on Snwo White and she must be brought back to life	The Prince acquires magical powers	The Prince uses his magical powers to bring Snow White back to life	The Prince wins the hand of Snow White
Mister Clean	The brand should help get rid of stains effortlessly	The brand demonstrates scientific legitimacy (active ingredients, scientist's recommendation, etc.)	The brand overpowers the stain	The consumer is once again blessed with a home that glows with cleanliness

encompasses a whole range of activities which overflow the field of merchandising and return to the uniquely personal ways in which individuals handle and exchange meaning and value beyond the strictly functional aspects of obtaining goods and services. Likewise, the perspective on branding has also developed, from an approach that considers it simply as a sign for differentiation and identification purposes, into a holistic concept in which the brand is considered a narrative tool whose function is to produce and transmit meaning. The value of a brand can, thus, be understood as a string of benefits covering all the points of contact (the look, the feel, the purchase, the preparation, the storage, the disposal, etc.) implied in the experience of consuming the product or service. The relationship can be read as a value chain broken down into different steps that are related to the creation and development of the brand value over time.

This value chain shows that the interaction between the brand and the consumer can be understood essentially as being temporal, dynamic and symbiotic. Indeed, rather than considering the consumer on the one hand and the brand on the other (or in other words, the subject

Table 5.2 Consumer-brand interactions as a value chain

Steps in the process of consumption	Sources of brand value for the consumer
Decision to purchase	• Reduces cost of information research • Enables rapid identification • Reduces complexity of decision-making • Provides reassurance and reduces the level of perceived risk • Facilitates reading of the product • etc.
Testing of the product/service	• Decreases the level of risk (physical, psychological, functional) • Ensures reproducibility of the experiment • Provides a means of expressing identity • Allows the expression of deep values • etc.
Post-purchase evaluation	• Provides satisfaction • Gives a recurring affective and emotional reference point • Helps combat the uncertainty of the environment • Provides a strong relational value • etc.

and the object in the characteristically Western manner of thought), the emphasis may be placed on the consumer–brand chemistry, even at risk of substantializing this relationship while abandoning a purely dyadic and transactional point of view.

The relational metaphor thus reflects a paradigm shift reflected in Table 5.1. The relational approach goes hand in hand with the abandonment of a strictly behavioral and decisional view of buying, and to comprehend consumption as a set of attitudes, emotions and representation likely to provide an experience. In a recent work, Regis McKenna also defines the brand as an "active experience," meaning that the brand has become a prism through which to view the world and, in some cases, a partaker in the familiar and emotional environment of consumers. The relational metaphor figures notably in the fact that some consumers use an emotional tone when speaking about their favorite brand. The cultural climate also seems to be quite favorable to the personification of the brand. Indeed, brand relationships can be understood as an extension or symbolic substitute for personal relationships in materialistic societies. The brand–person would sell to compensate for the phenomenon of the dissolution of social ties, providing uncomplicated relationships to feed (at least symbolically) the "empty self" to which the abandonment of tradition, community, and social ties has predisposed modern society. Marketing *orthodoxy* also emphasizes the power of brands to restore to society the value of ties by substituting brands, symbolically, in place of interpersonal ties. As Fournier has demonstrated very well, consumers do not buy a brand regularly based on its performance or perceived superiority; rather, they do so because they are involved in relationships with a collection of brands that bring meaning to their lives. These meanings may be functional and emotional, but all are deliberate and have a strong resonance with the identity of the consumer. (Fournier, 1998: p. 361)

Loyalty and relationship

Like it or not, the idea of a consumer–brand relationship is a throwback to the notion of loyalty. The traditional approach to loyalty reduced it, essentially, to a merely cognitive decision-making process with an eye to utility and resorted to probabilistic methods of analyzing purchasing habits through the analysis of sequences of purchases or of the feeding rate (the proportion represented by the brand among purchases budgeted by a consumer for a given category of products); therefore, the notion of loyalty has gradually lost its meaning by being progressively assimilated by a simplistic behavioral inertia. Well, watching consumers quickly shows that it is important to distinguish between an essentially passive loyalty linked to habitual purchasing behavior and a more active loyalty linked to a very favorable attitude, even a strong affection for the brand. The decision-making approach to consumption, by assigning to the brand a more or less strictly functional role, has notably cast into the shade an important aspect of the brand, namely the "talisman-like relationship which consumers maintain with the goods they consume" (Belk et al., 1989: 31).

Now, what is loyalty etymologically? If one follows the assertions of Emile Benveniste in his *Vocabularies of Indo-European Institutions*, one can understand the concept of personal loyalty as "the bond that is established between a man who has authority and the one who is submitted to him by personal commitment." The modern term derived from this root has undergone a great expansion from which several modern forms derive, some of which refer to pacts, alliances, agreements and sworn beliefs, while others, verbs or nouns, have the sense of "to inspire confidence, to reassure, to comfort," and also "to bind by a promise." Here, etymology clearly shows that loyalty is not merely a matter of behavior; rather, it points to a promise or, in other words, to a relationship.

The consumer–brand relation as a story

So why not envisage the consumer–brand relation as a story, given that a story is composed of a series of events arranged along a timeline? As Aristotle pointed out in the *Poetics*, a story must be unified and identified by interconnected events and must necessarily represent events that succeed each other along a probable causal sequence. The consumer–brand relation can therefore be read like a narrative whose organizational structure can be updated. To understand the minimal organization of the story that links the consumer to the brand, remember that a narrative is always based on a problem to be solved. The problems a consumer may experience are of several orders: hunger and thirst, the need to move, desire for escapism, and so forth. Thus, the narrative is triggered by a situation of dissatisfaction that becomes a motor (in the sense of motivation in psychology) for the consumer.

The narrative is, then, the process by which this problem of the consumer will be solved by the brand through a series of stages, or more precisely, of functions that pertain to the existence of a canonical narrative structure:

- a *qualifying* trial: the brand should show that it is endowed with the skills for solving the consumer's problem;
- a *decisive* trial: the brand should accomplish a set of actions in overcoming a certain number of trials that test its skills;

- a *glorifying* trial: the brand is recognized on the basis of its actions and accomplishments.

These three movements sketch the figure of the narrative schema, one of the main contributions of structural semiotics, which can be broken down into four stages:

- a *contract*: inside a system of values, the brand undertakes to carry out a program of actions;
- a *skills-demonstration* phase: the brand must show that it has the necessary skills to accomplish the program induced by the contract.
  - a *performance* phase that recounts the execution of the program and refers to the phase of experimentation as such of the product or service;
  - a *sanction* that recounts the comparison of the program accomplished and the initial mission. This sanction can be positive (the brand is glorified) or negative (the brand fails if it does not complete the mission).

Table 5.3 The narrative functioning of the consumer–brand relation

	Skills	Contract	Performance	Sanctions
Stage in narrative process	The brand displays skills and competencies	The brand commits through a brand contract to solve the consumer's initial problem	Implementation of brand contract	Confrontation of the result with the initial contract
Corresponding phase in the consumer–brand relation	Discovery of the brand contract (or promise) through communication operations (advertising, store visits, discussion with sales person, contact with the product, etc.)	Acceptance of the brand contract (purchase or purchase again the product)	Confrontation of the consumer and the product through consumer activities (storage, use, pampering, etc.)	Post-use behavior + buy again, attachment, prescription, etc. – abandonment of the brand, complaint, negative feedback

6
I/Materialities

The blandness and delights of a daily object

Marketing talks often about products, but seldom about objects. Moreover, when people evoke products, they are often referring to sign systems. The semantic approach makes a clear distinction between the material dimensions of objects (the signifier or the expressive level) and their idea-related dimensions (the signified or the contents level). This perspective analyzes objects in terms of their specifically ideological dimension, to the detriment of their corporeal and sensorial dimensions. Have the instrumental and symbolic dimensions that are traditionally associated with objects in our Western culture put paid to all other possibilities for ascribing coherence and meaning to objects – despite the fact that these other possibilities continue to crop up, as if by stealth, in people's daily lives? But how is it then that objects are still able to surprise us time and again, enchanting us despite the familiar place they have in our daily lives? By no longer focusing only on the symbolic dimensions of products and brands, the experientialization of consumption may pave the way for an approach that will do a better job of incorporating the specifically material embeddedness of our relationships with objects. Now is probably the time both to try and understand the infra-ordinary mode that surrounds us and also to transcend the saturation of the effects on our senses as well as the tyranny of symbolism. Both these factors have imprisoned objects in a register that tends to empty them of their meaning and emotionality, and very probably of their effectiveness. The present chapter aims to reveal insights into the objects that surround us on a daily basis, insights that will marginalize the commonplace and the spectacular and help show how our everyday experiences with objects epitomize a sort of constant iteration with the moral and physical constraints of daily living (Kaufmann, 1997). The idea argued here is that, to understand key issues in marketing, and to truly reacquaint ourselves with consumers' actual experiences, we have to go beyond the rhetorical and the spectacular fields that have become so intrinsic to commercialization.

The disenchantment of objects

The excessive semanticization of consumer goods has caused an irreversible shift in the analysis of objects. Whereas objects were viewed as material entities, now they are seen as system of signification. We could even say that, ever since Baudrillard's seminal work in this field, studies have continually analyzed the signifier in terms of the signified, thus destroying the material and sensorial dimensions of objects. It is clear that an object will at the very least speak to us and tell us about various ways in which it can be used.

This raises questions as to the role played by a specifically sensorial and corporeal experience in the choice and utilization of an object. After all, experiential marketing orchestrates a constant scenarization, which can readily intimate that signs have become the principal suppliers of meaning and therefore of enjoyment, reducing consumption or interaction to a semiotic experience. It is possible that marketing's undeniable capacity for theatricalization has been replacing senses with signs by obliterating the sensoriality and gesturality with which all experience is necessarily imprinted? We can this question around by wondering aloud whether an object is capable of provoking affection, feelings and emotions.

In actual fact, this constitutes one of anthropology's main criticisms of the semiotics of objects. An object cannot be reduced to a system of signs, because social significations are not only things that it conveys. In other words, an object will not always be bogged down in cultural and social significations that inexorably cause an a priori determination of its senses and functions. It can also be appropriated by individuals and strengthened using signification and personal values, even as it refers to something other than its utilization value or its value as a social sign. The big risk of equating an object with a quasi-language is that, once the signified has been identified, the signifier becomes surplus to requirements. After that, an object will no longer be seen as anything more than a simple system of connotative signs that run at high emotional temperatures (Eco, 1985). This kind of practice, from which a certain number of semioticians are not exempt, can nullify the very idea of objects being incorporated by individuals. In other words, structural and semantic approaches to objects can be criticized as being reductionist. This is because hey ignore materiality per se, in terms of its relationship both to the construction of the subject and to its objectification within action.

Reducing a material object to a sign or "quasi-word" means that material culture tends to be viewed as a "simple twinning of discourses" (Warnier, 1999: p. 124). In other words, by replacing objects with words, semiotics seems to be depriving itself of everything that is original about a substance, in particular its ability to structure and diversify instruments of action or its environment, thus shaping the subject in a way that cannot be reduced to mere discourse. At the same time, by manipulating objects, a subject becomes embodied, expressing itself through gestures and substance; hence, the irreducibility of the material expression, something that becomes particularly necessary whenever discourse no longer has the words to describe this. Even if some objects could be translated into words (as a result of their structural and communicational dimensions), their most opaque substrata rebel against notional and verbal expression, even though they represent a powerful factor for building subject and meaning.

And yet, modern humankind seems to suffer when faced with an object. At a time when technological progress has enabled almost all conceivable combinations of the forms, materials, and colors that are now possible, objects scarcely provide any more the kind of initial resistance that once explained their charm. The infinite malleability that design offers has detracted from the objects themselves insofar as the profusion of objects has tended to empty them of their signifying substance.

Objects become sorts of slaves, having lost their nobility, as we are told, in the service of humankind. They have become too obvious, too familiar and too docile. To what extent can they continue to surprise and amuse us? What awaits and threatens an object is real neglect stemming from the continuous rationalization of the production and consumption processes. This sort of disenchantment with the world of objects basically harks back to the mass production of objects and to the ensuing depersonalization of contacts (how can we have a personal contact with an object that is replicated ad infinitum?). As Max Weber pointed out, this process of disenchantment with the world is one in which spontaneity, idiosyncrasy and superstition have been erased and replaced by values such as effectiveness, predictability and replicability. Here, the consumption object appears to be abundant and at the same time there is a shortage of it. It is abundant because of the profusion of objects in individuals' daily lives (as mentioned previously, people supposedly encounter 20–30,000 objects in just one day). It is in to empty them of their signifying substance. Now, an object can exist only if it entertains a relationship of signification with its user. It must necessarily be imbued with values superseding its function alone. An object (with its substance and meaning) is able to scenarize consumption by projecting in into a universe that is rich with meaning and emotion. We feel that this is what imbues an experience with its full meaning, signifying here a transformation process as well as people's ability to use the power of objects to become something different.

Objects, between routine and surprise

People have relatively paradoxical expectations of the objects that make up their daily lives. In turn, these expectations evoke a repetitive flow of actions, taking a simple psychological approach that views an object in terms of its utilitarian purposes and that also expresses people's desire to be surprised and enchanted when objects become endowed with a certain mystery, magic and even an aura. An object takes part in a sort of reassuring routinization of gestures, incarnating a form that incorporates the object into daily gestures and ensures an embodiment in one's daily actions. Individuals wield undeniable control over the objects they use. This allows them to control their environment, notably their interpersonal environment. Thus, in terms of an object's instrumental functions, we should not forget the crucial value of freedom that is associated with material ownership and specifically makes it possible to predict a result and to experiment with causal efficiency and control (Furby, 1978). In short, the most salient benefit that an object offers is very probably the fact that it can be controlled, as this makes it possible to characterize ownership, regardless of the age of the person involved (Furby, 1978). Objects constitute benchmarks for an individual's identity and truth. Thus, routine is the vehicle that will enable the individual to live in an illusion of stability such as seen in devotion to household chores (Kaufmann, 1997).

Above and beyond the control function, an object contributes to emotional stability, as the environment it creates is a familiar one. Some children, for example, can eat only from a plate that is familiar to them. Similarly, some adults feel at home anywhere as long as they can listen to their usual music on their iPod: objects help to garnish an emotional screen that makes people feel secure. A child never feels alone when his/her teddy bear is around, and the same can be said on many adults with some of their favorite objects. Objects accompany us in many different ways (Tisseron, 1999), for example by offering children a training pitch where they can practice potentialities that will be of use to them for later interpersonal relationships, such as patience or the ability to test one's own limits when encountering an obstacle. An object can specifically mollify the tensions that are created by life in society. Objects also surprise us when they break down or when incidents occur that transform the continuous and monotonous thread of our daily lives into a major event. At the same time, even the most familiar objects can be imbued with different values, enabling an emotional release. Such values can be based on varying emotional registers such as contemplation, nostalgia, connection, self-projection, and so forth. To understand this intrinsic ambivalence in our relationship to an object, perhaps we should shift the starting blocks that determine our representation of an object or an experience (often by subjecting this representation to the sort of logic that applies to major events) and envision other modes for relating to an object.

From substance to interaction

If objects play such an important role in our lives, it is because they occupy a physical space, a symbolic space, a mental space (by filling our minds with dilemmas about choice, utilization, storage and rejection), and a temporal space – as well as a mixture of sensations and emotions. In other words, an object becomes an essential mediator between individuals and their daily environments, helping them to reconsider their surrounding spaces. Objects all summon up practices and rituals and, therefore, a specific type of corporeal experience. Objects present "ways of doing things," illustrated, for example, by the ritualized act of perfuming oneself – as stated previously, people do not perfume themselves at just any time, in just any place, and especially not in any way. The perfuming act can be broken down into a precise syntax of gestures that enable appropriation, even incorporation, of the product and the brand. This frequent ritualization of perfuming gestures reminds us that perfume brands are often "factitive" insofar as they induce specific gestural sequences.

We may also deduce that all sensorial experiences are inseparable from a specific corporal experience. In this way, one can notice that linen constitutes the backdrop for a type of eternal new beginning that can be attributed to the reproduction of gestures facilitating the transmission of ways of seeing things, as well as of doing things. From mother to daughter, household know-how is perpetuated by imitation and technical learning, until women begin to identify deeply with linen, an attachment materialized through simple gestures whose nature seems self-evident and natural. It remains that the experience of an object evokes, above and beyond any sensorial imprint, a universe of consumption that is emotionalized and socialized (Boutaud, 2004). In short, our relationship to objects always more or less mediates a relationship to someone else.

Psychotherapists have long recognized that our love for objects constitutes a replacement for difficult emotional relationships. One interesting example was found by Serge Tisseron (1999), who tells the story of a young man who used to greatly enjoy repairing old sofas. This activity was an extension of what he did as a child to "repair" his parents, whom he always saw as being broken down and used up. Having failed in this task, he tried to do better with sofas. The choice of this particular piece of furniture was symptomatic of his desires, as a sofa is a lap that people can sit on. Moreover, sofas have arms that can hold you, which is more or less the expectation that any child has of parents. As the young man's therapy sessions progressed, he began to concentrate on renovating the kind of veneer wood that is used to decorate early 20th-century sofas, discovering how gestures such as sanding, polishing, varnishing, and cleaning the wood's "skin" could help him to unconsciously work through early experiences in which he had been the object of too much hugging from his parents. This had happened because the young man's parents used him to give free rein to their own frustrated needs for closeness and contact. Once their son had grown up, they reacted to their own incestuous desires by adopting attitudes of coldness and distance that the child found all the more difficult to explain because this would occur after periods of excessive intimacy. What the young man was trying to heal through the various facets of his "do-it-yourself" activity were these two traumas, the invasive contact followed by the sudden distancing.

Objects as something in between

The psychoanalyst Donald Winnicott introduced the notion of a transitional object to designate a material object that is imbued with an elective value for an infant and a young child, notably at bedtime (a corner of a blanket or a towel that the child sucks on). The transitional object is halfway between the internal and the external world and specifically presupposes the existence of a transitional space. This idea of a kind of initial indistinction is reminiscent of certain studies of emotions and passions. For example, at the origin of an emotion, there is always a meeting. According to Sartre, "the emotion is a certain way of apprehending the world", one in which "the subject feeling the emotion and the object of the emotion are united in a synthesis that cannot be dissolved" (Sartre, 1943). As indicated by its name, "e-motion" is not a purely internal state, but more of a movement that brings the subject feeling that emotion out of him/herself, with the subject then being able to express him/herself by modifying his/her relationship to the world. Consciousness projects emotional significations upon the surrounding world and, in return, "vibrates at its most intimate level, 'living' this modification of the world and providing it with consistency through physical reactions that serve as its 'substance'" (Sartre, 1965: pp. 50–51). The being who feels the emotion is overwhelmed both internally and externally. Through its emotional power, an object plays an essential mediator's role that makes it possible to express some of its user's character or personality traits via a sort of mechanism based on an incorporation and marginalization of the individual's psychic life.

The emotional power of objects raises questions as to where they begin or end. Are objects defined in opposition to "living substances" or rather by their own functions? Should they be contrasted with humans? Can they occasionally supplement humans or become part of them? Furthermore, the distinction between subject and object is a relatively recent one. Its premises go back to Roman times (notably the distinction between *persona/res*), even though this has only really developed in what we call modern times. So what is the definitive definition of an object? Etymologically, object (*objectum*) means "thrown against," a thing that exists outside of ourselves, that is placed in front of us, and has a material nature. An object, insofar as it can become non-transformable, impenetrable, offering us smoothness and an indifferent nudity, is first and foremost something that resists.

Yet to understand the emotional power of an object over a subject, we need to hypothesize the existence of an exchange between subject and object, an idea that the Western mindset particularly dislikes. The same does not hold true in those traditions that recognize no such chasm. For example, Chinese thinking is based on a participation of both the human body and the human mind in the winds that blow through the cosmos. Poetry specifically (Liu, 1975) affirms the solidarity of the I (*wo*) with things (*wu*), as well as the inseparability between emotions of internal experiences (*ch'ing*) and the "setting" or the outside world (*ching*). Similarly, in the African tradition, emotion occupies an eminent position, not as the expression of personal feelings, but as an openness to the world. For a black African, a work of an art expresses confrontation, an embrace of a subject and an object (Senghor, 1977). Esthetic emotion supposedly has traces of this kind of distinction, or feels nostalgia for it. The differentiation of this state entails an investment in the object that specifically implies an exchange between the inside and the outside worlds, one based on a mediation of the body that feels something. What we mainly remember here is the continuity of the psychic processes that, in one and the same movement, invest the body as well as the objects that surround it. But does this psychological continuity not mean that we should in fact view objects as if they were our partners?

Objects as partners

The positions our Western cultures attribute de facto to objects exist in relation to a subject. But if we accept that an object entails an experience, would this not be tantamount to hypothesizing the reciprocity, or more precisely, the reversibility of objects? This would intimate that the consumption experientialization paradigm means that objects and brands constitute fully fledged actors in consumers' emotional and daily environments, much like relatives or friends. One significant analysis here is on the relationship that individuals can have with mobile phones: "[W]e sometimes touch them delicately as we would a dearly beloved friend" (Tisseron, 2000: p. 20).

Indeed, if the relational paradigm is to be something other than purely metaphorical, we must accept some symmetry in the exchange between an individual and an object. The wealth of the relationships we entertain with objects stems from their reversible nature, for example, from the fact that an object may only be an object yet, at the same time, is capable of mutating into a true subject partner. Take, for example, something that is "treated like a face, hence 'envisaged' or 'given a face', and which in turn faces us and looks at us...." (Deleuze, 1983: p. 126). What this means is that a "face-giving" process exists for objects, and that "even an object we use (a house, a utensil ... a piece of clothing and so forth.) will be given a face. We will say that they are watching me, not because such objects resemble a face, but because they are connected to the abstract machine of face-giving" (Deleuze and Guattari, 1988: pp. 214–5). Imbued with curative powers, an object becomes much more than an object. It is this person who remains alive, as long as the being who desired it continues to exist.

Blandness or an object destiny

Without a doubt, marketing has chosen spiciness over blandness. But how should we deal with the vital energy that an object may be carrying? After all, this is a principle that covers a number of sensorial modalities:

the power of a form, substance, color, space and movement. How can we ensure that this emotional condensation is ascribed (at least some) meaning in our Western universe, and that it can really reach us without making too many waves or setting off any fireworks, that is, without causing any major deviations from our usual modus operandi, which involves provoking, upsetting and disturbing the world that surrounds us? Is not the best deviance from the form the norm for us to remain quiet when everyone around is all up in arms, and to let our silence be heard in the generalized uproar?

> But even if we could isolate this silence in the general noise, something that would already be quite a challenge and a feat, this does not mean that it would be ascribed any meaning outside of its phatic power. (Boutaud, 2004: p. 88)

To achieve this, we mobilize an esthetic of blandness (Jullien, 1991) that allows us to imagine other categories conducive of a new vision of objects: the vague, the indistinct, the quiet, the transformative, and so forth. This prism helps us to realize the extent to which brilliance fades because its underpinnings are at best topical and ephemeral, whereas blandness expresses openness to all potentialities as well as to the propensity of things just to exist, even those things that are not yet visible or cannot be distinguished. Blandness engages a logic that tries to "infuse" meaning instead of exposing it and hanging it out for all to see. This is also a logic that revolves around an object's underlying ability to express itself through ellipsis and enigma, drawing on the efficiency that an object finds in a discrete existence, one in which it does not try to create any major effects – as if an object is all the more effective when people do not notice it or see it at work, only remarking on its effects. Instead of valuating that which is spectacular and lauding effort and risk, Chinese thought is attentive to the realm of the discrete, recommending a sort of efficiency that is non-confrontational and does not force things, a drive that advances seamlessly and without spending itself. Hence, its gray effectiveness, flowing through the course of daily objects that refuse to stand out. The better these objects perform, the less people notice them.

Meaning should be "infused" rather than exposed and hung out for all to see. Blandness corresponds to a particular experience of the world, one based on internal detachment. In the same way that spiciness binds us, blandness frees us. The former captures us and we are obsessed by it. The latter liberates us from outside pressures, sensations and artificial intensity. This elegy of blandness, which is a basic characteristic of Chinese thinking, could be understood as an antidote to Western culture's inherent ideology, which is based on an over-semanticization of objects. Considering an object's blandness also means trying to transcend the saturation of our senses' effects while overcoming the tyranny of the symbolic – both of which imprison objects in a register that tends to empty them of their meaning, emotionality, and very probably their effectiveness.

In search of the lost aura: the object in the age of marketing romanticism

In a 1936 article, "The Work of Art in the Age of Mechanical Reproduction," Walter Benjamin shows how art objects have lost part of their original meaning and authenticity because of their ever-increasing reproduction and diffusion. The reproduction of art objects goes together with the loss of authenticity, of uniqueness and of distinctiveness, which considerably reduces their propensity to surprise and fascinate and, thus, to illuminate. What Benjamin said about art objects in 1936 seems to apply exactly to today's everyday objects and especially to products, brands and discourses created and diffused by marketers. Due to an extreme process of standardization, these so-called objects seem to have lost their meaning, that is, their authenticity. The aim of this chapter is to draw a parallel between art objects and marketed objects that unables for the possibility for marketers to rethink and redesign "illuminating" objects.

Duchamp, du signe, du sens

In 1917, French artist Marcel Duchamp created a scandal by exhibiting, at a famous exhibition in New York, a public urinal, which was to become the very first *ready-made* object. Duchamp's artistic gesture intended to show that manufactured objects such as bicycle wheels, dustbins or chairs could arbitrarily be promoted as works of art and thus be exhibited in museums and exhibitions, depending on the discretionary power of the artist (Thevoz, 1980). This historical artistic posture is very significant as regards the status of the work of art in contemporary society. Duchamp's aim was to question the distinction (which had been made since the Renaissance) between the craftsman and the artist. This social mythification of the artist responded to a diffuse and collective aspiration, one which corresponded to the gradual dechristianization of Western societies that transferred their religious fervor to art. Museums have replaced places of pilgrimage and now – for the tourist industry – represent much more than a cultural alibi: a cultural tribute, a sacred legitimization (ibid.: 148). Duchamp therefore aimed at a substantial and self-deconstructive activity by promoting standardized objects as artistic. This blurring of genres together with a deconstruction of symbolic hierarchies illustrate the shift of art into industry, thereby leading to a collapse of the boundaries between art and everyday life. The correlated expansion of the role of art within consumer culture led to the famous "aestheticisation" of everyday life promulgated by Featherstone (1991) and others (e.g., Morace, 1990). This movement has been said to be one characteristic of the postmodern condition (Lyotard, 1979). Be it modern, postmodern, over-modern (!) or even none of those, the American philosopher John Dewey has pointed out the fact that art is not something special but a significant part of everyday experience and that real understanding of life is synonymous with aesthetic enjoyment. The aesthetic dimension has gained importance within the area of mass consumption, which means that visual and sensory aspects have gained increasing importance in terms of consumer preference and choice for many products: clothes, cars, kitchen appliances, and so forth. The consumer has shifted from *homo economicus* to *homo aestheticus* (Ferry, 1990) in the sense that sensory and aesthetic dimensions have gained much more importance in the consumer's choice than they used to. Together with this, our time is based on the concept of reproducibility, which goes together with the concepts of authenticity, authority and originality. There seems to be a loss of meaning in consumer objects, mainly because of the conjunction of two factors: (a) a societal move from craftsmanship to industrialization, which leads to the serialization of objects, and (b) a marketing approach based on the design of objects that respond most closely to consumer needs and therefore exclude any surprise effect.

The problem we want to raise here may thus be summarized as follows: How do we reconcile the necessary standardization of objects, which is intrinsically linked to the consumer society, and the need for objects that are still able to communicate an aesthetic dimension, even though they are widely reproduced and copied?

The object in the age of reproducibility

First, it is necessary to go back to the dilemma posed by industrialization and the necessity of reproducing identically any object across time and space. As Benjamin remarked, the object has lost in contemporary society the status of originality and of unicity. In his 1936 article, Benjamin interprets two kinds of art: auratic and mechanical. Traditional art, he argues, possessed an aura of authenticity, an aura that surrounded the original – non-mechanically reproducible – work, endowing it with qualities of "uniqueness," "distance" and "otherness." These auratic qualities of the original, humanly crafted work of art elicited a meditative response from the onlooker, which enabled him or her to transcend time and to perceive the beauty of the work of art as a quasi-eternal moment of completion. Benjamin traces this auratic dimension of art back to its magico-cultic origins in primitive history (Kearney, 1994: p. 164). He invokes the theological idea of a collective psyche (*animal mundi*), which could generate recurring archetypal images and thereby transcend the limits of normal time. He further identifies these auratic images with Goethe's *Urphänomene* (eternal forms that recur through history), Baudelaire's *correspondances* (an aesthetic conflation of spiritual and material meaning) and Leibniz's *monads* (the idea that each autonomous consciousness somehow pre-contains the totality of experience within itself in crystallized form) (Kearney, 1994: p. 164). The distinction made by Benjamin between handcrafted and technological art is expressed in two different kinds of experience: "auratic" *Erfahrung*, or integrated narrative experience, and technological *Erlebnis*, or atomised, fragmented experience. *Erlebnis* exemplifies the loss of the sense of traditional wisdom and communal narrative. Thus, the rise of radio and electronic media spells the death of linear, narrative coherence by promoting a form of dislocated information and simulation which communicates in isolated sensory moments – in a "shock of novelty," as Benjamin described it – subversive of the auratic qualities of contemplative distance and uniqueness (Kearney, 1994: pp. 164–5). Whereas *Erfahrung* provides an experience of the beautiful in which the ritual value of art appears through an authentic aura of the work of art, which depends on its being embedded in the fabric of sacred tradition, the technologically reproduced work demands an immediate accessibility:

> The social bases of the contemporary decay of the aura ... rests on two circumstances, both of which are related to the increasing significance of the masses in contemporary life. Namely, the desire of contemporary masses to bring things 'closer' spatially and humanly, which is just as ardent as their bent toward overcoming the uniqueness of every reality by accepting its reproduction. Unmistakeably, reproduction as offered by picture magazines and newsreels differs from the image seen by the unarmed eye. Uniqueness and permanence are as closely linked in the latter as are transitoriness and reproducibility in the former.... The adjustment of reality to the masses and of the

> masses to reality is a process of unlimited scope, as much for thinking as for perception. (Benjamin, 1936: pp. 216–7)

Mechanical reproduction emancipates the work of art from its traditional dependency on "authentic originality" and excludes no one from the art of communication. Dispensing with the idea of a single "original," the photographic print makes cultural experience available to anyone who wishes to participate:

> The technique of reproduction detaches the reproduced object from the domain of tradition. By making many reproductions it substitutes plurality of copies for a unique experience. And in permitting the reproduction to meet the beholder or listener in his own particular situation, it reactivates the object reproduced. These two processes lead to a tremendous shattering of tradition, which is the obverse of the contemporary crisis and renewal of mankind. (ibid.: p. 215)

Owing to the serialization process, the unicity of objects is seriously jeopardized and the value of authenticity (*Echtheit*) is virtually destroyed. But what is in fact the main difference between the original work of art and its multiple reproductions? What is changed according to Benjamin is not the original *per se*, but the relationship between the public and the original work of art, a kind of immaterial atmosphere which provides the original with a character of originality. A work of art is always created at a particular moment, in a particular place, in a unique manner, and this unicity explains in some way the mystery surrounding ancient works of art, which can be found in cultural places, churches and other sanctuaries. They seem to keep the secret of their past splendor and the effect they may have produced on the ones who contemplated them. Benjamin reminds us that, historically, art is linked to ritual and magical practices that our civilization seems to have forgotten. Any tradition is based on the transmissibility of authenticity; the aura of a work of art and the function of the rite are precisely to help this transmission of an old heritage (Jimenez, 1997: p. 360). Modern reproduction techniques no longer need this traditional mediation: they act according to speed and simultaneity. They are not concerned with an aura they can neither preserve nor communicate. Our era thus seems to be solely concerned with the functions of reproduction, exchange, exhibition and transaction. The progressive decline of the concept of aura means that works of art lose their cultural value and are attributed an exchange value, which makes them as negotiable as any other consumer goods.

The brand's dilemma

Brands are very interesting in this perspective because they, at the same time, glorify and annihilate the concept of authenticity, being based on a paradoxical combination of contradictory functions. The first role of brands goes together with a psychology of simplification in the sense that brands play a labeling function which reassures consumers by assuming a homogeneity of quality and consistency over time and space. A brand indicates that the endorsed product of service is identical wherever and whenever it is bought. The brand first acts as a label of authenticity which proves that the product meets all requirements and expectations and therefore eludes any surprise. The psychological and economic power of brands is based on an ability to reproduce, ad infinitum, a consumer experience. This ability of the brand to duplicate an experience in some way explains most loyalty patterns. On the one hand, the brand reassures consumers because they know who manufactures the product, where it comes from and so forth. Herein lies the main paradox of brands in the sense that the brand plays the role of a sign which guarantees the origin and authenticity of the offer through a possibility of duplication, whereas authenticity originally supposes unicity and the possibility of any duplication. The brand reduces the distance and originality and cancels any possible surprises, pleasant or not. On the other hand, a brand does not boil down to an authenticating function. Together with a simplifying function, the brand plays a complexifying function, in the sense that it has to surprise consumers and create emotional value. Consumption cannot be reduced to functional expectations because it also includes emotional and existential benefits which sometimes even exceed utilitarian expectations, as illustrated by Hirschman and Holbrook (1982). As emotions and affects a priori exclude standardization it is necessary for brands to innovate, that is to de-standardize, to surprise, that is, to break codes and rules. The brand has to innovate in order to inject value on the market, and it thus needs to surprise consumers with new products, images, messages, shapes, colors and so forth. The paradoxical role of the brand, as related to the concept of authenticity, may therefore be summarized in the following manner: a brand must erase all surprise (reassurance function) by reducing to the utmost the distance between consumers and the product (distance is here considered as both a physical distance and a psychological distance), and it must simultaneously create the greatest possible distance between consumers and products (innovative function) so that consumers are surprised. The paradox of the brand is that it must at the same time create and abolish distance. We would now like to tackle this "distance dilemma" by showing that marketers may still be able to create "auratic" objects.

A marketing versus an aesthetic credo

To assert that marketing is able to create enjoyable or aesthetic objects might seem at first glance contradictory to marketers' main mission and philosophy. The standard approach to marketing assumes that marketers should research the needs of their target markets and design products accordingly. Here is, for instance, the way a product is defined in a now very standard textbook: "[A] product is anything that a firm offers to satisfy the needs or wants of consumers" (Doyle, 1994: p. 34). The current ideology is that a company is successful insofar as it meets the current and potential needs of customers more effectively than its competitors. The marketer is therefore not concerned with the expression of aesthetic beliefs, built by nature on an "ideology of reception" (it is necessary to identify customers' expectations) and not on an "ideology of expression."

Moreover, value is not conceived as something which stands out from the manufactured product, but rather appears as constructed through a sequential process. This value creation process is very often decoded, analyzed and implemented through a temporal process (as illustrated, for instance, in the concept of value chain) in which the value of goods is collectively co-constructed, co-accepted and co-digested. In this perspective, value is essentially grasped as a programmed differential process (to be "valuable" means more or less to be "different"), which in fact often leads to a lack of creativity, inventivity and imagination. This credo is expressed, for instance, in one of the few "customer value basics" identified by Naumann: "[C]ustomer value expectations are formed relative to competitive offerings" (Naumann, 1995: p. 24).

The concept of differentiation, which has infused marketing practices, is in this perspective very interesting, because to be different always means more or less emerge to differ, to be different from other beings: it is as if any object could not emerge *per se* and could only exist in a differential network through a series of relationships of oppositions and resemblances with other objects. In this perspective there seems to exist no seminal object, but only a series of *simulacra*, as Baudrillard would say promoted to capture value on the market. This approach to value, which is nothing less than praise of a kind of anti-chaos order, necessarily raises the following question: Has marketing really lost (or simply never had!) a capacity to illuminate? This issue appears all the more problematic when one compares the marketing credo with the aesthetic credo. The latter is more or less based on the expression of a subjectivity through various forms and senses, which explains why the modern conception of art is very strongly linked to the notion of subjectivity. An art object is above all something made by an artist and which expresses a kind of interior voice. Also, this expressive gesture – the status and meaning assigned to a work of art – largely depends on its reception, that is, the social, economic, cultural and intellectual conditions under which the work of art is received (Jauss, 1978). This brief comparison sets out the question regarding the ability of marketers to design objects that can be enjoyed for themselves, not only because they meet consumers' needs. The issue we want to address now is whether marketing and aesthetics are really incompatible.

The need to romanticize everyday objects

The penetration of science and technique into our daily environment has eliminated most technical barriers to the production of objects. New forms and functions can now be used, thus enlarging the field of possibilities and the creative abilities of designers. An ever more-competitive environment has increased the use of new technical and creative possibilities in design. The conjunction of these two factors has led to three major challenges related to the status of objects in contemporary society:

(1) Consumer objects have experienced a crucial disjunction between matter and form. Matter – which is always considered the solid, stable, inert counterpart of ideas – has, thanks to huge technological progress, become pliable and capable of being molded into any possible form (Manzini, 1995: p. 222). New forms and functions are now possible. This phenomenon, often related to a dissemination of worthless products, leads to an impoverishment of sensory experience, to superficiality and to a loss of relationships with objects. It is possible, for instance, to consider that at the beginning of the 19th century, a four-person family would possess 2,500 to 3,000 objects (Branzi, 1988), including electrical appliances and decorative objects. As stated previously, a person is said to come into daily contact with approximatively 20,000 products. Design has an essential role in giving meaning to objects, doing so by the shapes, colors and materials of an object. As Lorenz reminds us, "in a world where many new products are similar in function, components and even performance, a product's design – its shape, its look, and above all its image – can make all the difference." The role of designers is to

semanticize, that is, to differentiate the product, in other words to make consumers love the product in the sense that love was defined by George Bernard Shaw: "a gross exaggeration of the difference between one person and everybody else."

(2) Consumers are immersed in an uncontrolled number of signs and confronted with the phenomenon of semiotic pollution. Designers have to invent products and designs that can survive in a consumption and societal environment saturated with products and signs.

(3) The reproducibility of objects inevitably leads to the fading of meaning of most everyday objects, which have become mere commodities and thus have lost their substance.

Design and the re-enchantment of experience

Design infuses every object in the consumer world and gives form to immaterial processes such as goods, services, and so forth. In a culture of "doing," it becomes essential to determine why and for whom things are designed and produced. Giorgio Vasari (1511–74), an Italian painter and architect and author of the famous *Lives of the Painters, Sculptors and Architects,* was one of the first artists to attempt a definition of painting through the concept of design. Drawing (*disegno*), he writes, means the art of outlining figures by means of appropriate curves. In most marketing textbooks the concept of "design" is either completely ignored, or fallaciously presented as a mere dimension of the product. The meaning of design is nevertheless much more profound. As an English word, "design," which appeared in 1588 as a modern derivative of the Latin *designare,* means to mark or point out, delineate, contrive. "Design" also comes from the French *désigner,* to indicate or designate, and can be defined as planning for action or miniature action. In a broad sense, Simon defines design in the following manner: everyone designs who devises a course of action aiming at changing existing situations into preferred ones (Simon, 1969: p. 55). It is interesting to note that the French word "design" has two antecedents, which cast light on its meaning: design is related to both *dessein* (project, invention of a plan of action, constructive forethought) and *dessin* (drawing). Design thus means both to plan out in systematic, usually graphic, form and to create or contrive for a particular effect or purpose.

Design can also be understood as the manipulation of content through form, and vice versa. Even though content is the raw material of design, form is, in turn, the reorganization of content, in the sense that "to form" is to fix visual relationships in a given space. Therefore, design is much more than simply to assemble, to order, or even to edit: "[I]t is to add value and meaning, to illuminate, to clarify, to modify, to dignify, to dramatize, to persuade, and perhaps even to amuse. To design is to transform prose into poetry" (Rand, 1993: p. 3).

Design activity is part a Promethean activity that consists in the production of both material and immaterial artefacts from which we build our everyday environment (Manzini, 1995). The designer's role is to make the world habitable in both utilitarian and existential terms. The increasing importance of design for consumers is related to the growing importance of images in contemporary culture, which become a persuasive means of motivating people to express themselves. The social exchange of goods is essentially a symbolic process that enables people to communicate through the medium of objects. With consumer society, objects lose their material and functional status by their integration into sign systems. Consuming is defined by Baudrillard as the organization of material substance into signifying substance: "[T]o become an object of consumption the object must become a sign" (Baudrillard, 1968: p. 277). Products have meaning not solely as objects, but also as elements of a vast sign system, through a process of semanticization. Consumers thus invest products and brands with personal and emotional values. There are basically two kinds of values associated with objects: utilitarian and existential. An object is seen as essentially utilitarian when it is perceived by the user as mainly serving particular functions (electrical goods, furniture, kitchen appliances and so forth.). The effectiveness with which objects fulfill these functions plays a large part in their evaluation, and much consumer behavior is directed at searching for information about such effectiveness. The role of design is to convey an impression of effectiveness, solidity, through appropriate features, colors, and materials. Objects may also have existential connotations as emotional value, importance to the individual and so forth. The design of products and signs necessarily has to take into consideration the various types of existential values related to the consumption of objects. These might include such values as social values (the product design might indicate that the user belongs to a given social category), emotional values (the product design has to arouse feelings and affective states) and epistemic values (the ability of the product to arouse curiosity and to provide novelty). The latter refers to the necessity for consumers to live new experiences through the use of products that provide innovative combinations of shape, materials, colors and so forth. The importance of these existential values is the choice of products and brands, and therefore how consumers perceive the design of products is also related to hedonic consumption, which has become a new paradigm of consumption. Hirschman and Holbrook (1982) have identified the main characteristics of this hedonic consumption process: that is, first, emotional desires prevail over utilitarian motivations in the choice of products and services; and, second, consumers may project onto a product a subjective meaning that by far exceeds the real attributes this product may actually possess. The consumption of products, thus, no longer refers to an act of destruction effected by the consumer, but rather to an experience in which the priority is given to affective factors.

Broadly speaking, the designer is a "modest demiurge... who takes charge of the daily environmental pattern in a hedonistic context where the measure of his action is the quality of life" (Moles, 1972). The work of a designer classically fulfills a series of functions that have been identified by Moles. These functions are:

(1) *Information*: the design of a product indicates what the product is and who the manufacturer is (i.e., who does what, where the product originates from, what is the product's reason for being, how much the product costs and so forth).
(2) *Propaganda*: the product design urges the consumer to use the product in such and such ways, and/or under such and such conditions.
(3) *Consonance* of consumers with their goals and expectations: product design as well as advertising can play an a posteriori role, after the purchase, in strengthening consumers in their choices in relation to their images of what has value.
(4) *Social consciousness*: product design often connotes signs of belonging to a given social class or socio-economic category.

These functions fall broadly into two main categories of functions, which are semantic and aesthetic. Any object always embodies both a denotative message and connotative message. Denotation refers to the fact that the object conveys information about its functions, what it stands for (semantic function), whereas connotation refers to an aesthetic dimension that conveys a subjective impression and emotion about the product (aesthetic function). Thus the tasks of the product designer is to understand what are the consumers' main expectations (functional and existential) of the products, and to design products accordingly. In other words, the designer's role is to design shapes and to use materials that schematize, strengthen and activate the desired and appropriate dimensions (solidity, resistance) valued by the target customers, given the fact that this functional dimension of the product is always accompanied by an aesthetic message.

From *exophoria* to euphory

It is widely accepted that the shape of an object more or less follows its function. The shape of objects indicates the possible use(s) of the object (what the object stands for), hence for instance the work of ergonomy. This conception of the object as a tool is very utilitarian because it considers an object's value as linked to its functional utility. The shape of the object indicates its use but also adds an unescapable aesthetic dimension (there is no innocent shape!), which may contribute to the redefinition of the object. In some way the shape of an object may by far overlap its function. There is a degree of freedom which gives the designer the opportunity to disconnect (sometimes quite radically) form and function. Let us consider, for example, the lemon squeezer designed by Philippe Starck and which looks like a rocket, or other cooking utensils manufactured by the Italian company, Alessi. These objects propose totally new approaches to such familiar household implements as bottle openers, kettles, pepper mills. By breaking the usual codes of representation, the designer opens the object to a plurality of meanings which contribute to re-semanticize the objects beyond their functional purpose. Thus the design on any object implies two dimensions: first, an *endomorphic* dimension, which guarantees that the object belongs to a certain class and organizes the invariable elements; and, second, an *exomorphic* dimension, which allows for radical formal innovation in the object category (Polinoro, 1989: p. 69). So all the stylization attempts at formal codifications, which do not entail the iconic convention establishing that a given object belongs to a certain category, can be said to be endophoric; on the contrary, all the iconic hybridization process and all the attempts to re-semanticize objects can be said to be exophoric. On the one hand, the endophoric axis limits, crystallizes and adjusts; on the other hand, the exophoric axis invents, diffuses and disorientates. The first axis makes the object recognizable and has a reassurance function, whereas the second axis de-structures the object and responds to new expectations. Let us consider for instance the kettle designed by Michael Graves for Alessi: this object is very strongly exophoric because of its very cone shape which destabilizes the idea of a kettle, but also because of the little bird sitting on the spout, which conveys the idea of lightness and defies the geometrical rigidity of the object. Looking at the kettle for the first time, one is disorientated by an object that seriously questions its identity as a kettle and searches for a new identity outside the functional aspect (Polinoro, 1989: p. 70).

The open object and the consumer as a reader

The exophoric work on the object leads us to question the identity of the object – that is, its potential belonging to a given a priori category. In other words, by playing with the exophoric dimension, the designer does nothing less than break the endophoric codes so as to open the object to new interpretations. The aesthetic code is in fact the result of a dialectic between the conventional code and the innovative message (Eco, 1968; Nöth, 1990: pp. 427–8). By their innovative character, aesthetic messages infringe upon the rules of their genre and thus negate the code. But at the same time, the new message creates a new aesthetic code: "[E]very work [of art] upsets the code but at the same time coding, i.e.[,] the creation of new rules on the basis of pre-established ones. Aesthetic overcoming generates a kind of semiotic 'surplus' on the level both of content and of form. By this surplus of expression and of content, the object becomes open to multiple interpretations. The essential feature of codes and ality of cultural subcodes, the aesthetic message has the character of an 'empty form', into which the recipient inserts meanings. The interpreter 'tries to accept the challenge posed by this open message and to fill the invisible form by his or her own codes'" (ibid.: p. 165). An object is always more than what it was originally designed for. It might even be re-coded by consumers using a code different from the one used by the creator.

There is thus no single meaning assigned to an object but, on the contrary, a plurality of meanings. An object is different from a tool in the sense that it is not limited to a mere utilitarian function. It might be embedded within an aesthetic dimension that gives it value beyond its functional purpose, and might even sometimes totally eradicate its semantic function. The meaning of an object is not a fixed property imposed by the designer, but results from a kind of negotiation between the designer/producer and the consumer/reader. This issue was addressed by Arthur Danto in his book, *The Transfiguration of the Commonplace*, in which he tries to explain why the facsimiles of Brillo soap pad boxes exposed by Andy Warhol in 1964 may be perceived as works of art, even though one can find almost identical objects in any supermarket:

> There was a certain sense of unfairness felt at the time when Warhol piled the Stable Gallery full of his Brillo boxes; for the commonplace Brillo container was actually designed by an artist, an Abstract

> Expressionist driven by need into commercial art; and the question was Warhol's boxes should have been worth $200 when that man's products were not worth a dime.... In part, the answer to the question has to be historical. Not everything is possible at every time, as Heinrich Wölflin has written, meaning that certain artworks simply could not be inserted as artworks into certain periods of art history, though it is possible that objects identical to artworks could have been made at that period. (Danto, 1982: p. 44)

The other part of the answer lies in the concept of interpretation. Danto contends that if there is no aesthetic difference between the commodity and the identical copy made (on purpose) by the artist, only interpretation helps to understand this "transfiguration" of a banal object into a work of art. Even though this approach is in many respects contestable, its main interest lies in the fact that Danto points out the importance of interpretation, that is, the reception of the work of art, whereas most aesthetic theories usually focus on either the production of the work of art or transcendent criteria imposed on the spectator. The point we want to make is that in some way the aesthetic status of the object lies in the viewer's eye as well as in the designer's gesture.

Walter Benjamin's "aura" and re-illumination of objects

Some objects may, through their design, redefine their original function and create an aesthetic experience that may sometimes be an emotional shock. In other words, some objects even though they are only objects, may have a real aura. First, what is etymologically the notion of *aura*? Aura was first used as a medical term given by the ancients to indicate a particular state of the body preceding either epilepsy (*aura epileptica*) or hysteria (*aura hysteria*). Aura is thus originally linked to a violent physiological experience. That is why the auratic experience differs from the experience of the beautiful. Burke (1991) made the distinction between the sublime and the beautiful in the following manner: the sublime is not only linked to aesthetic enjoyment but is also linked to a mixture of pleasure and pain. The satisfaction derived from the experience of the sublime results from an association of imagination and reason, but this particular feeling goes together with a sensation of danger, of something that seems horrible and terrible. The experience of the sublime arouses a physiological reaction. This type of reaction one might have in front of auratic objects such as the kettle previously mentioned. Aura is, hence, linked to a kind of transfiguration, and it also means a breath, or a sort of halo, which envelops or stands out from a person and can only be perceived by initiated individuals. In mythology the aura was used to describe some sorts of Sylphs, that is, subtle and aerial divinities which used to frolic with the Zephyrs. In artistic terminology, aura is used to manifest what stands out from a character and serves to underline exceptionality. The concept of the aura was widely developed by Walter Benjamin in a text on the "history of photography" (1931) and in the previously mentioned text, "The Work of Art in the Age of Mechanical Reproduction" (1936). "Aura" is defined by Benjamin as "a unique phenomenon of a distance however close it may be" (*ein einmalige Erscheinung einer Ferne, so nah sie sein mag*). These objects designed through a marketing process have an "aura" because they remain unapproachable and distant however close they may be. This is consistent with the etymology of the word object, ob-*jectum*, that is, something which stands in front of us with an evident resistance, something which remains exterior to us, with a definite property of strangeness and otherness (Sartre, 1943). Auratic objects are able to create proximity to and distance from the viewer. Proximity, because they may be used in everyday life and be appropriated by users; distance, because they question their identity as functional objects and may be considered as open aesthetic objects that provide a multiplicity of potential meanings. They do not show exactly and instantly who they are, and what they are designed for. Even though they are highly visible, such objects remain in a zone of invisibility. Their power goes beyond visibility, like a sixth sense, and this contributes to the creation of a sort of double distance between the object and the viewer. This distance is what creates an aesthetic and emotional shock, the shock being for Burke what distinguishes an experience of the beautiful from an experience of the sublime. The idea of *shock* is fully consistent with the original medical meaning of the concept of aura, which is a set of symptoms that precedes, and in some way announces, an epileptic crisis.

Such objects, in the sense that they offer a new perception of the world, are thus much more than beautiful objects. By being auratic, an object is enjoyed independently of its functional purpose; it offers nothing like a representation of consumers' expectations and desires. It does not resemble or imitate anything except itself. The object is not an object in the world but a real "breakthrough" in the world, one which lets us perceive another world (Grimaldi, 1983). Through the vision of the object, another world appears. Therefore, the aesthetic perception of the object is a metaphysical experience of strangeness and otherness. But through this strangeness appears a new vision of the world. The object remains inaccessible, unattainable, and this inaccessibility is exactly what makes us view the world differently, with much more intensity, through a kind a glorification of our everyday experience.

Proposals for a little philosophy of the toothbrush

Let us conclude this brief analysis with an object that illustrates the possibility of daily objects becoming auratic thanks to creative and ingenious designers. This object is a toothbrush designed by Philippe Starck for the French brand, Fluocaril. The object is first presented in a semi-opaque packaging, which plays very well with both visibility and invisibility, presence and distance. The object has all the recognizable features of a toothbrush and, still, it seems to look like something other than a toothbrush, a kind of old pen, for instance. Moreover, apart from its obvious aesthetic qualities, this toothbrush appears to be made of two parts: a brush and a stand. The stand is symbolically very important because it means that this object has gained autonomy, a physical autonomy in the sense that is does not have to be hung up, laid down or even hidden. The toothbrush might exist, per se, standing on its rack and thus become a decorative object. Hence, through a re-semanticization process, the object is viewed differently and it makes us see the world differently: in a sense it has gained some aura....

Is design the future of marketing?

A semiotic reading of innovation

While marketing never ceases to sing the praises of innovation, the veritable innovations that can be attributed to marketing are, in fact, quite rare. Anyone who regularly visits the aisles of supermarkets and other shopping centers notices rather quickly that the shelves are choc-a-bloc with products that find it increasingly difficult to evidence real singularity. This paradox of marketing that constantly speaks of innovation, and yet only offers it up along the edges, encourages us to pose the question of the relations between marketing and design: Is design an avatar, a rival sibling or an emergency exit for marketing from markets that have become trivialized?

The relationship between marketing and design is, first of all, orchestrated around the question of the modes of constitution and definition of the object. Where do objects come from? What and who are they for? These questions emerge from the tension specific to all objects between the criteria of style and aesthetics on the one hand, feasibility and profitability on the other. If we accept the historical precedence of the decorative arts over design, the designer could be summarily understood as a profane representation of the artist and whose remit is to provide a touch of aesthetic emotion in the all-too-quotidian routine of usage. But how do we conjugate this aesthetic aim with the sort of precedence of the expectations and preferences of the consumer naturally induced by the marketingization of entrepreneurial practices? Does the object therefore come from a singular gesture in an economy of the aestheticization of consumption choices, or does it derive from downstream demand (the expectations of the consumer)? Should we consider the object in the light of eminently artistic and/or aesthetic preoccupations, or in terms of the "silent majorities"? In other words, is the object guided by a creative gesture or by social demand that would presuppose a capacity in the individual consumers to evaluate, formalize and verbalize their preferences in terms of the shape, color, texture, and so forth of the products in their daily lives? And it is in fact this tension that perfectly illustrates the very notion of industrial aesthetic that brings to light the necessarily aestheticizing nature of the object and conditional on meeting the constraints of industrial feasibility at lower cost. Marketing often expects design to precisely reconcile these two poles by proposing objects that are "profitable" both for the consumer and for the company.

The difficulty with differentiation

The paradox of marketing is to make the object familiar to and appropriable by the consumer while at the same time bestowing on it a sort of resistance so that it does not don the cloak of self-evidence that would attach to it naturally from the flux of objects in which consumer society immerses us. While doing so, the task of marketing is to sustain the curiosity and interest of individuals for products by "endowing basically duplicable, standard objects with a coefficient of difference that captures attention and seems to destine them in advance for public favor" (Rosset, 1979: p. 64). In other words, marketing's main role is to sharpen the consumer's involvement with the products by attaching to certain brands imperfections worthy of justifying preference and purchase. Differentiation has therefore become the mantra of marketing, which precisely consists in distinguishing a brand from rival offers in order to optimally match the consumer's expectations in a profitable manner. This may be so but the ideology of differentiation relies on an over-investment of the figure of the *shopper* (the customer, as opposed to the consumer who *uses* the product), who is most of the time indifferent because of being disengaged from the act of purchasing (except for infrequent purchases presenting a high degree of perceived risk) as a result of lack of time and interest. Hence an inherent logic of hyper-visibility of the effect that aims to create a sort of excess domain participating both in the "not like others" and the "in addition" (Rosset, 1979). Now, this ideology of difference that results from the infusion of a resolute marketing spirit in the contemporary design of the products clearly and quickly displays two obstacles. The first consists in differing for the sake of differing, with an ideology merely of pure differentiation. This register of trivializing difference is sterile, for it models itself on competitive practices and aims to create soulless clones. This approach is destined to reach an impasse through time because of the saturation of the codes and the lassitude generated in the consumer by the repetition, ad infinitum, of pre-established codes – the arrogance and automaticity of which conceal only too imperfectly the absence of any real intent. This type of approach shows, through a superabundance of signs, the poverty of intent. The object no longer has anything to say, it no longer communicates or says anything about itself, the user or their environment.

The second obstacle consists in making the object match very (too!) closely the expectations of current or potential consumers. This is then a prostitutive approach to the object, whose prime and only function is to seduce (from the Latin *sēdūcere,* to lead apart, from *sē-* apart + *dūcere* to lead). The object can exist only in a relation of signification with the user; it must necessarily be invested with values that go beyond utility. The role of the designer is precisely to de-trivialize daily life by giving it meaning again, that is to say a real project for the objects in our surroundings. This is a question of no more and no less *poeticizing* the object to recreate complicity between the users and their life matrix. Such is no doubt the founding question of an innovative vision in terms of design. Such is also the nodal point of confrontation between marketing and design.

Analytical approach to the product

And so, what distinguishes the product from the object is precisely that the latter cannot be transformed, is impenetrable, offers up a smoothness, an indifferent nakedness. By projecting meaning on objects, consumer culture has repudiated this form of nudity, which is consubstantial with the object. In the Christian tradition, nudity equals nature. Nature is there to be modeled by man; nature is the rough substance, and man should turn it into a manufactured product, culture. In other words, nudity is entropy, and the negentropic activity of the human spirit must clothe it (Flusser, 2002). In total it is to some extent against this nudity of objects that man checks his own being, which consists in opposing the amorphous absurdity the world presents to him (Flusser, 2002). Is not the product precisely a way of clothing the object? The object engages a form of synthetic experience by opposition to the product, which prefigures a dislocation of the unity of the experience as a collapse of the experience. This passage is characteristic (in Walter Benjamin) of the modern consciousness which, at each instant, "is bombarded with unrelated data; automation and parceling of activities, prostitution of goods and people in merchandise, atomization of the masses, bursts of information" (Proust, 1994); now, it is precisely the marketing logic of differentiation that leads to an analytical approach to products. The pressing analytic vision in micro-economics (from which, we may remember, marketing derives) considers the product as a "bundle of attributes" to borrow the expression of the economist Lancaster). This approach led marketers to differentiate their products only on the fringes, by modifying one or other of the attributes according to trade-off methods. The irregularity can therefore no longer be attributed to the style, or way of being of the product but to irregularities cobbled onto certain salient attributes of the products – attributes which are so highly visible for the consumer and likely to engage or divert their choice. In this way, the idea of design conveyed by marketing relates above all to differential management of the product attributes. We recognize the Zippo lighter from the way it clicks, Frosties from their snap, crackle and pop when the milk hits them, and the Babolat brand by the two famous white stripes. But, for all this, the attributes of a product are not independent of each other in the consumer's perception mechanism. Very often consumers unwittingly operate perceptual inferences by deducing, for example, certain properties of the product from the qualities, in particular chromatic qualities and formal packaging qualities (or other vectors of brand representation), by operating a transfer of sensation from packaging to product (Pinson, 1986). Thus, the consumer has trouble recognizing the flavor of transparent syrup, hence the failure of colorless syrups. In the same order of ideas, we can quote the example of the withdrawal of green ketchup launched by Heinz. How can we assess the strength of the aroma of a coffee if not by the intensity of the colors? Would we believe coffee was decaffeinated if sold in a black packet? Would we eat yoghurt sold in bright red packaging? Would we buy a fizzy cola drink if the visual codes were not red and white, colors taken up by all the competitors of Coca-Cola (with the exception of Pepsi-Cola, which bases all of its message on the switch to blue)?

Taking into account the consumer's perceptual inferences, on the one hand, and the sedimentation of the codes due to the logic of mimicry on most markets, on the other, explains the development of conventions in the majority of product categories: omnipresence of red/white code for cola, brown and black for coffee, white for yoghurts and so forth. Marketing innovation is often played out against a background of metonymy, of gradual variation in tiny touches.

But then how can a brand display singularity in a conventional market? More precisely, how do we make design efficient again in a world consumed by mimicry?

The paths of differentiation

For the simple reason that a market exists polemically as a set of competing forces, the strategic action of brands is oriented one towards the other, so that the dominant model of competitive reaction is mimetic innovation. The "doxal" structuration of the market categories by which the leader often imposes a set of reference signifiers (reference values, motifs, figurative codes) that oblige the challenger(s) to either follow or subvert the norm. Thus, for example, some product categories have a strong isotopic effect: the laundry iron with translucent colors and a streamlined profile as if to signify both respect for the whiteness of the laundry and the rapidity of the gesture; vacuum cleaners with bright colors, robust, compact shapes that try to signify strength and easy handling.

Design is part of a psychology of simplification as it responds to expectations of bearing markers and reassurance in a semiotically oversaturated world, but it is also a part of a psychology of complexification in virtue of which the consumers expect something other than mere repetition of discursive schemas (colors, forms, materials and so forth). Brands should therefore all perpetually oscillate between redundancy and creativity, since perpetual balancing is set up between (a) conformity that, in matching the expectations of the recipients, reassures them by excluding the ambiguities that lead to a too-strenuous or random effort at interpretation, and (b) an originality that provokes the unexpected by transgression of the conventions and the horizon of expectations of these same recipients.

What is brewing here is, in the end, the question of the identity of the object – a question which, as we can see, is always more or less played out at the junction between two dimensions: the fact that, first of all, this object belongs to a certain world of products and possesses the visual and sensorial codes enabling it to be included in a given group and considered a prototype of its world; then, the fact that this object has individual features that distinguish it from the other objects in its category and gives it a *raison d'être*. The object therefore conjoins endomorphic and exomorphic dimensions. The endomorphic dimension ensures that the object belongs to a given product category (this is the axis of belonging and similarity). Each product world develops codes of color, materials and shapes that allow the market to recognize its purpose, that is to say its assignation to a given product category and therefore to a pre-defined type of use). But the object also exists in relation to an exomorphic dimension, which takes account of an innovation factor that breaks with the market codes (this is the dimension of differentiation and alterity). On the one hand the intensity that makes the perception more or less acute and corresponds to the form of breach of the conventions.

How then can we understand the role of design (and innovation) in the resonance of these two dimensions specific to the object? We can in fact identify three paths along which to progress. The first consists in giving preference to the codes of belonging by modulating the relationship of the product world to the norm. Here we must remember the formal and chromatic conventions of the product category by pointing out a small difference on the margin. We then concentrate essentially on the endomorphic dimension. By opposition, a strategy naturally emerges consisting of playing on the intensity of the breach by precisely signifying the rupture with the codes in force. This dimension, which we shall describe as exomorphic, can gradually invest modes of transformation or of revolution. In this latter case, it is a question of re-founding the codes of the category, which is often the case with a challenger brand. James Dyson's vacuum cleaner, for instance, which literally revolutionized the codes of color, shape and price – multiplying the sale price by three – of its product world with the success we are all aware of. In the same order of ideas, the Macintosh revolutionized the codes of the computer market in 1984 by proposing a friendly object (the cones and the mouse participating largely in the possible appropriation of the object by the lay user), which contributed to the creation of the personal computer. In the same order of ideas, the Renault Espace revolutionized the automobile market by proposing a vehicle designed from the inside out as a living space, creating the category of the people carrier. This transgressive approach has also been approached by the notion of "disruption," which refers to the brand's ability to smash the codes and conventions in force in its product category to create a veritable singularity. But here we touch on the logic of visibility, impact and upping the ante on codes, which quickly leads to excess. Danone's Activia brand broke with the codes of the yoghurt market by imposing the color green,

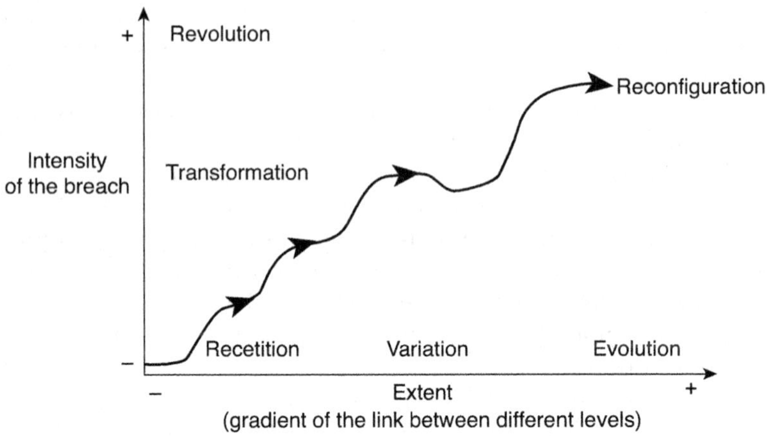

Figure 6.1 The paths to differentiation in marketing

while Badoit introduced the first red bottle to a water market traditionally dominated by blue and green.

And so on the one hand there is compliance with the norm in force, on the other the rupture in relation to the quantity on hand which, in the eyes of the consumer, can in the end justify design's pretention to value creation.

As breach is not admissible in a society that is averse to risk, marketing often reduces design to a reconfiguration function, a sort of middle way that consists in borrowing, modifying and re-orchestrating the codes of the product world. In this way we understand that a marketing society that has repudiated invention often seeks refuge in reconfiguration. Hence, the immense anthropological do-it-yourself project of signs that constitutes the market.

Promising indeed!

Beyond the prime opposition highlighted between marketing and design, could we not reconcile these two domains whose final function is to develop objects of meaning in order to make a real contribution to the user while at the same time creating value for the company? This is where the mediator that is the brand intervenes and creates an exit from the suggested dichotomy between imitation and creation. If we accept the idea that the brand always entails an implicit or explicit contract between the company and its current and potential customers, design should presage a reinforcement of the terms of this contract. It is not therefore a question of creating the different out of the simple pleasure of difference at all, but of renewing a contract of trust between the brand and its consumers. By innovating, a brand capitalizes on a contract of trust, which allows it to move forward and propose difference to its customers – that is to say, not necessarily something new, extraordinary or spectacular, but another vision of the world and therefore of the objects that people our daily lives. The contract at work in any innovation worthy of the name therefore naturally directs a promise made to the consumers, to the extent that etymologically, promise (from the Latin *promittere*) means literally "send forth", and figuratively "guarantee, ensure", or even "predict". The promise of innovation is therefore a sort of commitment and sometimes even an annunciation as it testifies to a strong anticipation of the expectations of the public with respect to a given object. Promise here means that the brand "naturally" matches the expectations of its customers, but also that, on the strength of the relation of trust created through time, it is capable of foiling their expectations, anticipating them by reconfiguring the conception the user may have of a given object.

Any brand that innovates (in the strong sense of the term) therefore applies to the letter the claim that one brand recently decided to champion: "Think different." This also means, by extension "feel different," "look different," and ultimately "live different." For, at the end of the day, what is successful innovation, if it is not always more or less a contract of life the brand offers its consumers? By reconfiguring the objects of our daily lives, it is a question of offering individuals (and not just consumers) a new perspective on things and, consequently, a new perspective on life.

A brand should not only reassure (which a label does) but also surprise: that is to say, deploy itself alongside a horizon of expectations. The Vuitton brand daringly smashed its own recognition insignia by adapting the famous "Monogram" canvas in the Graffiti range, a limited series that allows the brand to play with its own codes and display a certain contemporary dimension by means of the tag. This is a question of ensuring a balance between the brand's founding values and the adaptations of the values of creativity and boldness, which creates an effect of distance between the brand and its market. The brand management depends on the subtle balance between the expectation of a certain reassuring repetition (which aims simultaneously at resurgence, continuity and sameness) through a process of reproducibility and the unexpected, the surprise through a continuous process of innovation. It is precisely the capacity of brands to incorporate a dimension of alterity, temporality and unbalance that allows them to go beyond their simple function of label and increase the emotional and hedonistic nature of the consumer experience by weaving a sustainable relationship with their consumers. To be "taken by surprise" is what allows us to temporarily cease to be ourselves, helps us to fix our own boundaries, become aware of what makes us effectively us, which is how we can start to have trust in others. The dimension of surprise that design injects must boost this trust by allowing the brand to move forward and propose difference to its customers; that is to say, not necessarily something new, extraordinary or spectacular, but another vision of the world and therefore of the objects that people our daily lives. The Italian kitchen utensil brand Alessi is managed like a fashion brand, a sort of sounding box permanently nourished by the notoriety and creativity of reputed designers (Andréa Branzi, Michael Graves, Jasper Morrisson, Ettore Sottsass, Philippe Starck *inter alia*). Alessi produces experimental items that are free of the constraints of industrialization and produced in materials other than steel (related to their founding skills), such as Guido Venturini's phallic gas lighter the *Fire Bird* or Stefano Giovannoni's *Mary Biscuit* box. This capacity the brand has acquired of conjugating a long timeline with the commercialization of fashionable products that break with their own codes allow it to continuously sustain the curiosity of the consumer. In combining a logic of duration and the effects of surprise, does this not make the brand a kind of insect that crawls up and nips and titillates and tickles the body and the fancy of the consumer, a function which Daniel Marcelli showed holds an essential place in the organization of the human psyche (Marcelli, 2001)?

Delineation or segmentation?

So what can marketing expect from design if it is not to introduce a break, an exact delineation, that may generate discontinuity (if possible strongly visible) between before and after an innovation, so as to create a linear impact)? Now, indeed, delineation is different from segmentation. As segmentation depends on the organization of parts of a whole, delineation translates the density of presence, the strength with which one part is affirmed based on others. In innovation an almost irreversible break is produced in the value system: the subject confronted with the new system cannot return to the previous state that has lost all consistency and legitimacy. Innovation causes an offset, an incongruity against the expectation of change of the market and in particular of consumers. In short, innovation is an event that achieves more than it becomes. But it is necessary for the event to have visibility and be demonstrated by a noticeable result. The creation innovation assumes must not be strictly consistent with the content of the expectation: an invention that does not meet an expectation could not be considered an innovation. Innovation is different from a planned change due to a deficiency and aiming to fulfil this deficiency (Fontanille, 1998): innovative materials that remove an annoyance or secure new enjoyment. Innovation reveals an inconvenience or annoyance at the same time that it eliminates it. Innovation formulates the problem and, at the same time, its solution. Innovation thus creates the value; it transfers the value of an object to another; or it completes the value of the object by creating another dimension than the one envisioned at the beginning. So, change by innovation must obey a certain continuity because of the very fact that innovation is not revolution, and if delineation is required, the new system must appear in the lineage of the old. "In other words, over time innovation", delineation must add segmentation, meaning a principle more or less logical that affirms the continuity, the link between the new and the old (Couégnas and Halary, 2005). By a sort of retrospective causality, the consumer must be able to consider the new as the completion of the old. The new system is thus essentially created as a reconfiguration of the old one. A minimum identification must be possible between the different states, hence, precisely the importance of the visual identity that endorses the continual presence of the brand regardless of the onset. This form of change shows the problem and its solution at the same time. As an example, let us take ZAP yogurt, sold under the Yoplait brand and considered by professionals as one of the major innovations in yogurt in 1998. ZAP is not the product of a technological or food revolution. By introducing on the market a yogurt consumable anywhere, under any conditions, the Yoplait brand was able to resolve a problem of consumption at the same time as it revealed that problem. To meet the definition above, there is indeed the "replacement of a former situation" – inability to eat yogurt under satisfactory conditions of mobility– with a new situation –. The delineation of innovation, is the strength with which the new system is affirmed, therefore invalidating how things were before the innovation (Couégnas and Halary, 2005).

Design as an extension of the brand domain

The function of design is specifically to feed a brand project by offering objects that endorse a know-how, a vision of the world and of specific values. Design is precisely what makes it possible to actualize a project (by abstract definition), enabling the brand to be positioned as an expression of ethics and aesthetics. But there is the question of individualism and style. Just as Cervantes, Dostoyevsky or Beckett made a definitive tear in the literary fabric, brands like Nike, Apple and Alessi exist by their capacity to transcribe in an intangible manner a revolutionary vision of their world of product: Nike, in transforming sneakers into a trendy everyday urban accessory; Apple, in redefining the very idea of computers through friendliness and aesthetics; Swatch, in transforming the watch into a fashion accessory that also tells time, and so forth. Every big brand achieves a gap in reality that is emblematized in a product or discourse breaking away from the existing. Likewise the Caprice de Dieux brand created in 1955 broke from the current conventions on the camembert market by offering: pasteurized cheese (thus, with a predictable taste), an oval form (no longer round) and in the official red and blue colors, borrowing angel-type symbols (no longer monks or knights).

In his work *Disruption*, Jean-Marie Dru (1997) attempts to formalize a thought process of differentiation. The methodology consists of identifying discourse conventions that characterize a domain (personal-care products, alcoholic beverages and so forth.) and developing a discourse not presented in reaction with current convention, and doing so in order to renew the point of view and vision of the brand in its sector. We can thus consider three modes of transcending the commonplace, modes offered by design to marketing to escape the mimetic spectrum. On the one hand, reconfiguration that consists of overhauling existing market conventions; Badoit Rouge is a good example, transposing in the water market the red and white codes of the soft drink. On the other hand, the plastic inversion that is quite simply taking the opposite codes of the main competitor, which is very common due to the contradictory structure of most markets. As such, Pepsi Cola's entire strategy consists of doing away with the leader's red-white code by unveiling the color blue supporting proposed new forms of life. But this inversion of the visual also depends on the market to be considered a logic of innovation that transcends the commonplace. It thus remains to be considered the path of individuality that explains what design can bring to marketing.

The tricks of design

It is necessary for us to understand the singularity offered by design exit the mysteries of a liberating marketing since it is self-fulfilling and without conviction. Moreover, what is meant by *design?* Certainly, the term, fundamentally of English origin, indicates among other things "project, plan, draft, intention, objective" as well as "form, configuration, basic structure," but also "bad intention, conspiracy." There is, then, a sort of trick, a concealed fraudulence in the very idea of design (Flusser, 2002). So, we can also read *into design*: "engineer, simulate, give shape, sketch" and "strategically proceed." The designer is thus like a malicious conspirator in charge of setting traps. Design thereby demonstrates a true project, of a game on objects or even as Francis Ponge voiced a tribute to *l'objeu*. Now what is the game, if not precisely an offset within our common representations, shifting the gaze around the object, a way to reconsider the object with fresh eyes in its form as well as in its function(s). The game serves here thus as when we say: "there is play"; the object that used to be offer such evidence with clarity and routine and droning triviality, again resists the eye and the hand; playing with the object means thus being played by the object, being surprised and amazed by it. Thus it became a sort of manipulated thing without reference and without affect, once more an object endowed with meaning.

Taking an oblique, lateral look on things, not taking them with full force, relies on an assumed difference that further justifies the work of any designer. Why, in fact, introduce a new object, if varying could not remotely compare to the too-common round shape of objects.

This approach is apparently consistent with the marketing ideology that outlines consumers' expectations and develops objects to such expectations as accurately as possible. But, watch out, true design work, even if it cannot forget consumers and their expectations, must above all be able to know how to exceed and defy expectations and market conventions. Design must at the same time allow the brand to foresee and go beyond the only difference. If the work relies on observing consumption practices: how do we use the object? How do we look at it? How do we touch it? And so forth. It also nevertheless involves going beyond the consumer discourse on the object, foreseeing technological developments, eliminating the preconceived notions of the object (a ski boot must be heavy, a vacuum cleaner noisy, and so forth.) to give it revolutionary meaning. It thus does not entail matching your project with consumers' expectations (so where would the designer creator be in that case?), but reconsidering in a fresh new way the expression of the offer and demand. And it is undoubtedly why it is necessary to consider a real marketing approach to design; in the end, marketing is not a practice consisting of developing an object corresponding to pre-established expectations, but reconfiguring the relationship (practical, esthetic, emotional) that individuals maintain with objects; objects that are moreover essentially cultural since hopelessly marked by an era, a genre, a defined type of practices and uses. The designer is therefore the one who, by reconfiguring the object, can change relationships with the thing and bring about new expectations. So we can expect something else from a toothbrush other than just being a functional object "intended to remove pieces of meat from between the teeth" (Starck's ironic take); why would it not become in fact a fun, even esthetic object that may even become (why not?) a bathroom decoration.

The object, with material and meaning redefined, thereby becomes the bearer of a story, an undertaking. It specifically makes it possible to reshape consumption by projecting it in a universe full of meaning and emotions. Now, what does consuming mean? Is it not only the idea of using or destroying an object, but moreover a set of meaningful practices by which individuals handle objects to create meaning? The object is thus an identifying marker in that it creates meaningful universes that show fragments of the individual's identity. The object thus becomes an important mediator between the individual and his daily environment, and helps him reconsider the space around him. It reconfigures relationships between individuals: it makes the unpleasant pleasant, it reduces tension, it offers harmony. It is thus in this way not neutral, but an essential mediator of human relations, in particular in the family living space. The object is a relational entity that allows the individual to make the relationships that he maintains with his loved ones (but also with himself) more pleasant and harmonious. But the object is also the bearer of a brand project. Now what is a brand, if not an entity with meaning instilling objects with meaning and values? A brand is a story told on objects, on the user and on the world. If by brand, we mean not just a simple visual image affixed on objects to differentiate them from one another but, more broadly, a machine generating a universe of meaning and values, then the brand can be understood as a promise that offers customary terms on the object and real-life scenarios. What makes up the legitimacy of a brand is, moreover, a know-how, a type of story told on things and humans and the relationships between the two, meaning real-life scenarios.

The designer's work reinvests the object with new values. It first of all involves relieving it of its simple utilitarian value (taking a shower, brushing your teeth and so forth.) to welcome other types of assessments (emotional, esthetic, and so forth.). In this sense, we can say that the project here at work usually avoids the two risks inherent to any innovation, meaning humdrum repetition and refined differentiation.

Moreover, the etymological context of design encounters meaningful terms like "mechanical" and "machine"; now the Greek *mêchos* means precisely a disposition to fool, a trick, such as, for example the Trojan

Horse; or consider Ulysses called *polymêchanikos*, man of a thousand tricks. A machine would be thus – as in Old French – a device intended to fool in the same way as the mechanics is the strategy to dupe people. But also remember that *design* contains the substantive *signum*, the sign, but contains it so as to cancel it; in fact, to design means according to the etymology "de-sign" something, meaning simply removing its sign!

Against the unlimited semiotics that marketing offers too often by lack of ideas, convictions and projects, design would perhaps be the escape route of brands no longer focusing on the overabundance of visual images but on the full meaning of the objects that populate our daily life.

Which design philosophy?

Structure, function, symbol

Design helps objects produce meaning. It is this capacity to produce meaning (and thus the commercial value in a marketing logic) that at the same time sets it apart from a purely functional logic and from art for art's sake. The meaning is first of all the social meaning the object provides to invest real or virtual social relations. "This virtuality and this need for the social bears another name: symbolic. A symbolic object is an object that brings human beings together and from which relations between humans can be considered. (So) "fetish" objects – and thus the Christian missionaries emphasized that they were adored for themselves – are extremely "symbolic," full of social meaning, cult objects undoubtedly but hence establishing, through the face of the god that they represent and embody at the same time, a mediation between men. That is why the anthropologist industrial objects bear "social meaning, because most of them are dedicated to the circulation, communication or registration – in short to the relationship between one another."

Consumers do not need a car but to get around comfortably, unhindered and as a family; they do not have any further use for toothpaste but they want to have fresh breath, be able to smile freely and keep their original teeth as long as possible. A product or a place is defined thus by:

- ***material*** components (technological, physical quality, packaging and so forth): this has to do with its sensory attributes and qualities;
- ***functional*** components (what purpose it can serve): this is about its different uses;
- ***intangible*** components associated with imaginary representations: this is its symbolic dimension.

Design, draft, drawing (*design, dessein, dessin*)

What exactly is design? If we accept the idea that marketing is essentially a symbolic manipulation to increase the commercial value of commercial objects, the relationship with design becomes more than obvious. *Design* in fact means several things according to which we consider the noun – that expresses a scope of activities – the verb – that indicates an action – the adjective – that can influence the characteristics of an object.

Nothing can dispute that the term design derives from the term *sign* that itself derives from the Latin *signum* close to trace, impression, signal even omen. The Latin already received the term *designo, are* meaning to represent, draw, indicate and where the Italian *disegnare* (that appeared in the 13th century, probably derived), that meant to outline and shape a project. From there the two essential dimensions are clearly expressed that give the term design its meaning (which, remember, appeared in English in the 17th century in the sense of plan of a work of art but emerges in the French language in 1959!), meaning on the one hand *dessein* (in the sense of project) and *dessin* (in the sense of graphic and material representation). Design is thus simply all of the tools that give shape to a project.

Design is thus not, as a falsely naive vision might have us believe, a work only on the form of the object, but more fundamentally is the harmonious expression of a form and intent. Thus the intent of said object must be defined or outlined. It is feasible then to replace this specific approach with the object within more general philosophies of the object.

Semiotic approach of philosophies of design

We can consider the object in two ways: as a utensil, a means, or otherwise as an end, a "style of our being." This distinction between what is called in semantics a practical program and a life program discerns four modes of assessing the object or place:

- **A utilitarian assessment**, characterized by its extremely concrete and utilitarian intent; the object is valued and sought out for its practical value, its functionality, comfort, performance, efficiency or even its ease of use;
- **An additional critical assessment** of the above that corresponds to a logic of distancing, calculation and comparison; the object is here subject to evaluation criteria inspired by external elements

and sought out for the quality/price or quantity/price ratio, savings, safety, pledges of security;

- **An existential assessment** that is the exact opposite of the previous approach; it corresponds to the "superior" expectations of individuals, such as self-fulfillment or even the esthetic meaning: the object becomes a vector for exceeding and accomplishing something that lets the consumer express his identity, his search for adventure or his life plans;
- **An additional fun assessment** of the above that essentially has to do with emotions and sensations or even luxury: the object must above all be a source of emotion, pleasure, distraction, refinement....

To this approach by the values potentially invested in the object (for which the semiotic square of assessments offers once again an interesting typology), we suggest communicating a second level of analysis dealing with the forms and functions of the object. We can in fact consider that design directly or indirectly promises a certain discourse on the "reality" of the object, meaning it manifests its intent or more accurately the functions immediately assigned to it.

If we accept the idea that design, as it expresses a draft and a drawing, refers to a basic ratio that is inherited in form and function, we can thus consider at least four ways to understand the ratio between the object's form and functions by reproducing the analysis implemented by Floch (1990) to offer a typology of advertising strategies. Highlighting the values potentially invested in the object, it is feasible to express a second level of analysis dealing with the object's forms and functions. We can in fact consider that design directly or indirectly promises a certain discourse on the "reality" of the object, meaning that it manifests its intent or, more accurately, the functions immediately assigned to it. If we accept the idea that design – as it expresses a draft and a drawing, a project and form – refers to a basic ratio that is inherited in form and function, then we can consider at least four ways to understand the ratio between the object's form and functions. We will in fact discern according to what the role of design represents or even builds the function of the object. Using a semiotic square, we can thus highlight the different creative approaches in matters of design.

Referential design

The form can thus adhere very closely to the functions assigned to the object; we can talk about reference design insofar as the role of design is to produce a form the main virtue of which is to show very precisely the function of the object. Here we have a very utilitarian approach to design supported by an index function that merely shows what purpose the object can serve. That is, for example, the entire meaning of the functional project, but also of a school like the Bauhaus, the dedicated formula of which was "form follows function." A brand like Braun can represent of this approach insofar as it has always advocated a "new culture of the (desired) honest and human product, free of any misleading decoration. The form of the device is determined by its sole function" (Barré-Despond, 1996: p. 92).

Substantive design

Substantive design takes the object at its root, highlighting its substantial and defining qualities. There is clearly a refusal of decoration and lavishness, since the form must be fully erased to highlight the substance of the object. This design is thus based on an economy of meaning and means. A representative of this approach is unquestionably Martin Szekely known specifically for his aversion to artistic visions. So, he affirms regarding the glass designed for Perrier: "an object is designed

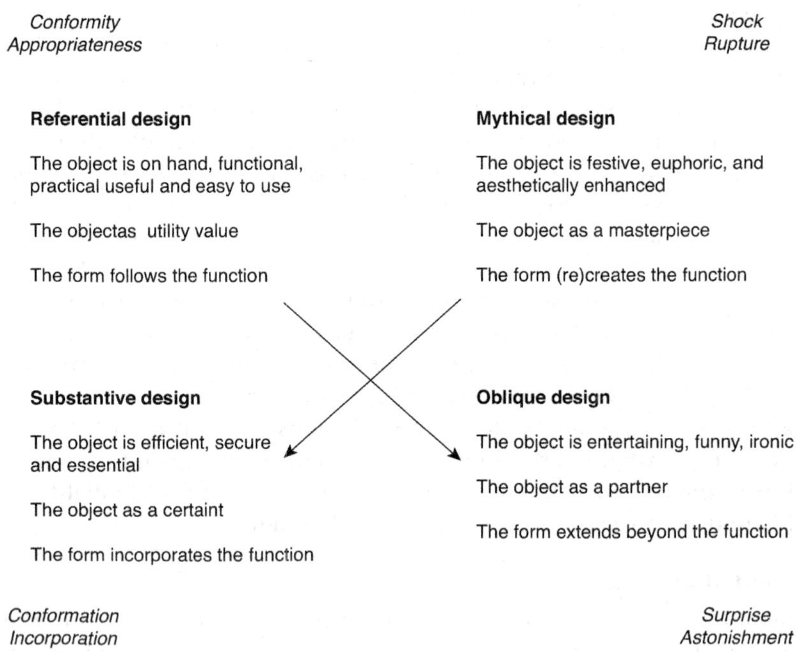

Figure 6.2 Semiotic approach to the philosophies of design

of itself.... It is the use, drinking[,] that determined this simple form of ancestral goblet." Design refers almost here to a desire to no longer drawn: so he again said regarding glass dishes: "These dishes are reduced to the strict material... I want to build with nothing. An object must only separate man from the ground, allow him to sit, to eat.... Not more."

Mythical design

Mythical design, for which Philippe Starck is undoubtedly the most illustrious representative, recreates the object. This design can be understood as the exact opposite of substantive design in that it manifests a radical innovation on the form and clearly brings out the exomorphic dimension of the object on its endomorphic dimension. There is, moreover, a negation of the object in its common acceptance. Starck explains, regarding the toothbrush designed for Fluocaryl: "I created this toothbrush because it is a straightforward non-product. Everyone needs a toothbrush, and they almost all look alike. But I said to myself that if the first thing that you encounter in the morning [is] bright and enjoyable, that would be as if every day you open the window of the bathroom on a summer landscape" (in Lloyd Morgan, 1999: p. 11). This game allows taking the object from its practical value by "[conferring needs,] a fifth dimension, a depth that gives an ordinary object the possibility to talk about something else." (in Lloyd Morgan, 1999: p. 21).

It has to do with innovating and making innovation visible, even if this does not necessarily challenge the obvious intent of the object. We are, here, essentially in an approach de break. It has to do with breaking as clearly as possible from the current codes and shower the user this break. There is thus something essentially visionary in this approach. This approach aims to consider that the object must not only communicate feelings and emotions, but also and especially violate. The object plays essentially on the poetic function of Jakobson by introducing an offset between the form and the presupposed function of the object. This is free of any obvious intent to become a poetic object that serves as for itself independent of any utilitarian or practical function of allegiance. It has to do with releasing the object of its practicality and attaching to it an essential esthetic function. The object thus becomes something other than what it was supposed to be – from the point of view of consumption – it becomes worthy of interest for itself, free from being taken as a pure object of esthetic emotion independent of a predetermined use. It is the entire meaning of André Branzi's statement: "for men, building a house, means making a place and objects with which it is possible to establish relationships associated not only with their use and functionality, but also psychological, symbolic, poetic relations" (Branzi, in Alessi, 1998: p. 64).

Now, this is not about doing away with the intent of the object; we can in fact consider that achieves here precisely a re-routing of the intent of the object from function toward existential. It has to do with reinvesting an object – often considered ordinary – with emotional values. We find ourselves here toward a true desire to re-engage the object and likewise everyday life. It has to do with recreate by a distance between the object and horizons of expectations thus it was subject – and that are expressed through in particular established codes concerning the form, materials and colors in particular.

Oblique design

Oblique design aims to look at the object in an altered, ironic way. It has to do with denying a purely referential approach for the object, in considering that the form exceeds the function of the object, and that design precisely tries to signify that the object is not reduced to a set of functionalities. The form here is only a carbon copy of the function assigned to the object. The meaning of the object is not already there; it is a project to be built. It has to do with rubbing the thing to take the world head on to make it more meaningful, get rid of the blandness that inevitably plagues it. It is thus nothing more or less than a play on objects or, even as Francis Ponge stated as an accolade of *l'objeu*: Now what is the game, if not precisely an offset within our common representations. [I]s shifting the gaze around the object a way to reconsider the object with new eyes in its form as well as in its function(s). The game serves as here thus like when we say: "there is play"; the object that used to be offered such evidence with a sort of clarity and routine and droning triviality, again presents a resistance to the eye and the hand; it no longer appeared in fact on the body in its regular bills. Playing with the object means thus being played by the object, being surprised and amazed by it. As if [it] became a sort of manipulated thing without reference and without affect, it becomes again once more an object, meaning cultural artefact given meaning. Oblique design aims to look at the object in a new way, to reinvest it with new values, which requires break the current conventions in the sector. It is precisely this approach that invests the object with a story or, more exactly, a tale since it has to do with thus rebuilding the reality of the object by offering a new interpretation of the object that offsets it from the current horizon of expectations. It thus has to do with play at the same time on the endomorphic and exomorphic dimensions of the object, and, by breaking the codes of the sector, shift the terms of the interpretative contract between the user and the object. It has to do with nothing more and nothing less than re-offering a new contract between the brand and the consumer, and it is at that price that innovation can achieve truly without being a pure differentiation. Oblique does not mean random but a specific project aiming to change the system of understanding (too) common of the object in everyday life. It is moreover an established fact that the meaning of an is never lodged in the recesses even of this object, since an object with meaning always has several possible meanings, like in particular Umberto Eco demonstrated in *Les limites de l'interprétation,* they are not however infinite. So, we can never say of an object with meaning what it absolutely means, even if it is possible (by the negative) to consider that it does not mean resolutely. We can, for example, say assuredly that a toothbrush, even equipped with arms and legs, does not represent a pear, a dinosaur or a dog. There are thus multiple meanings attributed to an object with meaning but not at all random or infinite. These meanings are shaped ultimately actively by the individual who is in front of the object, was it on a store shelf or even in its bathroom. This process refers to the idea of "active cooperation" offered by Eco (1985). The object is just as much developed by the user as by the designer. It is through a process of cooperation with the object that the individual will develop a meaning that makes sense for him. The vision that the user (or the potential user) will develop depends on the relationship that he has developed over time with the object (frequency of contact, emotional connection to the object and so forth.) but also its expectations towards the product category considered. The user develops thus, without moreover necessarily being aware of it, expectations with respect to any product of current consumption, whether these expectations are in terms of forms, colors, materials or functions. These expectations refer to the current conventions on the market but also to specific expectations that cannot be expressed by the existing offer. Innovation in matters of design refers precisely to the perception of an offset or dysfunction between the existing offer and the expectations of individuals. Designing an object is always more or less attempting to cancel out this discrepancy and to resolve this dysfunction.

The relationship to the user ends up necessarily modified. We test his intelligence and humor. Oblique design functions on a wink and provocation. It tries to break the monotony with the difference and to romanticize the object to recreate a friendly connection between the user and the object. It has to do with nothing more and nothing less than re-establishing a full and meaningful relationship between man and the object so that the latter again becomes an identifying marker bearing projects of the use, values and aspirations of the individual. The object is thus relieved of its simple utilitarian value (taking a shower, brushing your teeth and so forth) to allow it to collect other types of assessments (emotional, aesthetic and so forth.) The object with material and meaning thus redefined thus becomes the bearer of a story, a project. It allows in particular to reshape consumption by projecting in a universe full of meaning and emotions. Now what does it mean to consume? It is not only the idea of using or destroying an object, but on the contrary a set of meaningful practices by which individuals create meaning by manipulating objects.

7
Embodiments

Is French design siding with objects?

It is paradoxical that French poetry, through the intermediation of Francis Ponge, managed to side with things, while French design seems to have sided with images and signs, through being forced to deal with a sort of semiotic diktat and the hypertrophy of the figure of the designer. How then are we to describe, circumscribe or even approach the idea of French design? Is it even possible to define the characteristics of the French approach to design? Is it even possible to speak of French design or should we be talking about French designers? It would appear that this list of questions poses a certain problem, as it is tricky to try to envisage common ground between the work of someone like Philippe Starck and that of Martin Szekely, for example, or the work of Roger Tallon and that of Marc Sadler. If we are to believe what we read in mainstream magazines on the subject, French design can be characterized by the "art of plundering the past to constantly reinvent itself," or even, to quote the photographer Mario Testino, we can recognize French design by its "blend of precision, elegance and sophistication that always harbors an element of surprise, bold ideas and an impeccable 'savoir-faire'." However, does the same not apply to Italian, Swedish and Japanese design? Decidedly, whatever we say about it, design is always a question of balance between the past and the present, between stability and disruption.

For example, where should we go looking for French style? In recurrences? And what do we mean by French? Is it a question of the designer's nationality, the culture he or she belongs to, where he or she trained, his or her influences or the brand he or she works for? Quite quickly, we see that the path is strewn with obstacles that prevent us from trying to outline a form of "Frenchness" in design, most notably in terms of style. Pinning down the identity (or at least the markers) of French design is problematical inasmuch, as Nathalie Heinich says, as "the concept of identity has no meaning unless it is envisaged as a construction and not as a substance: there is no such thing as identity per se, only diverse operations that can confer a being with a collection of relatively stabilised properties." Identity can only be understood as "the result of an ensemble of operations through which a predicate is attributed to an object."

Even more than "Frenchness," it is the very idea of design that becomes an issue here. In effect, the understanding of the term is not the same according to whether or not we are considering the strictly technical and professional meaning of the term, the representation given by interiors and furniture stores or the implicit way the term is understood by the general public. So, our approach to design (and all the more so to French design) will differ if we are considering the term from the point of view of the Saint-Etienne Biennale, the trendy design stores in the Marais district in Paris or a lecture in a design school. In addition, a number of levels of observation can be envisaged according to whether we are examining the object, the process, the style, the designer, the brand or the common representation of design.

Brand versus country of origin

In Du style, a decidedly instructive piece of writing, Joan DeJean shows how the "Sun King" (Louis XIV) – who in addition to being a charismatic monarch, was the world's first-ever fashion victim and an unconditional fan of luxury and elegance – transformed France into a hub of refinement and prestige. By claiming for France – and more precisely for Versailles, which was for a long time a cutting-edge trend laboratory – the "savoir faire" and skills in domains such as diamonds, champagne, chic cafés, luxury boutiques, Louis XIV managed to create what can be termed the "country-of-origin effect," which meant a level of expertise that was recognized, specific and therefore exportable in areas reputed for excellence which, as such, naturally attached to France. Of course, the legitimizing effect of national origin remains in place today in most of the domains mentioned above, but is it the case for what we have agreed to term design? There are certain icons of French talent in design. For example, Seb's pressure cooker and toaster, Citroën's 2CV and DS and so forth. We are obliged to admit that the majority of "design objects" attributed to France are architectural objects (such as the work of Jean Nouvel, Christian de Portzamparc or Philippe Starck internationally), or objects whose notoriety has been obliterated by the designer or the brand. Thus, today design is only attributable to a country through the (often joined) brand and designer – and this is not only true in France. Of course Nokia telephones and B&O hi-fi equipment illustrate, respectively, Finland and Denmark, but they are above all, emblematic representatives of global brands that have lost the beneficial effect of the country of origin due to the fact that they cross national borders with standard products that have rapidly become the prototypes of a global culture.

The designer as king

So, design in France is not so much a question of objects or national style as it is of people. The preeminent factor of valorization and legitimization of objects is the designer's name: designers themselves increasingly tend to brand themselves in order to valorize their own "source effect" and market position. To be honest, what are the stand-out features of design in popular culture if not the media-savvy designers themselves (Roger Tallon, Philippe Starck, Ora-ïto, Matali Crasset), categories of objects (furniture, cars, interiors) and brands (Renault, Moulinex, Apple, etc.). In the same way that Paul Bénichou highlighted a form of sacralization of the writer at the turn of the 18th century, French culture, near the end of the 20th century, was all about the canonization of the designer. However, while French culture has always managed to define groups in artistic fields such as painting (the symbolists, the Parnassians, etc.), literature (la Pléiade, the Nouveau roman, etc.), and in cinema (the Nouvelle Vague, etc.), it is much more difficult to operate this type of segmentation in the area of architecture or design where the names of the designers themselves take precedence over the "schools."

Not only that, the level of diversity in object design that seems, at first glance, to characterize French design means that it is all the more difficult to outline an identity that would demand a definition shared by a broad range of stabilized, even institutionalized individuals. French design does not function collectively (unlike *Droog* design in the Netherlands); it is essentially a *design d'auteur,* which entails the glorification of the designer whose work is essentially singular and personal. This results on the one hand, in incessant flirting between the function of designer and that of artist – to the extent that the design objects can often be found on sale in the museum shop, where they are also on show as works of art – and on the other hand the primacy of individual style over collective style (whether it be national, regional, etc.). The function of the object is to render the style of the designer recognizable so that it is automatically attributable.

There is also the double phenomenon of co-branding, where the object is valorized through the association of the prestige of the designer's name with the prestige of the brand (an approach originally developed by the Italian brand, Alessi, and since taken up by Philips, Moulinex, etc.). The name of the artist is often used as a trademark that highlights the singularity of the object and, above all, enables a price markup beyond what the brand alone would have been in a position to charge. This occurs to such an extent that the design is seen as the creative gesture of an artist who must brand and sign the object, scattering tiny crumbs of recognition through the design. The signature on the object is essential. So French design is triply a design of branding inasmuch as it is a design that serves brands, a design that transforms the designer into a brand and a design that demands that the designer use strong identifying markers so as to maintain a form of "authorial" fiction. French design is both recognizable and media-friendly, thanks to identifying marks that are not those of a culture or a collective but are the identifying marks of the auteur. The narrative of the object is thus often eclipsed by a narrative made up of scattered clues as to the designer's identity.

Design, son of a pitch?

The late arrival in France of specialist design-training courses, while in other countries such as the United States and England, dedicated design-management courses had been in existence for a long time, means design in France is defined by default at the crossroads of decorative arts and industrial aesthetics. So we could think that design has remained quite close to the decorative arts, and for many people that is really part of interior decoration, unlike some cultures (notably Nordic) where it tends more towards science and engineering. It must be said that one result of the late development of design schools in France has been that the constitution of a structured field was only recently made possible. Design was relegated to the category of the beaux-arts, and this obliterated the close links that have to exist between the formal and the functional. Because it was reduced to a merely decorative function, design in France suffered from its close links to categories of products that were visible and spectacular. Even though French culture remained for a long time impervious to pop art and the blend between popular and artistic culture, design typifies the movement of the aestheticization of daily life taken to the extreme in French culture. So a schism occurred between on the one hand, a form of design that works on life forms and is based on the efficiency of the object (illustrated by the work of Szekely, Dubuisson and Boisellier), and on the other, a flashier design based on the "spectacularization" of the object (the work of Starck, Crasset, Garouste and Bonetti). So this still-evident hesitation in French culture with regard to pop art has repercussions today on the social function of design. Rather than playing with a possible permeability between popular and artistic culture, design in France has remained (at least in the minds of the general public) a way of marking social differences. Its close links to art are used as a lever to justify the higher price tags on the objects. As a result, design's essential function is one of demarcation that ensures a certain visibility and a certain stability of the categories by which individuals are classified. This is why, in the horizontal logic that prevails in democratic societies, design is sure to have a long life, as it remains one of the only means left through which social demarcation and the promotion of social identity is possible. As a result, one important social function of design in this context is to show that an object incorporates design through a rhetoric of effect and showing. In addition, while it may claim a societal role at times, the ostentatious character of French design inevitably brings us back to an economic model that valorizes the object: (a) through the joint effects of the fame of the brand and the designer and (b) through the emphasis on its aesthetic function. While Nordic design has often given precedence to ergonomics and the democratization of the product (as can be seen by the success of Ikea), design in France is still seen (again in the minds of the general public) as a way of making objects more expensive. So design is seen to be a form of ruse – as is marketing, even though nothing in their respective definitions would lead one to find this link – that corresponds perfectly to the etymological root of the word design with terms such as "mechanic" and "machine," not forgetting that the Greek *mechos* designates a means to fool, a trap.

This ruse relies in part on a capacity to over-evaluate the aesthetic function of objects relative to their technical dimension. In this, one of the characteristics of French design is that it is seen by the majority of consumers to be synonymous with marketing. This means that only in exceptional cases (Martin Szekely springs to mind) is French design associated with substance; it is seen to be more founded on the metaphysics of the effect. This is why, in France, design is seen as an advertising continuator. And one of the most remarkable characteristics of French design is its propensity to propose a mythical approach founded on the extreme difference between its form and its function, as if to remind us that the function of an object is but fiction. Design signsm the apology for branding founded on the pre-eminence of image over use. In fact, herein lies the ambivalence of a designer such as Starck, who can proclaim "a product that gets to its end with a minimum of means"; "I like to get to the root of things" is something he repeats regularly, but at the same time he shows a willingness to take the object away from its use by conferring on it "a fifth dimension, a depth that gives an ordinary object the possibility to say something else." (Starck quoted in Morgan, 1999: p. 21). It is this split between function and form, between use and image, that enables the creation of an intrigue that draws in the consumer.

This is why in today's post-advertising society, Philippe Starck plays the symbolic role that Jacques Séguéla played in the France of the 1980s. The object is treated as a medium that enables the designer or the brand to address the consumer directly. If French design is relational, it is not about the relationship between the end user and the object; instead, it is about the relationship between the designer and the consumer through the collusion, complicity and diversion that have made advertising so successful. In fact, it is a form of advertising that aims to valorize brands through a particular medium, the object, the product. The object is not taken into consideration alone; it is a loudspeaker for the designer and the brand. This "marketization" of design results in a corresponding glorification of the consumer and a permanent discourse on the benefits to the consumer (enjoyment, emotional satisfaction, possibility to show off, etc.) as the justification for the innovation. This results in a design culture that considers the object in terms of a result and a sum of effects rather than a process of elaboration. Only very recently has the sports store, Decathlon, begun to display the technical backdrop of the products with in vitro tests and displays of products taken apart. This emphasis on the result produced rather than on the act of producing is linked to the common disdain in France for the engineering sciences. As such, the object is reduced to effects of showing and ostentation that only serve to underline the hyper-investment in its decorative or emotional functions. Only in France will you find interior decor or furniture stores that are called Design stores. This showy culture of design is in fact summed up quite well in the very French expression: "ça fait design!" ("that's very 'design,'" where the term is used as an adjective) which, in the end, merely reduces design to its effects. So design is implicitly considered to be a visible, noticeable, even spectacular intervention that deals solely with the formal and color-based aspects of objects, most of the time underestimating the technical and social issues that are at stake.

Hyperbolic effectiveness

The metaphysics of presence imposed by such a strong culture of the object has a number of consequences. As it is often the result of the brand effect (whether this is a commercial brand or the brand incarnated in the designer himself), French design relies very often on a valorizing and relatively spectacular conception of the effect of the product. This is why French design has often gone for taste over blandness, notably through the saturation of effects (diverting codes, coexisting contradictions, extreme semanticization, etc.). We could almost say of design what Clément Rosset says about marketing: that it "aims to give perfectly reproducible and standard objects a coefficient of distinction that grabs the attention and seems to make them sure to find favor with the public before they even begin" (Rosset, 1979). So the French concept of design is essentially Promethean, inasmuch as the designer is seen as a sort of magician capable of creating transformations and conferring power (speed, omniscience, safety, comfort, etc.) on the consumer. This means an inherent hyper-visibility of the effect that tries to create a sort of domain of excess that defines itself not as real but as a supplement to the real, participating both in the "not like the others" idea and the idea of something "extra" that is absolutely in line with the way French design is anchored in the decorative. So French design constantly plays on the exomorphic dimension of the object that signals a split from the accepted conventions. This is how design is considered a creative act, and the designer is seen to be a cross between an artist and the Almighty. The object is the means of showing uniqueness. So, fundamentally, the tropism of French design is discontinuity – relative to others, to the past, to the surroundings as the object must explode onto the stage as a contrast and so forth. The effect is often considered, as a result, both visible and spectacular. It throws up benefits that are directly perceived and appreciated by the consumer. It is in this way that French design is mythical in obedience, inasmuch as the myth is, above all, a narrative about origins. So, while Scandinavian design places the object in its natural and human environment, French design plays more on the effects of rupture or reconfiguration. But how can we express this fundamental discontinuity if not as a form of dramatization of objects?

The dramaturgy of the object

If we think about certain cultures such as the Dutch, who take their concept of design from their pictorial heritage, we could probably conclude that the French cultural representation of the object is based on the theatre. Are not the effects of narrative, image, scriptwriting and intrigue that are so characteristic of a certain type of French design a perfect metaphor for the theatre? French design envisages only the object; this leads to the importance of intermediate structures such as interior-design magazines and so-called design boutiques. French design is that which transforms the object into an intermediary, meaning a subject. The object becomes an actor, it talks. It finally acquires the status of a character, which brings us to the notion of the actor product developed by Bertrand Barré to signify the active role played by design in the seduction process at the point of sale (Barré, 2009). Actually, a characteristic of French design is the way in which it works against the tide of the first, slightly forgotten, meaning of the term. As Vilém Flusser reminds us, design means literally to de-sign, which means to remove the sign dimension from the object to give it, perhaps, a capacity for resistance that forms its ontological base (Flusser, 2002). French design is the opposite in a constant procedure of semanticization that exemplifies objects. The object humanizes itself as the market relationship becomes more dehumanized, caused notably by the change in shopping habits (the progressive disappearance of salespeople in hypermarkets, online shopping, etc.). It is not by chance that French culture gave rise to the hypermarket model and, also, it is that culture that gives objects a voice as if to overcome the dis-intermediation of the contemporary shopping process. This explains the importance, on an economic and symbolic level, of anthropomorphic objects in the French landscape. The theatricality is needed to give objects a voice. This is impeccably carried out by the various paratexts (Genette, 1997) used by a great number of French designers to give their work meaning. This results in a form of extraneousness of design that wraps the object in a flow of words aimed at justification, explanation and valorization.

The image trap ...

In-depth reflection on French design leads us to the possibility that it is perhaps easier to outline what it is not. While outlining Scandinavian or Japanese design is within the realm of possibility, with regard to a French philosophy of design, it is simpler to outline its contours by default, as if in opposition. It is perhaps possible to define the imprint of French design, indented, relative to its other. By clearly taking sides with image over use, is French design not now trapped by image? Has French design become, for example, the antithesis of the vision of the object as deployed by Dutch culture. As Jean-Louis Schefer shows us, Dutch painting is remarkable in that it renders objects "conductors" like the all-powerful flow of the low tide. The renewal of painting subjects that emblematized this culture is "an abandonment of the tragic base of European culture. This catalogue that has the good sense to clean up painting... is a private version of the great catalogue of culture, i.e. of all of the emphasis, all of the pathos of the great German Italian traditions, etc." (Schefer, 1995, p. 20) Is this not close to the metaphysical and symbolic clean-up that corresponds to the etymology of de-sign? This acceptance of substance and the optical cleansing of their individuality – which leads to a form of equality of all things under the sun – plays essentially with "an attenuation of roles, drama and, [as] we can see, the magnification of a social and community based virtue" (Schefer,, 1995, p. 28). The object is there to fluidify relations. It is discreetly efficient. It is a question of making human relations work. Roland Barthes says: "Let's look at Dutch still life: the object is never alone, and never in the centre; it is just there, in the middle of other objects, painted between two uses, part of the disorder of the movements that seized it, then rejected it, in a word, used. What can be the justification of such an assembly if not to lubricate the eye of man inside his domain, and to slide the eye over objects whose enigma has been dissolved and so are nothing more than easy surfaces? The use of an object can only help to dissipate its capital form and on the contrary over bid on its attributes" (Barthes, 1964).

Nordic cultures of the object seem to have proposed another form of intelligibility of the object, one that enables it to express itself in ellipses and enigmas by taking its effectiveness from discretion and not "looking" to have an effect. It would seem that the Nordic culture of design is more attached to transformation that, unlike an impact that is local and short-lived, is always global and progressive – so it does not stand out. So it is not noticed – we do not see it working, we just see the effects. Instead of valorizing the spectacular, of highlighting effort and risk, Nordic design is attentive to the discreet, recommends an effectiveness that does not attack, does not force, that is both without effort and without resistance. This leads to a grey efficiency running through things, an efficiency that does not stand out and is all the less remarkable while it is working. It is object design more than relations and a design of impact rather than of fluidity. In opposition, French design culture derives from a logic of effects and, as such, of "against." It follows the sort of deviant marketing that tries to mark the position of the designer and the brand by creating a sort of mental imprint in the consumer's mind, leading to the importance of markers that can be attributed to the brand and/or the designer. While Nordic cultures have rinsed the object of its semantic dirt, French design essentially functions through semanticization pushed to the extreme. Against the flow of this fluidifying power of goods and uses, French design takes on the resistance included in the etymology of the word literally. An object is anything found on the road, what was thrown there (Latin *ob-jectum*,

Greek *problêma*). The object is constituted on the aspect of resistance to the individual (as illustrated by the German *Gegenstand* that opposes beings of thought or reason), and sends us back to the subject. This form of resistance, in addition to the fact that it relies on a logic of effect more than on actual substance, finally sets the question of human relations to one side. But this is exactly the ethical issue of French design. Indeed, usual objects are "in intermediary functions (media) between me and others. They are not simply objective but also inter-subjective, not just problematical but dialogical. The question of the form to give them can thus be put in another way: can I give my projects a form so that they accentuate the communicational, the inter-subjective, rather than the objectival, objective, the problematical?" By emphasizing the objective side, French design may have missed the inter-subjective factor altogether, which can only lead to a shrinkage of the free space due the "irresponsibility of objects conceived solely for the attention given to the object itself".

The grandesigner (the great designer)

Philippe Starck definitely occupies a place of his own in the world of design by the objects and places that he designed and that bewilder us, as well as by the discourse of legitimization which he continuously balances with his work as a designer. To understand the principles and issues of his philosophy of the object, we will attempt to highlight the main characteristics of what we suggest calling a *mythical approach* to design, in considering Starck's different productions as well as the various accompanying paratexts (Genette, 1987).

The economy of the sign

Obviously, this favors the *exomorphic* dimension and takes root in the desire go against current conventions or, more specifically, to conduct a new semantic analysis on the object in increasingly competitive markets. Starck champions in fact a purely decorative vision of the object: "I am favorable," he said to the economy, "in the psychoanalytical sense of the term. The economy of everything. A product that *succeeds with a minimum of resources*. I want to *expect things at the root*, at the moment when division is no longer possible. The simpler the object, the more difficult it is to make: decoration always compartmentalizes something else." (Starck quoted in Lloyd Morgan, 1999: p. 17). However, despite this desire to return to the essential defining properties of the object, the Starck project takes root in a permanent desire to make the object less commonplace by stripping it down, as much as possible, to its sole practical value, even if the visual images associated with it are changed as a result. It is, moreover, what can negate the object in its common acceptance; as he explains concerning the toothbrush designed for Fluocaril, "I created this toothbrush because it's a *straightforward non-product*. Everyone needs a toothbrush, and they almost all look alike. But I said to myself that if the first thing that you encountered in the morning on a shelf was bright and pleasant, that would be as if *every day you open the window of your bathroom onto a summer landscape*" (quoted in Lloyd Morgan: p. 11). This game precisely allows the taking from the object its practical value by "(conferring needs) a fifth dimension, a depth that gives an ordinary object *the possibility to talk about something else*" (quoted in Lloyd Morgan, p. 21).

So, despite the claim of a non-decorative design, the Starck project refers to formal innovation that translates a project to re-define the object or place, an exact corollary of shifting values usually invested in them. In this acceptance, designing an object refers to re-defining its functions and thus defining the components; hence, as we will next see, the permanent need to develop paratexts that continuously justify this project.

The Starck program quickly reveals a paradox, insofar as its discourse constantly oscillates between the four modes of assessment, reinforced in particular by a tension between a critical and utopian assessment of the object. Likewise, Starck affirmed that, "at a hotel, it's above all the quality of the pillowcase" – thus even visiting the Mondrian is nothing other than "living, with angels, inside a sunny cloud" or even the pool room at the Hudson is "a haunted mansion where each door reveals an extraordinary scene." In Starck's discourse, continuously developing is a round trip between the lavish and the modest, the spectacular and the ordinary. This internal contradiction of the discourse that continuously expresses opposing modes of assessment is, in fact, as we will see, the basic engine of the Starck dynamics.

The contradictory virtues of utopia

Remember that the economic virtue of the Starck design is to increase the perceived value of the object in order to increase its economic value. It is thus a game on the practical value to change the object's exchange value and symbolic value. By shifting the mode for assessing the object to essentially fun or existential, the designer's work consequently increases the perceived value of the object, meaning in its price The assigned objective of this type of design is obviously to create economic goodwill. Now, in a culture of consumption in which consumers are more and more dedicated to marketing processes that create goodwill, it is difficult to demonstrate this objective – hence, the development of paratexts, the function of which is two-fold: to legitimize the object by projecting it into a tale (and, in particular, a tale of origins) but also to express other modes of assessing the object and in particular an ethical assessment (see for example the importance of the *moral market* for Starck) that will serve as ultimate justification for the goodwill of the economic object. Hence, the tripod on which the object is based for Starck: the esthetic value, the ethical value and the economic value. It is in this sense that we can understand the credo presented by Starck to "find, collect, correct, or create when necessary, objects that are honest, responsible, respectful of other people. Objects not necessarily *pretty*, but *good* objects." (Googoods catalogue for La Redoute, 1998). The apparent denial of the object's esthetic value (consistent with an anti-decorative discourse) in fact legitimizes its ethical value and likewise establishes economic goodwill.

The Starck project thus focuses on building the object's value that develops from a permanent tension between critical and existential values, meaning, in semiotic terms, between a practical program and a life program. So, at the same time it displays a desire to develop *non-products* for *non-consumers* in order to dis-alienate the consumer and at the same time, which can appear contradictory, a desire to design "objects that are honest, responsible, respectful of other people [so that] a *new relationship* between man, production and objects may appear." This paradoxical coexistence explains in particular the permanent oscillation of the strategies for legitimizing the Starck object between practical values and aesthetic values, that the play, *Richard III*, perfectly illustrates "stretched with hot brown leather, that straight on looks like the traditional Club armchair, but the entire back part has disappeared, revealing only a metallic structure". Straight on, it is completely bourgeois, but empty as soon as you turn it around: I love this bit of hypocrisy", explains Starck" (Good Goods catalogue, 1998).

So we can indeed talk about a utopian project from Starck, insofar as Utopia builds an ideal imaginary functioning mode on the pure totality; no Utopia is in fact conceivable "without associating in a limited place everything that man can ideally think and experience." The ideal nature of the utopian world in particular automatically takes on a part of internal contradiction, as utopia perfectly illustrates the triumphs of the systematic mindset by resolving contradictions in an integrating discourse. The internal consistency of any utopian discourse is thus, paradoxically, conditioned by a necessary resolution of contradictory games. The program thus fulfills the same functions as the myth as defined by Levi-Strauss: "a means to symbolically resolve inconsistencies, contradictions or conflicting unthinkable or unbearable situations, by including them in the layered structure of a tale.". We thus now need to understand what specifically is covered by the notion of *mythical design*. In other terms how do we consider the Starck project, in particular in the specific relations that it continuously builds between the form and function of objects and places?

The Annunciation, or the story of the hidden God

Starck's program could be understood as suffering from direct and transparent exposure; it ultimately emphasizes in the form of a strong declaration in the manner of God, who would appear hidden. Beyond the re-affirmed unending importance of the hidden, the anonymity in its words "others look for the form. *I am looking for more anonymity,"* an exhaustive consultation of certain convergent devices of the Good Goods catalogue will specifically show that Starck's program truly functions in the manner of an Annunciation. Now, what is the Annunciation if not highlighting inconsistency to a scope of expectations? Mythical design, as we have seen, is specifically based on reconfiguring the scope of consumer expectations by emphasizing the object's exomorphic dimension. It is based on a distortion/reconfiguration of the object and functions on the model of imparity, meaning discrepancy, displacement and detour. Moreover, the Annunciation generally renews visibility (the Annunciation specifically refers to what is, but does not yet appear) as illustrated, for example, by the T-shirt for pregnant women that shows on the outside what is inside. This visibility is indeed obviously associated with the idea of advent and illustrated in particular by the predominance of white and the nativity theme in the Good Goods catalogue. But the most troubling element is undoubtedly the presence of Mary, which Starck specifically tells us is "the humility given to the object": the object becomes "almost nothing," the "least possible," it becomes a messenger; the object likewise becomes an intercessor, and in a religious perspective must "disappear so that there is no longer any way to track the order. It is limited to touch, looks, voices" (in the same way as the visual images of the Annunciation). The presence of Mary obviously calls the angel who is none other than Dr. Skud who, Starck tells us, is a "little guardian angel." Finally, as in the Paintnigs rom the Renaissance, each object is accompanied by a *festaiuolo*, a sort of narrator who prepares the reader and instructs on what happens in the table. The *festaiuolo* has moreover a restricting role in the Renaissance by making ready the spectator, not only of what happens at the table, but also of what must happen before the table. That is precisely the role of the paratexts accompanying each object that has at the same time a descriptive and prescriptive role.

The designer-God, or the meaning of life ...

We can thus legitimately wonder if the culmination of this essentially mythical approach to design does not secretly refer to a deification of the designer. The visionary role of the designer can be observed on several levels. Through the creation of names (Palapala, Dr. Skud, Moosk, etc.) and the designer's underlying capacity to give voice to objects or at least bring them to life by creating objects in the style of subjects (the example Starckeyes made on the model of the human body) or even by developing animated or humanized objects. The visionary power can then be seen in Starck's self-affirmed capacity to transfer powers to the consumer as the StarckNacked illustrates that "could be this magic wand that gives the woman the freedom to choose who she wants to be, where and when she wants."

Finally, the visionary nature of Starck's approach, experienced essentially in the *factitive* nature of objects, meaning their capacity to get users to act in a certain way by introducing gesture sequences and even emotional schemes. The power of the visionary is transformed into governing power on bodies and souls in the Foucauldian sense, where power is precisely the capacity to act (indirectly) on others' behavior. Governing, here, means structuring others' potential fields of action by organizing, in particular, the ways individuals have to see the world. Most Starck objects have a very strong prescriptive power that goes well beyond commercial life, as the TeddyBearband illustrates: "[A]s a supporter of unique love, I dreamed of a single toy, a sort *of preparation for sustainable commitment.*" The object is prescriptive insofar as it incites us to act, do and think in a certain way. We thus better understand why the Starck project is indeed utopian insofar as utopists are not only people who mend the world; they further embody a visionary desire to create true prescriptive worlds based on expressing the need for the desirable and the claim of an obligation to be. This prescriptive power is built through creating a sort of consumer community (which it is becoming difficult to escape); that is what the series of T-shirts seems to present that by successive transitive relations by affirming "We are God," letting doubt be cast on the identity of "us" that can in turn describe Starck or even the consumer community thus established. This "us" in turn is all and no one person (Starck?) or even what is not yet a person (hence, the resurgence of the theme of the Annunciation). The designer comes hidden and secretly flows into the object like thickener into a sauce: "[C]onsidering the object as a manifesto is suicidal and means it will not be integrated. *It is necessary to stir the creation into the object like milk into a sauce,* if we want to know how to talk to people." (Good goods, 1999). This notion of thickening/thickener is predominant because it underlies a religious metaphor insofar as the implied desire here is to bring individuals together (on condition of community) and to connect these individuals to God (Starck?). This community continues, moreover, by the sacrament of communion brilliantly illustrated by OAO organic wine, which demonstrates well that "we are what we eat" (Good Goods, 1998). So, the Starck object is not an end in itself, but implies a system of intercession, metaphorical communion between a visionary designer and consumers who endeavor, by marking their bodies, minds with a certain number of ethical and esthetic precepts. This marking is moreover persistent in the recurring tattoo theme (see in particular the photo of Starck tattooed with his objects or slogans) or even in a product like the skin watch, as if the Starck mindset was incorporated literally in the body and mind of its consumers. There is thus a prophecy, not as much of Starck the man as of the Starck brand, that by its formidable ability to be everywhere at once applies to all objects; it functions as a halo embodying objects and infusing them with a mindset, a way to see the world, to act, think, love.... Through the brand, the designer infuses his mindset on all objects and places as by transubstantiation. There is thus a certain magic but also perhaps a mystique to the Starck object, stigmatized as a "non-object" and at the same time deified as an essential and corresponding fundamental; this process is thus not without recalling the mystics who "punctuate their tales with 'almost nothing[,]' with sensations, encounters, daily tasks. The fundamental is for them inseparable from the insignificant. That is what underscores the trivial. Something moves in everyday life. The mystical discourse transforms details into myths; it clings to it, expands it, multiplies it, and deifies it." Is that not precisely what Philippe Starck tries to design with objects and places?

Sensory misery: the difficulties of sensory marketing

What is the role of marketing and brands in the (de-)formation of consumers' tastes? Pragmatic, sensory, multisensory: these are adjectives that marketing often takes pride in. But does not this sensory overload betray fundamentally the sensory and symbolic vacuum of a consumption society that has dissolved the material meaning into the dregs of what gives meaning? What is this "flavor of the world" that David le Breton speaks of so specifically, as multisensory marketing is revealed?

In looking at this dichotomy of making daily life more esthetic and establishing typical tastes, is not the main sleight of hand of marketing, *in fine*, to convince each consumer that he is a connoisseur and an expert, while bombarding him with products with standardized tastes? It would seem that most brands are subject to a question posed by Kant in his criticism of judgment, meaning: How do we maintain a universality of taste without which the principle of this common perception would not be subjective?

As a result of the countless ways technical progress manipulates perceptions, there is a sort of deterioration of products, insofar as their abundance tends to devoid them of their meaningful substance. The sociologist Max Weber showed the sort of dereliction that lies in wait for the industrial object, a predictable object without magic or surprise, the object of an industrial society characterized by the continuous rationalization of the production and consumption processes. This frustration with the world of products is that of a world wherein the inequity of the artisan world and superstition were erased in favor of values such as efficiency, predictability and reproducibility. As products have often become too obvious, taste too familiar, too predictable, is it not the role of marketing to increase their pleasure-seeking value to arouse consumers' interest?

Sensory enjoyment, tactile enjoyment

From the original linguistic deficiency of the common language to express the sensory, marketing has for a long time been met by a process of metaphorical semantics. Is this not so in marketing perfume, often reduced to strong visuals and spectacular scripting to often glamourous convention? In fact, the communication of perfume brands only very rarely has any connection to the ingredient or material, but more in methods such as exoticism, seduction, social status – methods that have nothing to do with the composition of the product. Marketing essentially deals with the olfactory senses indirectly, by building emotional value mainly from the rhetorical. Via packaging, a brand name, or calling to mind a fairyland, the constant scripting of products for which that marketing uses visual images as the main way to convey meaning and enjoyment, thus reducing the sensory to a semiotic experience. In other terms, will not the undeniable capacity for dramatizing brands end up substituting the visual image for senses?

This indirect approach to the sensory is explained by the mediation device characteristic of marketing. But the brand or product, which one do we play as a last resort in an act of consumption?

There is no doubt that products procure sensory-type enjoyment. However, the society of consumption is associated with relentless semantics that cloak material objects with meaning and thus with a power of suggestion often disconnected from the object's material nature. Meanings are in fact a form that gives meaning. They make deposits that render it intelligible. So, brands function as strong devices to express from a sensory point of view (by which the product touches our sensory experience) and an intelligible and thus abstract plan that projects the item into an imaginary dimension. The brand thus entwines meanings with our sensory perceptions. It is precisely the cultural dimension of the brand that shapes an individual "sensory organization." In fact, faced with the infinite possible sensations at any time, big brands define specific ways to make selections. They present, between consumers and the world, a screen of meanings, values, that motivates each person to exist in the world and communicate with those around him. This mediation ensures the fictional transition between a sensory level and an intelligible level. The power of a brand is first of all working on the mental representations of products by developing a positioning, meaning by installing the product in a certain way in the minds of consumers. Now, as the famous founding adage of modern marketing says, "positioning is not what you do to the product but what you do to the mind of your consumers" (Ries and Trout). Thus, we ultimately put the sensory with the psychological and mental. Consumers' perception of products depends largely on the way in which business narrates its products and brands through semantics. Semantics means that we attach the product's imaginary dimensions (values, a symbolic universe, a lifestyle, etc.) to its material dimensions (its texture, color, volume, etc.). Brands thus first of all offered a framework to categorize our sensory experience. Consistent with the idea that sensory perceptions reveal not only a physiology but also a cultural orientation allowing a margin to the individual sensibility. To that effect, Claude Levi-Strauss said, "[F]ood that is good to eat is first of all food that is good to think about." Generally speaking, we can defend the idea that a product good to consume, is first a product good to think about, meaning integrated in a network of culturally established associations. Now, it is essentially brands that help create this framework of thinking and perception of products. In other terms, "sensory formations form a prism of meanings on the world (that) are first of all the projection of meanings on the world" largely conveyed by marketing. Accordingly, we can understand the brand as a mechanism of transformation that makes goods pleasant to think about and thus consumable, and that may or may not make certain forms of sensory experiences desirable. In fact, what is a product, if not a cultural and marketed object stemming from an industrial process transforming various ingredients scattered in a cultural artefact, meaning comparable to understandable perceptual categories because culturally made (pants, yogurt, a suitcase, a car, etc.)? So, whether it is transforming milk into Nestlé yogurt, bottling Evian mineral water, making animal skin into Hermès or Vuitton bags, the marking is similar to magic transforming the natural into the cultural (and thus consumable). In the case of McDonald's, nature has been transformed: products are recomposed into products with individual shapes and names (Chicken McNuggets, Filet-O-Fish, etc.), animals are cartoon characters. The brand thus involves a largely prescriptive system that will often sustainably adjust our sensory experience by substituting, most of the time, tactile enjoyment for sensory enjoyment.

Analytical versus synthetic

However, it is important to understand the emotional power of products, not to reduce them to systems of visual images. A product is not constantly stuck in cultural and social meanings: it can produce individual appropriation by giving meaning and personal value. This emotional power of products makes so much more sense if we consider their resolutely multisensory nature. The so-called increase in power of experiential consumption compels marketing to further delve into the private sphere of the consumer by developing operating modes associated with touch, taste and olfactory – as witnessed for example in the development of *logolfs* (olfactory logos) or even the development of tactile design. In other terms, the issue for marketing is to leave the banks of the senses of far away (sight, hearing), to capitalize on the close senses (touch, taste), as well as the olfactory that acts as an intermediary. Now, focusing on the symbolic dimension of brands has somewhat spoiled the study of strictly material anchoring of the consumption experience. Moreover, the material anchoring of consumption is considered most of the time only in its ocular dimension, leaving only very little place for a strongly multisensory approach. Consumption of the product is thus often a synthetic experience that combines various sensations and, in most cases, the sensation of pleasure created by handling the product is global and spread out, not separate from what is immediately sensory or even of what emanates from connections with others or even childhood memories. The sensation of pleasure falls within a composite imaginary made from body to body with the object, of anchoring family ties and friendships, personal memories. Everything seems like a mixture and is concentrated in a pleasant and general perception. But what is truly in the apparently composite and emotional nature of the sensory experience of products? As Candau asserts, "there is no simple truth to a mono-sensory act, due to a multisensory process of stimuli by which individuals preferentially associate certain colors with certain scents ([for example,] the color pink more with strawberries rather than mint). One famous experience showed that the olfactory and flavor description of a white wine artificially colored red is influenced by this coloring" (Candau, 2007). An important mechanism explaining consumers' perception of products is, moreover, that of perceptual inferences by which the consumer deduces certain properties of the product from other attributes of the product or qualities – specifically chromatic and formal of the packaging (or other vectors representing the brand). This sensory transfer mechanism is the mechanism determining most of our sensory relationships with products.

Taking into account the consumer's perceptual inferences, on the one hand, and the settling of conventions due to mimetic logic on most of the markets, on the other hand, explain the development of conventions in most product categories: omnipresence of red/white for cola, brown and black for coffee, white for yogurt, etc. Now these conventions are positioned on all of the sensory attributes of products, which develops a taste matrix characteristic of most of the industrial food products.

From this come the often stereotyped expectations of consumers with respect to most product categories: is a household cleaning product not perceived as more effective if it is lemon scented, Landes pine or lavender? But it would be risky for a manufacturer to launch such a product with a strawberry or banana scent without undertaking significant costly work of educating the consumer.

The dictate of the exclamation

There are very few brands that have been able to develop an individual structure or gustative grammar. Now, despite the extremely subjective nature of tastes, the brand plays a preponderant role in a consumer's choices. That is what blind tests show: they reveal consumers' inability to recognize products that they consume regularly, and the significance of a placebo effect. In fact, a brand's market power is very often associated with its strong psychological impact on consumers' decision-making. So, affixing a brand on a product has a very clear influence on the perception that consumers have of that product. Studies show that, when blinded, smokers are absolutely unable to recognize their own brand of cigarettes. Likewise, comparative tests on the cereal market highlighted preference rates for Kellogg's ranging from 47 percent blindly to 59 percent when the brand is identified. Conducting blind tests very clearly demonstrates that perceptual differences are all the more intensified when brands are identified by the consumer, which illustrates the brand's capacity to create perceptual differences.

Though we recognize Nutella by its unique taste, a Ferrari by the sound of its engine or Frosties by the noise made when the milk is poured in a bowl of them, it is rare to find such brands with immediately recognizable sensory attributes. How can a brand thus display sensory individuality in a market broken off from conventional logic? Most brands thus try to enter into a logic of intensity to make an attribute stronger and more unique, in a logic of effect, impact and the overstatement of conventions that quickly lead to excess.

We see here breaking the dictate of an analytical approach of products explained in part by the fact that the main theories of marketing and consumption originate in the microeconomic mindset and in the conceptualization of the product like a "basket of attributes" (bundle of attributes according to the now famous expression of Lancaster). This analytical vision of products had led to the development of multi-attribute models and trade-off methods overused by the main marketing research firms. This approach decomposes a product into distinctive (meaning visible and determining for consumers) attributes in order to offer methods to choose the product according to which the consumer favors one or more attributes, decides to prioritize them or not, and so forth. We easily understand that this relevance of multi-attribute models (filling even a number of manuals on consumer behavior) has largely contributed to an analytical approach to products. The product is thus rarely considered holistically but synthetically. To this we can add the approach of the famous Unique Selling Proposition (USP) developed in the United States in the 1950s and still largely in vogue in many markets.

The idea is that, in a competitive market, a brand would do well to focus on a single sales proposal often based on its superiority regarding a given attribute. This logic is completely characteristic of the anthropological experience of the sensory by which "we pause on a sensation that makes more sense than the others and opens mysteries of memories and the present (even if) we encounter infinite stimulations at all times and descend into indifference" (Le Breton, 2006: p. 14).

This attribute that is valued at the expense of others may be the sparkle of soda, its fruit content, its coffee taste. Hence the propensity of brands to utilize strong identifiers that are as many statement brands, recognizable in this "forest of indices" as there are markets. These statement brands that historically refer to visual indices may today become olfactory (logolfs) or even tactile brands. The reign of the USP has undeniably led to typifying sensory regimes called to mind by products as well as process of grammaticizing the sensory, as Bernard Stiegler in particular highlighted (Stiegler, 2004 and 2005). To that effect, experiential marketing has an almost aesthetic aim, as defined in particular in the 18th century by Baumgarten. As he wrote, "the more a perception includes distinctive brands, the stronger it is. That's why an obscure perception, but including more distinctive brands than a clear perception[,] is stronger than the latter. Perceptions that contain in fact the greatest number of distinctive brands are called palpable. Thus palpable perceptions are the strongest.... Terms whose meaning is palpable are empathic." (Le Breton, 2006).

This characteristically empathic logic functions essentially by a mechanism of saturation of the effect and conventions. Now the historic development of marketing was two-fold; on the one hand, the overload of the meaningful by exaggeration and stereotyping that allow external recognition of the brand (the sensory attribute as an element of distribution and legal defendability), and on the other hand the exaggerated nature has become the main source of assessing objects in a society inundated with visual images. The reference here is thus a question of overemphasis on the sensational sensory in which brands compete to be understood within a joyless, linear economy saturated with clone products. This "one-up" logic is sensory emphasis always for "more taste," "more sparkle," in short more sensations! Hence, the tendency for brands to saturate certain senses simultaneously like, for example, using salt and fat or fat and sugar to even further increase the individual's addiction to the product. But does that mean that we are in an exclamatory logic that seems, however, to require a differential logic? What does an exclamation really mean? "I feel something, meaning I 'internalize it,' and I express what I feel, what I externalize: let's call this path an exclamation.... [M]oreover, what I 'internalize' was expected: only what meets my horizons of expectations affects me [and]... paradoxically, what truly affects me, and what surprises me, beyond what I understand, arises as the unexpected even what I expected. It is necessary to talk about exclamation of an exception whereby the selection is externalized as a meaning showing *the excess that constitutes the sensory as it is individual*" (Stiegler, 2005: p. 68). There is only exclamation as of the moment when "the sensory appeared, ,, individual and unique [and the individual] perceives it as *sensational*: sensational means here incomparable, and thereby circulating its excess through the circuit of an exclamation that is also an outcry" (Stiegler, 2005: p. 69). It is thus the incomparability that triggers the exclamation and the true capacity of delineation of brands, that is, its capacity to forge its own conventions.

That is why in the end marketing maintains an ambiguous role with respect to the civilized process as described by Norbert Elias, since it again shows what was culturally switched in secret or in silence, meaning the sensory crash, exposure and almost systematic extravagance characteristic of a society of consumption called pornographic by Jean Baudrillard. In the consumer's silence is a propensity of marketing to overwhelm the senses by emphasis and hyperbole and that cancel the strict balance of the sensory experience. It is in this logic that contrasting and opposing experiences come into play. Is not this so, for example, in matters of form between sofa beds with contrasting shapes but soft cushions like down comforters, or even in angular automobiles with passenger compartments designed like a cocoon? Food has been served for quite a long time as a game between hard and soft textures; for example, chocolate chips in ice cream, lollipops that are hard outside but have soft chewing gum inside. So the "Ivoire" cake of pastry chef Pierre Hermé offers the taste buds a dialogue between the crispy (cream puff pastry and fine layer of white chocolate with *fleur de sel* on top, caramelized flaky pastry on the bottom), the smooth (cream, candied fruits, rice pudding), starting from the principle that "contrasts in textures trigger the pleasure to eat." These contrasting effects are found in other industries such as cosmetics with, in particular, the development of scrubbing products, exfoliants with abrasive microbeads that are supposed to leave the skin "soft and younger-looking." In the automobile industry, the importance of touch in particular produced the "slushy" material, soft to the fingers but grainy in appearance that lines dashboards.

We can thus think that this hard–soft divergence reconciles opposites, meaning the use of "hard" as structuring and protective as a counterpoint to the "soft" tactile, calming, even vaguely regressive (Normand, 2004: pp. 180–2). But in the end is not the slack the (non-)response given by most brands, with simplistic interference and false mixtures (see, for example, the list of ingredients we can enjoy in ice cream from Häagen-Dazs, coffee from Starbucks, etc.)? At the onset of "McDonaldization," this interference made it difficult to differentiate flavors and thus ideas.

Despite the diversity, it seems to promote a subdued universe that standardized everything to cater to as many people as possible: tastes, shapes, smells, textures and mindset. This hint of weakness is not without remembering the stagnation and generalized sterility of the dining space highlighted by Jean-Paul Aron. (Aron, 1997: p. 32).

The brand that thought with its fingers

Among the operations listed by Montaigne, there are few that are not carried out by brands. Indeed, are not brands among the first to promise, cry out, pray, deny, doubt, instruct, command, and so forth? What brands do is more or less what we do with our hands. But what of the hand, or hands, of brands? If we accept that a brand can have a face, a voice, an identity, its own charisma, what about its hands? While brands are the offspring of the Industrial Revolution, they seem to increasingly want to flirt with the world of craftsmanship. While our post-industrial society keeps shifting the stakes and the borders of the spheres of production and consumption, it would appear that the issue is no longer the porosity between art and craftsmanship as it was for William Morris for example, but of the proximity between industry and craftsmanship. As such, the hand has become a major rhetorical figure in the communication and advertising of certain brands (most notably in the luxury sector) that wish to remind, suggest, and infer their artisanal skills. But what should be understood behind the resurgence of "handmade" as a communication code for certain so-called luxury brands?

The aim is to propose a reflection on the role and functions of the hand in the different communication and advertising approaches of a brand that claims craft-based skills such as Hermès. The point in this approach is to remember the position of the brand within a material culture. Brands have been examined from the angle of symbolic approaches linked to representations and evacuating the body and gestures for a long time. Having to undergo the famous "value-sign" concept, brands have often forgotten the carnal dimension of consumer goods and their capacity to transform men. This is why, the title of this text is a nod in the direction of Marcel Mauss's body techniques and also to Jean-Pierre Warnier's work on material culture (Warnier, 1999).

The hand and the signature

First of all the brand encounters the hand through the signature, and the possibility it provides for testifying to the traceability of an object. Artisans, who from ancient times were the first to distinguish the objects they produced, did so by marking them with an identifying sign (the ancestors of the signature or the monogram). So there is a connection between the hand and the product, as if the hand lent value to the object through a signature that is both indicative and symbolic. Firstly, the hand is that which enables the artisan to make his mark on the object thanks to a sign that, while it is eminently symbolic, is also indicative inasmuch as it indicates a commitment from the body. In the same way, what do we mean when we say that the brand works like a tracer? A good tracer is one that refers directly back to the object and does not result in too many flights of fancy. In chemistry for example, a tracer must be light, fine, mobile and abundant. Traceability means the journey back from consumption to production. The brand is essentially a footprint, a tracer, and refers to a game of hide-and-seek, meaning the question of presence and absence. Thus, while Mr. Armani is not physically present in his stores to sell his suits or perfumes, he is present symbolically. In the same way, Nestlé or Danone are represented at the point of sale of the products through their logos on the products. This question arises notably for brands whose original designer is dead. For the myth to function, the Chanel client must accept the idea that Coco Chanel has left her imprint on the clothes, the perfume, the accessories, that she has signed them in some way. The brand is thus founded on the symbolic process of representation, in as much as it substitutes the absence with a material presence. All brands are thus linked to the fiction of a presence and only exist through a relationship. The brand is that which enables a relationship to grow between the designer, the artisan or company, and their clients. It provides a link between an object and a manufacturer who is not present and who often owns production sites hundreds of kilometers away. The brand thus attempts to repair the physical distance through a symbolic and indicial proximity that enables it to prove a certain level of skill. This imprint is all the more important as the original encounter, the contact between the artisan and the object, has often disappeared in our industrial culture. Certain brands have in fact kept this gesture, imitating a manual signature –the first Apple Macs or even Kellogg's cereal packets that have a handwritten signature as if to signify the founder's commitment and ensure a form of fictional continuity. The handwritten signature enables the creation of a space–time fiction, meaning that the products are made "like they always were" and that there is in fact a line of continuity between the founder, the factory and the product. The hand, by imprinting a trace on the packaging, thus enables the contiguous relationship to be created which through metonymy, ensures the quality levels of the product.

Human activity passes through the hand and it would appear that in order to re-legitimize themselves; brands attempt to recreate a fiction through which the products of craftsmanship also have a soul.

The brand: the foot or the hand?

The ancestral link that binds the brand to the hand is also metaphorical, like a game. As Frank Cochoy showed us in his take on the history of marketing, the point of marketing is essentially to discipline the market and involves above all a game of "hitting the other persons hand faster between the different players in the market" (Cochoy 1999). The issue is to determine who has control of the process of creating value, the manufacturer, wholesaler or retailer. As such, the brand has enabled industry to take back control of the value harnessing process by short-circuiting the commercial intermediaries and setting up a direct relationship with the consumer through the symbolic intermediation provided by the product, the packaging, the merchandising and the advertising. But this game of "main chaude" can only work once a brand can claim a certain skill. What a client buys from a brand is ultimately the power to do what he or she is not capable of doing or does not want to do themselves.

The philosopher Michel Serres associates the brand with, not the hand, but with the foot. He links the brand to the verb "to walk," thus referring to the footprint in the sand left by the sandals of the prostitutes of Alexandria so that their clients could find them: "The whores of Alexandria used to carve their initials in mirror image on the soles of their sandals so that by reading the footprints in the sand, the potential client could recognize the person desired and follow the direction to their room." This trace, this identifying sign on the sand, was used to create demand. So the brand is a question of hands (with derivatives linked to ingeniousness and skill that today pose a problem in the economy of sub-contracting that brings all products down to a sort of average qualitative level) and a question of feet, of footprints.

The syllogism of the hand

The use of the hand as a rhetorical tool is part, first of all, of a collection of beliefs that are spread over all of the general consumer markets but also of so-called luxury goods and notably using a form of syllogism that can be outlined as follows:

(1) An artisanal product has more value than an industrial product;
(2) An artisanal product is handmade, and so
(3) A handmade product has more value than an industrial product.

This implied syllogism – never said out loud – is based on a series of cultural oppositions that are part and parcel of the post-industrial society: hand versus machine, artisanal versus industrial, predictable versus unpredictable, and so forth. The issue here is not to discuss the relevance of these cultural oppositions – inasmuch as neo-craftsmanship has gone beyond these oppositions and put them into practice, but to emphasize the figure of the hand in order to try to understand what it can mean in the communication and advertising mechanisms of a brand that is trying to valorize artisanal skill and knowledge.

The hand as a way to legitimacy

What characterizes the hand is its extraordinary plasticity. It can carry out any type of work, as Bergson reminded us in *L'évolution créatrice*. This is why it is a major weapon in the construction of the skills/knowledge rhetoric. The assertion of an artisanal skill base aims essentially to enrich a claim of competence and as such reinforce the authority of the brand that finds itself weakened by the industrial system. Weber's work on authority led him in fact to distinguish three types of authority: *traditional* authority, *rational* authority and *charismatic* authority. Traditional authority is based on the existence of traditional rules and procedures the memory of which is generally the responsibility of a specific social group to whom members of society pay respect for the venerable character of the duly conserved institutions. Rational authority exists thanks to the existence of the laws of nature, whose eternal determinisms impose themselves on all those who, through reason, have access to the science needed to discover them; in this case, the legitimacy of the brand is based on consumer perception, on its technical superiority over the competition.

Charismatic authority exists thanks to the presence of something or someone sacred, a presence most often incarnated by a charismatic leader and attested to by the level of faith all members of society have in this leader; it is thus based on the devotion of subjects to the heroism and exceptional powers (for example the ability to accomplish miracles) of the leader as well as to the normative order he or she sanctions.

All three types of authorities have existed, but Weber presupposes that Western society illustrates the progressive triumph of rational authority and the progressive elimination of the two others. In the modern world, as Weber reminds us, "it is no longer possible to resort to magical means to implore or master the spirits, as the savages once did who believed in the existence of such magical powers." This rationalization of authority structures has led to the possibility of envisaging what Ritzer was the first to refer to as the "McDonaldization of the world," where Western civilization has restructured itself around values such as efficiency, predictability, calculability, controls, and so forth. Beyond the issue of perceived value, what do we hold against industrial products, if not their mercantile dehumanization, but also and above all the predictability that has become wearing. But for Weber, one of the springs behind the extreme rationalization of the Western world leads to what he refers to as the disenchantment of the world. This process of disenchantment of the world is one where spontaneity, idiosyncrasy and superstition have been wiped out in favor of values such as efficiency, predictability and reproducibility. The brand was born in an industrial regime that seems to have taken all power away from the hand in the creation of the product. The passage from object to product in the 19th century ensured a fiction of experiential reproducibility in which it was possible to duplicate a product infinitely, thanks to the machine. Mass production went hand in hand with a form of experience control that enabled the consumer to reduce the perceived risk.

Objects immediately lost their emotional value because of mass production which, in theory prevented any personal or authentic relationship developing between individuals and objects. Mass production and the profusion of objects resulted in the contemporary object losing its aura and becoming banal. So this profusion of objects made possible by infinite combinations of materials, shapes and colors, was mirrored by a sort of impoverishment of objects, inasmuch as the profusion of objects tends to empty them of their meaningful substance. So there would appear to be a sort of suffering on the part of modern man in relation to the object, inasmuch as the object no longer opposes this original resistance that once made its charm and that Sartre, for example, described so well in *L'être et le néant*. Merchandise seems to have become too obvious, too familiar, and too docile. Scitovsky covered this point about an '*économie sans joie*' to describe the disenchantment linked to the consumer's erroneous orientation that notably finds a correlation with the apparent disappearance of the magical and magnetic character of the object in the pre-industrial society. In other words, how is it possible to envisage having a personal contact with an object that is produced ad infinitum like any product? How can we bring brands that are bogged down in rational legitimization back to life?

The rhetorical use of the hand ultimately consists of getting rid of the regime of industrial legitimacy to attempt to articulate a traditional legitimacy (with the repetition of manual gestures that underlie the very notion of craftsmanship) that can indeed shift away from the rational sort of legitimacy that is the preserve of industrial work and a pseudo-charismatic legitimacy that expresses the aura of the brand shining bright through its own handiwork.

As such, the hand serves to appease our relationship to *teckne*. While artisanal *teckne* can seem imperfect as it is not totally reproducible, industrial technique can seem to rage against us with over-powerful, inexorable and destructive forces. As Dostaler and Maris (2009: p. 39) remind us, "technique takes rarity back a step and tempers our anguish, but at what price!" So that for Freud, our (notably technical) culture is to a great extent "responsible for our misery: we would be happier if we abandoned it and went back to primitive forms (Dostaler and Maris, 2009). This brings us to the notion that capitalism carries a mortifying energy inside itself, a sort of death wish. The hand represents the figure that shows the reassuring skills by shifting the emphasis from the anguish-laden technical context. A deep analysis of the presence of hands in advertising for a brand like Hermè would show quite easily that the hand is never completely closed, it is either semi-open, holding or letting go of a harness or lightly touching an object in a deictic role, or it is open to liberate a flow, a fluid. The representation of the hand seems to participate in a beat, a life impulse, against the very principle of control, of enclosure and control.

On the romanticism of merchandise

The emergence of the hand can be attributed to the sort of disenchantment that has inexorably followed in the wake of industrial products. The sociologist Colin Campbell has notably developed a provocative theory according to which the Romantic Movement played a critical role in the birth of modern consumerism. In his attempt to follow on from Weber's thesis on the boom in modern capitalism and the inexorable movement toward rationalization, Campbell defends the idea that, in the same way the puritan work ethic promoted the spirit of capitalist production, the romantic ethic promoted the complementary spirit of consumerism. But first of all, what is romanticism if not, as Campbell says, "an impulse toward chaos" and "a way of feeling, a state of mind, in which the sensibility and the imagination take over from reason; it tends toward the new, toward individualism, revolt, fleeing, melancholy and the imagination." Campbell adds that "other characteristics of this way of feeling would be; a dissatisfaction with the contemporary world, a perpetual anxiety with life, a preference for the strange, the curious, a penchant for dreams and dreaming, an attraction to mysticism, and a celebration of the irrational." While the traditional hedonist tries to repeat experiences he or she knows to be pleasant, the modern hedonist experiments with a hiatus between desire and consumption with the joys of dreaming about new experiences. But with what do we reproach the industrial product, if not its predictability? The predictable character of the industrial object is two-sided: on the one hand it enables the individual to control his or her consumer experience, as the brand means a form of implicit contract of the reproducibility of the experience; on the other, the individual has the right to expect new emotions, new feelings and as such a form of irregularity. The controlled irregularity that characterizes neo-craftsmanship enables one to envisage a sort of predictability within the unpredictability.

The infinitive creator

The growing metamorphization linked to growth in the marking phenomenon contributes in a certain way to discrediting the capacity of brands to truly give meaning to objects and consumption, but also and above all to claim a real skill base due to the overuse of *badging*. This gap grew notably as a result of the distancing of the enunciative and productive structures that often lead the brand to be nothing but a discursive and metaphorical bubble disconnected from the so-called reality of the object badged. This leads to a split between the brand's strictly material dimension and its narrative dimension, creating a disengagement between the brand's image value and the functional value of the objects branded. This disengagement is at the heart of the notion of brand legitimacy inasmuch as it can indeed lead to a weakening of brand legitimacy. This can in part explain the artisanal temptation of industrial brands. But the brand then finds itself in the trap of the famous "fiction–auteur" as depicted by Michel Foucault, to the extent that all products need to be brought back under the same roof in terms of expression, and that is the brand. So the hand then plays the role of transmission and continuity between players that are scattered. The brand must first be given a body and, it is indeed, through these famous body techniques that the brand can express a culture that is no longer just symbolic but material.

The question of the auteur and the authority comes back to the fore here, as it cannot be a body with numerous hands. But is it a question then of valorizing "the hand" or "the hands?" Is it not striking that in the work by Olivier Saillard (2012), *Petit lexique des gestes d'Hermès*, the verbs corresponding to the various gestures are all in the infinitive? The writer explains the meaning of *abat-carrer* (to soften the edges of a piece of leather), *décreuser* (to degum), *chipoter* (to poke), *gratte-bosser* (to brush with a scratch brush), *insculper* (to mark with an awl), *liéger* (to cork), *palissonner* (to smooth and soften leather), *putoiser* (to unify colors using a brush known as a putois) and so forth. The idea is to make things attractive through an understanding of the gestures: Think in the infinitive: "There are things that we would love even more if we knew the name. Or the verb, as the name is sometimes a verb. Without a name, love remains unfinished, suspended and without support. One needs to know the name in order to fully love. If one knew the name, one could dream, say and look at everything one loves again, see things one had never seen and love them, things that the name itself might not necessarily reveal" (Fournier, 2000: p. 249).

Inasmuch as the use of the infinitive form testifies to the fact that the artisan is absent as a subject and is subsumed by this sort of "great commander," that is the brand. While they describe the gestures linked to specific skills that are very precise and carefully handed down, these words forged in the workshops are often absent from dictionaries, and as such they make up a unique vocabulary. This obviously shines a light on the god-like power of the Hermès brand, which does not hesitate to stabilize the neologisms linked to the hand in order to display a technical skill base backed up with technical excellence. This work (in-beweoth meanings of the term) opens onto an infinite and generic universe. One could of course argue that the infinitive form is important in a brand's discourse, inasmuch as Fournier (2000: p. 9) reminds us in the evocatively titled *L'infinitif des pensées* (thinking is done in the infinitive), because of the fact that "all thought is in the infinitive and can be expressed by using only infinitives[;]... verbs are (conjugated) alone without worrying about nouns or adjectives." The creation of a true language through the brand would thus impose an ideology manifested implicitly by the infinitive form of the discourse. Fournier catches a good glimpse of this, the god-like power of the infinitive mode, when he tells us that "the infinitive provides us not only with an ethic and an aesthetic, but also a non-substantive metaphysic." As Fournier shows us again, this infinitive logic is an issue in itself, as "when one gives oneself to thought without worrying about nouns or adjectives, one misses subjects altogether. And also their substitutes, attributes, pronouns, articles, adjectives, adverbs. One is no longer in the assertion nor the representation... but with substantives[;] it is not only the subjects that one doesn't mark and that one neglects in the infinitive language, it is also the objects" (Fournier, 2000: p. 9). The paradox of Hermès is thus to manufacture singularity with the infinitive, and to do so through a trick of the light that is in fact the rhetoric of the sleight-of-hand. One could indeed think that craftsmen are merely the fingers of the giant hand of the brand.

The appropriation of a lexicon of gestures enables the creation of a "sum of little," essentially traditional legitimacies that in return enable the creation of a fiction of charismatic legitimacy around a brand that, while it is certainly patronymic, it is in fact is subsumed to a collective identity. Of course, through his gestures, the artisan does appear in the film "Les mains d'Hermès," in which the brand displays the skills of its craftsmen, but the issue is to show not the singularity of the individual but the generic nature of the gesture. In other terms, the gesture is specific to the brand but not to the artisan, who is a mere officiant

From the hand to the *chanson de gestes* (epic poems)

The issue here is the appropriation of a territory that, while it cannot be strictly manual, is necessarily symbolic. The fiction of singularity that the very idea of the brand presupposes comes from the semanticization of terms that are, in fact, not in the dictionary. By encouraging a book on the gestures specific to the brand, Hermès invents a specific language to signify that it corresponds to particular gestures and as such to a singular skill base. This is how the notion of the *chanson de gestes* was used to speak of the expert handiwork dealt with in *Les gestes d'Hermès*. But, we should remember that *chansons de gestes* are epic poems of a particular form that recount glorious acts of the past. The *geste* is to be seen here as a "shining accomplished action" of a warlike or fantastic nature. And, as Paulin Paris reminds us, the term *geste* "ordinarily usurps the meaning of race or family among our earliest poets. They could be the *geste des Loherains*, the *geste des pairs de Vermandois*, etc."; the *chanson de geste* was thus a means for the leading families in the Middle Ages to praise their familes, to the exclusion more or less of others, which is not without meaning when we look at a family-based brand like Hermès.

In addition, the *chanson de gestes* is characterized by the fact that it excludes the narrativity, the linear nature of the narrative, playing on a perpetual movement of *ressac*, repetition and echo. But the gestures in question refer to social customs that belong to each culture. Thus, as Schmitt (1992) remarkably pointed out, from the 4th to the 8th centuries, in a society where the Church was affirming its power, gestures enabled the elaboration of behavioral models for which measure (*temperantia*) and humility (*modestia*) were essential. The gesture was also the symbol of God's hierarchy, which had to be respected. It was in the monasteries that the medieval reflection on the body, soul and gesture was carried out, and the three examples of gestures to follow were found in the Bible.

The result is that the *chanson de gestes* proposed by Hermès contributes to the establishment of a sort of culture of gestures through the figure of the hand, but also of materials and beliefs. Thus, the verbalization of the gestures enables us to envisage a real culture of craftsmanship that is the brand's own and that, like a religion, insinuates itself through ways of speaking, thinking and doing.

The gesture also calls for a change in anthropological perspective inasmuch as it is no longer a question of establishing a visual relationship, but also a tactile relationship with the client. The finesse of the hand's mechanics and its organic complexity give it plasticity along with other powers, among which is the subtlety of touch (which Diderot considered to be the most philosophical of our senses, and through which Condillac began the edification of the sensibility of its famous status), followed by the power of expression. The sense of touch is strongest in the hand, more precisely in the fingertips. The pleasure of touch and tact accesses a number of different sensitive qualities, as Aristotle pointed out in his *Treaty of the Soul*: temperature, hardness, roughness.... Making touch a *tact*, is to get physically closer to the client by going from a feeling of distance to a feeling of closeness, but it is also, as Bergson might say, sending the intelligence of the hand to the head.

This emphasis on the tactile leads to a sort of eroticization of the relationship with the object that only the hand can have, because of the finesse of its touch: human beings owe the distinctive trait of the caress to the sensitivity and freedom of their hands. Unlike the other parts of the body through which we give and experience pleasure, it is the hand itself that experiences or gives this pleasure. Indeed, the hand has the power to be both touching and touched. Through the hand, a bijective and complicit relationship that is the preserve of amateurs (lovers) is created.

The hand to provide a voice

So the brand appears like a Leviathan, spreading through the extension of activities into new product universes, ensuring the link, the coherence, between these different professions – and doing so by a sleight-of-hand. The hand is, thus, the material and symbolic device through which the continuity is maintained between the disjointed worlds (professions, activities, materials). The hand thus appears as the ultimate figure of the brand's identity inasmuch as the identity is essentially that which reconnects the disconnected. Is the hand not that which assembles and reconnects the fingers to enable gestures? But, while we have often said of the face that it is the ultimate sign of personal identity, have we ever heard this about the hands? However, the hand is unique in appearance and skin texture, as opposed to a knack for something that can be shared by anyone.

Behind this predominance of the hand, a form of humanization of the brand develops. Thus, as Matisse reminded us, "the hand is but the continuation of the sensibility and the intelligence." The hand provides a body and, as such, a face for the brand. In fact, while the hand does not have a direct share of human intelligence, the observation of evolution seems to show that the industry of the *Homo faber* made the development of his faculties possible. The hand supports the word, for example, for deaf mutes. If we are to believe Rousseau or Condillac, the first human language was gestural. In fact, the pointed finger is the archetype of all designations: the hand is the first deictic; it is the hand that shows things first.

So there is a link between the hand and the word. It is in fact probable that the liberation of the hand led to the emergence of the word. As Grégoire de Nysse wondered, "If the body had no hands, how would the articulated voice form inside of it?" as manual technique gives the freed face the ability to express itself diversely. This gives us the fact that "the hands freed up the mouth for the service of the word." The idea is that, to show its face, the brand will in fact use the hand, which will enable the liberation of a full discourse free of the artifices of the industrial market. Taken by the hand, the brand abandons the banks of the discourse and the image to dock at the banks of the voice and the gesture. Is there no better illustration than the hand that comes from nowhere in the advertisement (2002) for a white tuxedo? In addition to the sobriety that characterizes this press advert (no title, no signature), let us examine the hand. First of all, the image presents two hands but does not actually show any (both hands are hidden: one gloved, the other in the pocket), reminding us of the game of hide-and-seek involved in the rhetoric of manual things. The hand implies that artisanal work is there and not there, visible and ostensible. So this means it *represents* (the hand is the presence that signifies an absence, that of the other hands) but also *displays*, as if the hand made an absence present but in a non-figurative way.

The hand is thus a figure of visual rhetoric that brings out both the metonymy and the metaphor. The metonymy functions on the mode of resemblance through contact and expresses the deictic function. It is a visual link, showing a quasi-physical contiguity between the product and the artisan to highlight the manual skills involved. The metaphor relies on the shift and the gap, as it aims to signify that the object was conceived using an artisanal process. So we are located in the furthest distance (the metaphorical hand) and the most reduced (the metonymic hand).

The hand thus incarnates the plural body of the brand inasmuch as the brand has an eternal body (the soul of the Hermès brand) and a flesh body that lives through those who officiate (notably the craftsmen and women) and are both plural and ever-changing. The hand incorporates multiple bodies. It operates the connection between the material and spiritual bodies of the brand. It also represents the past and the contemporary extreme of the brand. The gloved hand is holding the tux jacket as much as it is displaying it. It is both the hand that executes, thus the symbol of the famous Hermès hands, that which subsumes a plural, and so in turn the tailor, sewer, salesperson, and so forth.

While the brand is purposely under-coded, it is the hand that speaks, to tell the lover (*amateur*) of the carnality, the agility, the magic of the gestures but also the control, the authority, the acticity. The hand/brand manipulates the object but also the relationship with the world, with others and with itself. It leads the mind astray by replacing it.

The gourmet "Last Supper" or the pastry liturgy: on Pierre Hermé

Pastry-making is always figuratively connected to religion. First of all because pastry is close to bread used for communion, worthy of the greatest respect and truly sacred since it is dispensed by the grace of God. But also because pastry shops were traditionally set up in front of churches as if pointing to a sort of secret religiosity of the cake – that underlies for example the name just as much as the architectural composition of the *religieuse*. This little something sacred and ritualistic is moreover demonstrated in the cake with cathedral architecture (the tiered cake, the vacherin, the bûche) that piles layers, textures, tastes and that often ritualizes the being together. Pastry-making is has a function extremely connecting and even religious. But what can be sketched concerning an artisan culture of cakes, does it still make sense in a brand economy that replaces doing by having things done and substitutes machines for hand-making pastries? Taking the example of Pierre Hermé, we will try to show how the pastry artist is perhaps in a position to guide us on routes other than "religion in crumbs" characteristic of brands of products for mass consumption.

Desecration/the sacred

Whether the food brand is a social link is one thing, but that the food brand might access any state of grace is in itself another issue, for the simple fact that the brand society functions according to the model of desecration and permanent contact. If the industrialization of pastry-making puts us in permanent contact with commercial images, what is in the end a sweet tooth in a brand society that has substituted the visual for the taste (? Food often just exhibits its exposure value recalling its status as an industrial or, at least falsely crafted, product. There is like a pornography in the food object that contributes to the decline of the aura so finely predicted by Walter Benjamin since the 1930s, and associated with a desire to make things spatially and humanly "closer" to yourself by taking away, in particular, their uniqueness (Benjamin, 2000, III: p. 278). The serialization of food products results in a sort of standardization of the unique that cancels out the distance, and thus foreign, dimension of the food, and that substitutes uniqueness and the long-term relationship with a pastry. It is in this way that the brand reassures us, indicating a reproducibility of the experience and reminiscing about the eating experience still to come. In this over-presence of the food item, there a lack of meaning characteristic of a "joyless economy" in which the invading presence of products and the continuous varying of practices of consumption throughout the day inevitably brings about disillusionment; the eater nibbles all day long and, never being hungry, never draws from the food the physical satisfaction that tests the one who breaks the fast. How, then, do we arouse the desire of bruised taste buds in the era of food glaciation so precisely denounced by Jean-Paul Aron? Against the disillusionment of a joyless food economy, the response can be only the removal of pleasure. Is it not about pushing the fire of desire, thereby to illustrate, as Corneille says in *Polyeucte,* the simple fact that "desire increases when the effect wanes?" Against humdrum repetition that drains desire, should not the food brand try to break the cycle of repetition, decorum and opportunity? Thus Pierre Hermé surmised: "pastry-making where there would be only two different pastries to sell, that would change every day and never return," but also "a boutique, where we would only do things to order by interpreting customers' eating desires and cravings." Tending towards a uniqueness of the pastry, it is completely logical that the Hermé boutique was designed on the model of the museum through a scenography that gives a cake the status of a work of art and the strictly commercial circle. Cakes are no longer this pleasure-menu item that we are allowed to have when exiting church: this quickly swallowed mouthful becomes a promise of beauty, an esthetic object that we contemplate, eat with the eyes and not only with the mouth. The museum phenomenon of the pastry reintroduces from a distance (and thus from desire) but also from a temporal dimension. The sacredness of the pastry comes from this distance effect that shrouds it with an aura and a magnetism characteristic of the glorification of an artist's work in an era of technical reproducibility. We return to a status of the cake before merchandise, a state that is more than the craftsman state: it is the cake as art. It is in this way that we can understand the sort of pastry-making religiosity that results. Here, we mean religiosity, not "according to the nondescript and vague etymology of *religare* (which connects man with the divine), but of *relegere*, that indicates the scrupulous attitude and attention to detail that must reign in relations with the gods, the anxious hesitation (the act of 'reviewing') encountering forms –and formulas – that it is necessary to observe to respect the separation between the sacred and the irreverent. *Religio* is not what unites men and the gods, but that [which] wants to keep them separate." (Agamben, 2005: p. 93) It is, thus, negligence, meaning a free and "distracted" behavior that goes against religion, more than disbelief and indifference.

Visionary

Relaunching the machine of desire thus requires revisiting products and conventional forms by dulling the senses but also the uses. A world like pastry-making is often thought of according to a categorizing and combinatorial logic, which combines elements (colors, materials, shapes) making up a whole in culturally established forms: the baba, the napoleon, the Saint Honoré and so forth. It is most often part of a technical mindset of crafting, meaning, in a manner of thinking, the material according to the logic of composing pre-existing ingredients. Pastry-making and baking are industries governed by simple syntax in the image of the ordered display in a shop window. In that sense, pastry-making is almost always a standard form and that is why it arouses no desire, no surprise. Like charcuterie, it derives from a technical logic that organizes the composition according to expected main lines, simple structures (stacks, flakiness, etc.) and basic operations (fodder, embossing, topping, etc.). Hence, relatively systematized product names, whether it is the cake, the pitivier, the brioche, the Bundt; pastry-making is often an exercise in skill to best reproduce a standard form to hoist the product up along a taste scale. Pastry-making is thus often like painting, reproducing a model with strong constraints. But it is quite different for the pastry artist who is able to downplay expectations, to foresee them by reconfiguring the ingredient and formal uses and associations. But is not that also characteristic of any brand worthy of the name? A great creator is someone who is able to re-categorize a universe of objects and any great brand always uses a visionary logic by redefining the genesis (in the literal sense) of its universe. That is what pastry artists aspire to, by a continuous desire to transcend the commonplace, breaking down food, as much as possible, into the practical mental and taste categories, even if this means consequently changing the visual images traditionally associated with it. The Hermé pastry-making action refers to formal innovation that translates a project of re-defining dishes, words and uses. Creating is also innovating in the ways of making, certainly, but also saying and naming the elements. The systematic baptism of creations refers to this simple idea according to which what is not named or not nameable can really exist as an esthetic taste experience. It has to do with meditating on, and especially, understanding what we are going to eat. As in communion, the sign precedes the food in the mouth. Is it not, moreover, one of the characteristics of food, that food which is good to eat is first of all food that is good to think about? This is what Pascal Quignard reminds us of, when he says: "I am unable to eat something if I don't know the name of it.... The names – those are the first things in your mouth – unlock the chewing experience" (Quignard, 2001: p. 145). Now, it is undoubtedly not the same experience to eat a rose macaroon, rose cream, lychee and fresh raspberries and to savor an Ispahan! However, if there is nothing simpler and more human than desiring it, it is no less difficult to give the desire a voice. Semantic innovation from which brands come also revolutionizes the eating experience to which we are invited. It has to do with re-categorizing our mental categories to increase the strength of the eating promise and experience. Thus, making us understand that we eat, the brand reminds us how much we eat – first of all and always – the spoken word. Thereby projecting a semantic universe on an eating experience, the brand also makes us to better see the world. In fact, the brand makes us see, it makes a certain taste esthetic visible. It desensitizes our taste buds, asleep from having chewed too much. Meaning the importance of food scripting and the correct ways to say and do. Now, the power of the sacred act relies precisely on the convergence of a myth – hence the importance of paratexts (Genette, 1987) that, for Pierre Hermé, are always a tale of origins of the pastry – and of rites. Ritualizing service and offering gestures instills a form of ritual grammar that makes the product sacred by removing from it the too-common round shape of sweets. That is why the brand reaches a religious dimension, insofar as we can define religion as that which takes things, places, animals and people from their common use to transport them within a sacred sphere. Thus there could be no religion without separation so that "any separation contains or keeps to oneself an authentically religious core" (Agamben, 2005: p. 92).

References

Aaker, D.A. and Keller, K.L., 1990, "Consumer Evaluations of Brand Extensions," *Journal of Marketing*, 54, January, 24–41.

Aaker, D. and Biel, A. (eds), 1993, *Brand Equity and Advertising. Advertising's Role in Building Strong Brands*, Hillsdale New Jersey, Lawrence Erlbaum Associates Publishers.

Aaker, J.L., 1997, "Dimensions of Brand Personality," *Journal of Marketing Research*, 34, 3, 347–56.

Abelson, R.P., 1976, "Psychological Status of the Script Concept," *American Psychologist*, 36, 7, 715–29.

Ackroyd, P., 1999, *The Life of Thomas More*, London, Vintage.

Adès, J. and Lejoyeux, M., 1999, *La fièvre des achats. Le syndrôme des achats compulsifs*, Paris, Synthélabo.

Agamben, G., 2005, *Profanations*, Paris, Rivages. Translated as *Profanations*, New York, Zone Books, 2007.

Ahtola, O.T., 1985, "Hedonic and Utilitarian Aspects of Consumer Behavior: An Attitudinal Perspective," *Advances in Consumer Research*, 7–10.

Ahuvia, A., 1993, "I Love It! Towards a unifying theory of love across diverse love objects," Unpublished PhD dissertation, Evanston.

Alessi, A., 1998, *L'usine à rêves. Alessi depuis 1921*, Cologne, Könelman.

Ali, S., 1977, *Corps réel, Corps Imaginaire*, Paris, Bordas.

Allport, G.W., 1937, *Personality: A Psychological Interpretation*, New York: Henry Holt.

Anapadurai, A., 1986, *The Social Life of Things. Commodities in a Cultural Perspective*, Cambridge: Cambridge University Press.

Antoni, M., 2013, *Le luxe déchainé. De l'hernanisation des marques de luxe*, Lormon, Le Bord de l'eau.

Anzieu, D., 1991, *Le Moi-peau*, Paris, Dunod.

Aron, J.-P., 1997, "De la glaciation dans la culture en gégéral and dans la cuisine en particulier, in, *Cultures, nourriture*", Internationale de l'imaginaire, Nouvelle série – no. 7, Actes-Sud.

Assael, H., 1992, *Consumer Behavior and Marketing Action*, 4th edn, Boston, PWS-Kent Publishing Company.

Assoun, P.-L. 1980, *Freud et Nietzsche*, Paris, Presses Universitaires de France.

Attfield, J., 1996, "Barbie and Action Man: Adult Toys for Girls and Boys, 1959–93," in Kirkham, P. (ed.), *The Gendered Object*, Manchester, Manchester University Press, 80–9.

Audi, P., 1999, *Supériorité de l'éthique*, Paris, PUF.

Augé, M., 1988, *Le dieu objet*, Paris, Flammarion.

Babin, B.J. et al., 1994, "Work and/or Fun: Measuring Hedonic and Utilitarian Shopping Value," *Journal of Consumer Research*, 20, March, 644–56.

Bailly, J.-C., 1998, *L'apostrophe muette*, Paris, Hazan.

Ball, A. and Tasaki, L., 1992, "The Role and Measurement of Attachment in Consumer Behaviour," *Journal of Consumer Psychology*, 1, 2, 155–72.

Barber B., 1996, *Djihad versus McWorld. Mondialisation et intégrisme contre la démocratie*, Paris, Desclée de Brouwer.

Barjansky, M. and Krief, Y., 1980, "La marque : nature et fonctions – applications possibles," in *Publicité et communication – Expériences et recherches*, I.R.E.P., 5–79.

Barrier (sous la dir. de), 1999), *Les métiers de la sémiotique*, Limoges, PULIM, 61–73.

Barré-Despond A., 1996, (sous la direction de), *Dictionnaire international des arts appliqués et du design*, Paris, Editions du regard.

Barthel, D., 1989, "Modernism and Marketing: The Chocolate Box Revisited," *Theory, Culture and Society*, 429–38, 6 (August).

Barthes R., 1995, "Les choses signifient-elles quelque chose," 1962. *Le Figaro Littéraire*, Texte reproduit dans *Oeuvres Complètes I*, Paris, Seuil, 13 octobre.

Barthes, R. 1985, "Sémantique de l'objet," lecture given in September 1964 at the Fondation Cini, in Venice, later published in *L'aventure sémiologique*, Paris, Seuil, 249–60.

Barthes, R. "Arcimboldo, or Magician and Rhetoriqueur," in *The Responsibility of Forms: Critical Essays on Music, Art, and Representation*, trans.: Howard, R., 129–48. Berkeley and Los Angeles, University of California Press, 1985.

Barthes, R., 1977, "Introduction to the structural analysis of narratives," in Barthes, R., *Image – Music – Text*, New York, Hill and Wang, 79–124.

Barthes, R., 1967, *Système de la mode*, Paris, Seuil.

Barthes, R., 1964, "Sémantique de l'objet," Colloqium at the Cini Foundation in Venice, reprinted in *The Semiotic Challenge*, 1988, University of California Press, 179–90.

Batra, R. and Ahtola O.T., 1990, "Measuring the Hedonic and Utilitarian Sources of Consumer Attitudes," *Marketing Letters*, 2, 2, 159–70.

Batra, R. et al., 1993, "The Brand Personality Component of Brand Goodwill: Some Antecedents and Consequences," in Aaker, D. and Biel, A. (eds), *Brand Equity and Advertising*, Lawrence Erlbaum Associates Publishers, 83–96.

Batra, R. et al., 1993, "The Brand Personality Component of Brand Goodwill: Some Antecedents and Consequences," in Aaker D. and Biel A. (eds), *Brand Equity and Advertising*, Lawrence Erlbaum Associates Publishers, 83–96.

Batra, R. and Ahtola, O.T., 1990, "Measuring the Hedonic and Utilitarian Sources of Consumer Attitudes," *Marketing Letters*, 2, 2, 159–70.

Baudrillard, J., 1968, *Le système des objets*, Paris, Gallimard. Trans.: *The System of objects*, London, Verso, 1996.

Baudrillard, J., 1970, *La société de consommation. Ses mythes, ses structures*, Paris, Denoël. Trans. *The Consumer Society. Myths and Structures*, London, Sage, 1999.

Baudrillard, J., 1972, *Pour une Critique de L'Economie Politique du Signe*, Paris, Gallimard. Trans. *For a Critique of the Political Economy of the Sign*, St. Louis, Telos, 1981.

Baudrillard, J., 1980, *De la séduction*, Paris, Galilée.

Baudrillard, J., 1981, *Simulacres et simulations*, Paris, Galilée. Trans.: *Simulacra and Simulation*, Ann Arbor, University of Michigan Press, 1994.

Baudrillard, J., 1992, *L'Illusion de la fin*, Paris, Galilée. Trans.: *The Illusion of the End*, Oxford, Polity Press, 1996.

Bayley, S., 1987, *Sex, Drink, and Fast Cars: The Creation and Consumption of Images*, New York, Faber and Faber.

Beaglehole, E., 1932, *Property: A Study in Social Psychology,* New York, Macmillan.

Beaudé, P.-M., Fantion, J. and Vannier, M.-A. (dir.), 2004, *La Trace entre absence et présence. Actes du colloque international de Metz,* Paris, Le Cerf.

Beaune, J.-C., 1998, *Philosophie des milieux techniques. La matière, l'instrument, l'automate,* Seyssel, Champs Vallon.

Belk, R.W., 1988, "Possessions and the Extended Self," *Journal of Consumer Research,* 15, September, 139–68.

Belk, R., Sherry, J. and Wallendorf, M., 1989, "The Sacred and the Profane in Consumer Behavior: Theodicy on the Odyssey," *Journal of Consumer Research,* vol. 16, 1–38; June.

Belk, R., 1991, "The Ineluctable Mysteries of Possessions," in Rudmin, F.W. (ed.), To have possessions: A handbook on ownership and property. (special issue). *Journal of Social Behavior and Personality,* 6, 6, 17–55.

Belk, R., 1992, "Attachment to Possessions," in Altman, I. and Low, S.M., *Place Attachment: Human Behavior and Environment,* vol. 12, New York, Plenum Press, 37–62.

Belk, R., 1995, *Collecting in a Consumer Society,* London, Routledge.

Benjamin, W., 1972–89 [1931], "Kleine Geschichte der Photographie," *Gesammelte Schriften,* Tiedeman, R., and Schweppenhäuser, H. *et al.* (eds), Frankfurt/Main, Suhrkamp, vol. II, 1, 368–85; French translation in *Etudes Photographiques,* 1, November (1996), 7–39.

Benjamin, W., 1972–89 [1936], "Das Kunstwerk im Zeitalter seiner technischen Reproduzierbarkeit," *Gesammelte Schriften,* Frankfurt Suhrkamp, vol. I, 2, 471–508; translated as "The work of art in the age of mechanical reproduction", in *Illuminations,* Hammersmith, London, Fontana Press, 1992, 211–44.

Benjamin, W., 1979, *Correspondance,* edited by Scholem, G. and Adorno, T.W. and translated into French by Petitdemange, G., 2 vols., Paris, Aubier.

Benjamin, W., 1991, "L'œuvre d'art à l'ère de sa reproduction technique," in *Ecrits français,* Paris, Gallimard, 117–71.

Benjamin, W., 1997, *Sur l'art et la photographie,* Paris, Editions Carrés.

Benjamin, W., 2000, *Oeuvres I, II et III,* Pàris, Gallimard.

Benveniste, E., 1969, *Le vocabulaire des institutions européennes. Tome 1: économie, parenté, société,* Paris, Editions de Minuit.

Bernard, M., 1995, *Le corps,* Paris, Seuil.

Berthoz, A., 2009, La simplexité, Paris, Odile Jacob.

Bertrand, D., "Confiance politique et fiducie," in Fontanille, J. and Barrier, G. (eds), *Les métiers de la sémiotique,* Limoges, PULIM.

Biel, A.L., 1993, "Converting Image into Equity," in Aaker, D. and Biel, A. (eds), *Brand Equity and Advertising,* Lawrence Erlbaum Associates Publishers, 67–82.

Blackston, M., 1993, "Beyond Brand Personality: Building Brand Relationships," in Aaker, D. and Biel, A. (eds), *Brand Equity and Advertising. Advertising's Role in Building Strong Brands,* Lawrence Erlbaum Associates Publishers, 113–24.

Boltanski, L., 1990, *L'Amour et la Justice comme compétences,* Paris Métailié.

Bonnaffé, E., 1873, *Les Collectionneurs de l'Ancienne France. Notes d'un amateur,* Paris, Aubry.

Boudon, R., 2002, *Déclin de la morale? Déclin des valeurs?,* Paris, PUF.

Bouretz, P., 1996, *Les promesses du monde. Philosophie de Max Weber,* Paris, Gallimard.

Boutaud, J.J., 2004 "De la difficulté de communiquer un concept polysensoriel, Kenzoki de Kenzo," in Boillot, F. and Grasse, M.C. (eds) Olfaction et patrimoine: quelle transmission? Aix-en-Provence: Edisud, 79–89.

Boutaud, J.-J., 1999, "Analyses sensorielles: pour une sémiotique du goût," in Fontanille, J. and Barrier, G. (sous la dir. de), *Les métiers de la sémiotique*, Limoges, PULIM, 61–73.

Boutaud, J.-J., 1998, *Sémiotique et communication. Du signe au sens*, Paris, L'Harmattan, coll. Champs visuels.

Bouveresse, J., 2004, *Robert Musil. L'homme probable, le hasard, la moyenne et l'escargot de l'histoire*, deuxième édition, Paris, Editions de l'éclat.

Bowie, A., 1990, *Aesthetics and Subjectivity from Kant to Nietzsche*, Manchester, Manchester University Press.

Bowlby, J., 1958, "The nature of child's tie to his mother," *International Journal of Psycho-Analysis*, 39, 350–73.

Bowlby, J., 1969, *Attachment and Loss. 1: Attachment*, London, Hogarth.

Bowlby, J., 1973, *Attachment and Loss. 2: Separation: Anxiety and Anger*, London, Hogarth.

Bowlby, J., 1980, *Attachment and Loss. 3: Loss: Sadness and Depression*, London, Hogarth.

Branzi, A., 1988, *Pomeriggi alla media industria*, Milan, Idea Books.

Brémond, C., 1986, "Propp," in Sebeok, T.A. (ed.), *Encyclopedic Dictionary of Semiotics*, Berlin, Mouton de Gruyter, T.2, 771–3.

Brémond, C., 1966, "La logique des possibles narratifs," *Communications*, 8, Paris, Seuil, 60–76.

Brémond, C., 1970, "Morphology of the French Folk Tale," *Semiotica*, 2, 247–76.

Brémond, C., 1973, *Logique du récit*, Paris, Seuil.

Broadie, S.. 1991, *Ethics with Aristotle*, Oxford, Oxford University Press.

Bucci, A., 1992, *L'impresa guidata dalle idee*, Milan, Domus Academy Press.

Buchanan, R. and Margolin V. (eds), 1995, *Discovering design. Explorations in design studies*, Chicago, The University of Chicago Press.

Buell, V.P., 1986, *Handbook of Modern Marketing*, New York, McGraw-Hill.

Cabat, O., 1989, "Archéologie de la marque moderne," in Kapferer, J.-N. and Thoenig, J.-C., *La marque, moteur de la compétitivité des entreprises et de la croissance de l'économie*, McGraw-Hill.

Callot, M., 1997, *La matière émotion*, Paris, PUF.

Campbell, C., 1987, *The Romantic Ethic and the Spirit of Modern Consumerism*, London, Basic Blackwell.

Canto-Sperber, M. (ed.), 1996, *Dictionnaire d'éthique et de philosophie morale*, Paris, PUF.

Cassirer, E., 1972, *La philosophie des formes symboliques. T.2 La pensée mythique*, Paris, Editions de Minuit.

Cassirer, E., 1977, *Substance et fonction*, Paris, Editions de Minuit.

Chatman, S., 1974, "Rhetoric and semiotics," in Chatman, S. et al. (eds), *A Semiotic Landscape*, The Hague, Mouton, 103–12.

Christopher, M. et al., 1991, *Relationship Marketing*, Oxford: Butterworth-Heinemann.

Cikszentmihalyi, M. and Rochberg-Halton, E., 1981, *The Meanings of Things: Domestic symbols and the Self*, Cambridge: Cambridge University Press.

Claeys, C., Swinnen, A. and Van den Abeele, P., 1995, "Consumers' Means-Ends Chains for 'Think' and 'Feel' Products," *International Journal of Research in Marketing,* 12, 3, 193–208.

Cochoy, F., 1999, *Une histoire du marketing. Discipliner l'économie de marché, Paris, La Découverte.*

Collot, F., 1997, *L'émotion chose,* Paris, PUF.

Comte-Sponville, A., 2003, *Le capitalisme est-il moral?,* Paris, Albin Michel.

Conein B. et al., (textes réunis par), 1993, *Les objets dans l'action. De la maison au laboratoire,* Raisons Pratiques 4, Editions de l'Ecole des Hautes Etudes en Sciences Sociales.

Cooper, P., 1979, "Symbiosis: the consumer psychology of branding," *ADMAP,* November, 578–86.

Costjens, J. and M, 1995, *Store Wars. The Battle for Minspace and Shelfspace,* New York: Wiley.

Couégnas, N. and Halary, M.-P., 2005, "Objets d'innovation, logique des sensations: le design selon Marc Sadler," in Fontanille, J. and Zinna, A. (sous la dir. De), *Les objets au quotidien,* Nouveaux Actes sémiotiques, PULIM, Limoges.

Courtine, J.-J. and Haroche, C., 1988, *Histoire du visage. Exprimer et aire ses émotions (XVIème siècle – début XIX ème siécle),* Paris, Rivages.

Courtine, J.-F et al., 1988, *Du Sublime,* Paris, Belin.

Cova, B., 1995, *Au-delà du marché: Quand le lien importe plus que le bien,* Paris, L'harmattan.

Cova, B. and Kassis, J., 1994, "Plurality of the social link and confusion in consumption," Proposal for the Sixth Annual Conference of the Society for the Advancement of Socio-Economics, Jouy en Josas, July.

Cova, B. and V., 2001, *Alternatives Marketing,* Paris, Dunod.

Coward, R., 1984, *Female Desire,* London, Paladin.

Crozier, R., 1994, *Manufactured Pleasures: Psychological Responses to Design,* Manchester, Manchester University Press.

Csikszentmihalvi, M. and Rochberg-Halton E., 1981, *The Meaning of Things. Domestic symbols and the self,* Cambridge: Cambridge University Press.

Cyrulnik, B., 1989, *Sous le signe du lien. Une histoire naturelle de l'attachement,* Paris, Hachette.

Cyrulnik, C., 1995, "Les objets d'attachement," *La naissance du sens,* Paris, Hachette, 70–90.

Dagognet, F., 1983, *Corps réfléchis,* Paris, Odile Jacob.

Dagognet, F., 1985, *Rematérialiser,* Paris, Vrin.

Dagognet, F., 1989, *Eloge de l'objet, Pour une philosophie de la marchandise,* Paris, Vrin.

Damak, L., 1996, "Corps du consommateur et design produit: recherche d'une similarité ou d'une complémentarité," Thèse pour l'obtention du titre de Docteur ès Sciences de Gestion, Paris, Université Paris-Dauphine.

Damish, H., 1980, "L'alphabet des masques," *Nouvelle Revue de Psychanalyse,* no. 21: "La passion," printemps, 213–31.

Danto, A., 1982, *The Transfiguration of the Commonplace: A Philosophy of Art,* Cambridge, MA, Harvard University Press.

Debray, R., 1994, *Manifestes médiologiques,* Paris, Gallimard.

Debray, R., 1996, *Cours de médiologie,* Paris, Gallimard.

Debray, R., 2001, "Truismes," *Les Cahiers de Médiologie*, "Automobile," no. 12, deuxième semestre, 30–31.

de Brentani, U., 1993, "The Effects of Customization and Customer Contact on the Factors Determining Success and Failure of New Industrial Services," in Baker, M.J., *Perspectives on Marketing Management*, vol. 3, Wiley, 275–98.

de Certeau, M., 1985, "Practices of Space," in Marshall Blonsky (ed.), *On signs*, Baltimore, The Johns Hopkins University Press.

de Certeau, M., 1994, L'invention au quotidien, 1. Les arts de faire, Paris, Gallimard, Folio. Trans,: *The Practice of Everyday Life*, Berkeley, University of California Press, 1984.

de Chernatony, L. and McWilliam, M., 1992, *Creating Powerful Brands*, Butterworth-Heinemann.

de Chernatony, L. and McWilliam M.H.B., 1989, "The varying nature of brands as assets: theory and practice compared," *International Journal of Advertising*, 8, (4), 339–49.

DeJean, J., 2006, *The essence of style. How the French invented haute couture, great cuisine, chic cafés, refinement and élégance*, Free Press.

Deleuze, G. and Guattari F., 1972, *L'anti-Oedipe. Capitalisme et schizophrénie*, Paris, Editions de Minuit. Trans.: *Anti-Oedipus: Capitalism and Schizophrenia*, Minneapolis: University of Minnesota Press, 1983.

Deleuze, G. and Guattari F., 1980, *Mille Plateaux. Capitalisme et schizophrénie 2*, Paris, Editions de Minuit. Trans.: *A Thousand Plateaus*, Minneapolis: University of Minnesota Press, 1987.

Deleuze, G., 1983, *Cinéma 1; L'image-mouvement*, Paris, Editions de Minuit. Translation: *The Movemen-Image*, Minneapolis: University of Minnesota Press, 1986.

Deleuze, G. 1983, *Nietzsche and Philosophy*, The Athlone Press. Translated from *Nietzsche et la philosophy*, Paris, PUF (1962).

Deleuze, G. 1988, *Spinoza: Practical Philosophy*, San Francisco, City Lights.

Deleuze, G., 1962, *Proust et les signes*, Paris, PUF. Translation: *Proust and Signs*, University of Minnesota Press, 2004.

Denzin, N., 1992, *Symbolic Interaction and Cultural Studies*, Oxford, Blackwell.

Deroche-Gurcel, L., 1997, *Simmel et la modernité*, Paris, PUF.

Derrida, J., 1991, *Donner le temps 1. La fausse monnaie, Galilée.*

Derrida, J., 1978, *La vérité en peinture*, Paris, Flammarion.

Derrida, J., 1977, *Adieu à Emmanuel Lévinas*, Galilée.

Derrida, J., 1972, *Marges de la philosophie*, Paris, Minuit.

Derrida, J., 1967, *De la grammatologie*, Paris, Minuit.

Derrida, J., 1967, *L'écriture et la différence*, Paris, Seuil.

Didi-Huberman, G., 1992, *Ce que nous voyons, ce qui nous regarde*, Paris, Editions de Minuit.

Dittmar, H., 1992, *The Social Psychology of Material Possessions: To Have Is to Be*, New York, St. Martin's.

Dichter, E., 1964, *Handbook of Consumer Motivations*, New York, McGraw-Hill.

Dodds, W.B. and K.B. Monroe, 1985, "The Effects of Brand and Price Information on Subjective Product Evaluations," *Advances in Consumer Research*, 12, 85–90.

Dolich, I.J., 1969, "Congruence Relationships Between Self-Images and Product Brands," *Journal of Marketing*, 6 (February), 80–4.

Domecq, J.-P., 2004, *Traité de banalistique*. Paris, Mille et une Nuits.

Domecq, J.-P., 2004, *Une nouvelle introduction à l'art du XXe siècle*, Paris, Flammarion.
Dorey, R., 1981, "La relation d'emprise," *Nouvelle Revue de Psychanalyse*, no. 24, 117–40.
Dosse, F., 2007, *Michel de Certeau. Le marcheur blessé*, Paris, La Découverte.
Dostaler, G. and Maris, B., 2009, *Capitalisme et pulsion de mort*, Paris, Albin Michel.
Douglas, M., and Isherwood, B., 1978, *The World of Goods*, New York, Basic Books.
Dru, J.-M., 1997, *Disruption. Briser les conventions et redessiner le marché*, Paris, Village Mondial.
Dufour, D.-R., 2008, *Le divin marché*, Paris, Denoël.
Dumézil, G., 1968, *Mythe et Epopée*, Paris, Gallimard.
Duvignaud J., « L'usage des richesses », in Georges Bataille, L'Arc, n°32 (1967) et 44 (1971), republished by Editions inculte, 2007.
Eco, U., 1962, *Opera Aperta*, Milano, Bompiani; French translation: *L'Oeuvre Ouverte*, 1966, Paris, Seuil.
Eco, U., 1972, *La structure absente*, Paris, Mercure de France.
Eco, U., 1976, *A Theory of Semiotics*, Bloomington, Indiana University Press.
Eco, U., 1979, *A Theory of Semiotics*, Bloomington, Indiana University Press.
Eco, U., 1979, *Lector in fabula*, Milano, Bompiani; French trans.: *Lector in fabula. Le rôle du lecteur ou la Coopération interprétative dans les textes narratifs*, 1985, Paris, Grasset & Fasquelle.
Eco, U., 1985, *Lector in fabula. Le rôle du lecteur ou la coopération interprétative dans les textes narratifs*, Paris, Grasset.
Eco, U., 1985, *La guerre du faux*. Paris, Grasset.
Eco, U., 1962, *Opera Arte*, Milan, Bompiani.
Eco, U., 1968, *La struttura assente*, Milan, Bompiani.
Eco, U., 1990, *I Limiti Dell' Interpretazione*, Milano, Bompiani; French translation : *Les Limites de l'interprétation*, 1992, Paris, Grasset and Fasquelle.
Eco, U., 1992, *Les limites de l'interprétation*, Paris, Grasset.
Edelman, B., 2004, *Le sacre de l'auteur*, Paris, Seuil.
Edgell, S. et al (eds), 1996, *Consumption Matters. The production and experience of consumption*, Oxford, Oxford Blackwell.
Egan, C. et al., 1992, "The Importance of Brand Names in Industrial Markets," in Baker, M. J., *Perspectives on Marketing Management*, vol. 2, Wiley, 307–24.
Ehrenberg, A.S., 1986, *Repeat Buying: Facts, Theory, and Applications*, London, Charles Griffin and Co.
Eldenberg, M., 1997, *Le plaisir de l'objet. Nouveau regard sur les arts décoratifs du XXème siècle*, Paris/Montéal, Flammarion/Musée des Arts décoratifs de Montréal.
Esposito, R., 2000 *Communitas*, Paris, PUF.
Everaert-Desmedt, N., 1988, *Sémiotique du récit*, Editions Universitaires, De Boeck Université.
Falk, P., 1994, "Consuming Desire," in P. Falk, *The Consuming Body*, London, Sage, 93–150.
Featherstone, M., 1991, *Consumer Culture and Postmodernism*, London, Sage.
Featherstone, M. et al. (eds), 1991, *The Body. Social Process and Cultural Theory*, London, Sage.

Featherstone, M., 1995, *Undoing Culture. Globalization, Postmodernism and Identity*, London, Sage.

Feher, M. et al. (eds), 1989, *Fragments for a History of the Human Body*, New York, Zone Books, 3 vols.

Ferry, L., 1990, *Homo Aestheticus. L'invention du gout à l'âge démocratique*, Paris, Grasset.

Flechter, A., 1964, *Allegory. The Theory of a Symbolic Mode*, Ithaca, NY, Cornell University Press.

Floch, J.-M., 1995, *Identités visuelles*, Paris, PUF. Translation; Visual identities, Bloomsbury Academic, 2001.

Floch, J.-M., 1988, "The contribution of structural semiotics to the design of a hypermarket," *International Journal of Research in Marketing*, 4, 233–52.

Floch, J.-M., 1989, "L'apport de la sémiotique structurale au design d'un hypermarché," *Recherche et Applications en Marketing*, 4, 2, 37–59.

Floch, J.-M., 1990, "J'aime, J'aime, J'aime ...," in J.-M. Floch, *Sémiotique, marketing et communication. Sous les signes, les stratégies*, Paris, Presses Universitaires de France, 119–52.

Floch, J.-M., 1990, *Sémiotique, marketing et communication*, Paris, PUF. Trans.: *Semiotics, Marketing and Communications: Beneath the Signs, the Strategies*, London, Palgrave Macmillan, 2001.

Floch, J.-M., 1995, *Identités visuelles*, Paris, PUF. Trans.: as *Visual Identities*, Continuum International Publishing Group, 2000.

Flusser, V., 2002, *Petite philosophie du design*, Belfort, Circé.

Fontanille, J., 1998, "Ce qu'innover veut dire," *Sciences Humaines*, no. 88, novembre, 36–9.

Forty, A., 1986, *Objects of Desire: Design and Society from Wedgwood to IBM*, New York, Pantheon.

Foucault, M., 1970, *The Order of Things*, New York, Random House.

Foucault, M., 1975, *Surveiller et punir*, Paris, Gallimard. Trans.: *Discipline and Punish*, New York, Pantheon, 1977.

Foucault, M., 1994, "Qu'est-ce qu'un auteur?," in *Dits et Ecrits I*, Gallimard, Paris, 819–37. Translation "What Is an Author?" Twentieth-Century Literary Theory. Vassilis Lambropoulos and David Neal Miller (eds). Albany: State University Press of New York, 1987, 124–42.

Fournier, C., 2000, *L'infinitif des pensées*, Paris, Editions de l'Eclat.

Fournier, S., 1994, "A Consumer-Brand Relationship Framework for Strategic Brand Management," unpublished Phd Dissertation, University of Florida, December.

Fournier, S. et al., 1998, "Preventing the Premature Death of Relationship Marketing," *Harvard Business Review*, 42–51, January–February.

Fournier, S., 1998, "Consumers and Their Brands: Developing Relationship Theory in Consumer Research," *Journal of Consumer Research*, vol. 24, 343–73, June.

Fournier, S. and J.L. Yao, 1997, "Reviving Brand Loyalty: A Reconceptualization within the Framework of Consumer Brand Relationships," *International Journal of Research in Marketing*, vol. 14, 451–72.

Fournier, S., 1994, "A Consumer–Brand Relationship Framework for Strategic Brand Management," PhD Dissertation, University of Florida.

Fox, A., 1993, *Utopia. An Elusive Vision*, New York, Twayne Publishers.

Fox, S., 1984, *The Mirror Makers. A History of American Advertising and Its Creators,* New York, Vintage Books.

Fraenkel, B., 1992, *La signature. Genèse d'un signe,* Paris, Gallimard.

Francastel, P., 1956, *Art et technique aux XIXème et XXème siècles,* Paris,, Editions de Minuit.

Frondizi, R., 1971, *What is Value? An introduction to axiology,* 2nd edn., La Salle, IL, Open Court Publishing Company,.

Furby, L. 1978 "Possession in Humans: An Exploratory Study of Its Meaning and Motivation," *Social Behavior and Personality,* 6: 49–65.

Gabriel, Y. & Lang T., 1995, *The Unmanageable Consumer: Contemporary Consumption and its Fragmentations,* London, Sage.

Gauchet, M., 1985, *Le désenchantement du monde. Une histoire politique de la religion,* Paris, Gallimard. Trans.: *The Disenchantement of the World. A political History of Religion,* Princeton, Princeton University Press, 1997.

Genette, G., 1987, *Paratextes,* Paris Seuil, Translated as *Paratexts, Threshoslds of interpretation,* Cambridge University Press, 1997.

Girard, R. 1977, *Des choses cachées depuis la fondation du monde,* Paris, Grasset. Trans.: *Things Hidden Since the Foundation of the World,* (1987), London, Athlone.

Giard, L., 1994, Introduction to Michel de Certeau, *L'invention du quotidien,* t.1 Folio, Paris, Gallimard.

Giard, L., 1994, "Des moments et des lieux," preface à M. de Certeau et al., *Les arts de faire, L'invention du quotidien III, habiter, cuisiner,* Gallimard, Folio, 1994.

Gilmore, G.W., 1919, *Animism,* Boston, Marshall Jones Company.

Gilson, E., 1964, *Matières et formes. Poétique des arts majeurs,* Paris, Vrin.

Girard, R., 1965, *Deceit, Desire, and the Novel,* Baltimore, Johns Hopkins University Press.

Girard, R. 1972, *La violence et le sacré,* Paris, Grasset; English translation: *Violence and the Sacred,* 1977, Baltimore, The Johns Hopkins University Press.

Godin, C., 1997, *La Totalité 4. La pensée réalisée,* Seyssel, Champ Vallon.

Godin, C., 1998, *La Totalité 2. Les pensées totalisantes,* Seyssel, Champ Vallon.

Godin, C., 2000, *Faut-il réhabiliter l'utopie?,* Nantes, Pleins Feux.

Goldman, L., 1964, *The Hidden God: A Study of Tragic Vision in the Pensées of Pascal and the Tragedies of Racine,* London, Routledge and Keegan Paul.

Gordon, C., 1991, "Governmental rationality: an introduction," in Graham Burchell et al. (eds*), The Foucault Effect. Studies in Governmentality,* Chicago, The University of Chicago Press.

Gottdiener, M, 1995, *Postmodern Semiotics. Material Culture and the Forms of Postmodern Life,* Oxford, Blackwell.

Goux, J.-J., 2000, *Frivolité de la valeur. Essai sur l'imaginaire du capitalisme,* Paris, Blusson.

de Grazia, V. and Furlough, E. (eds), 1996, *The Sex of Things: Gender and Consumption in Historical Perspective,* Berkeley, University of California Press.

Greimas, A.J., 1983, *Du sens II,* Paris, Seuil.

Greimas, A.J., 1983, *Structural Semantics: An Attempt at a Method,* Lincoln, University of Nebraska Press. Trans. of: *Sémantique structurale,* 1966, Paris, Larousse.

Greimas, A.J. and Courtès, J., 1979, *Semiotics and Language. An Analytical Dictionary,* Bloomington: Indiana University Press.

Greimas, A.J., 1966, "Eléments pour une théorie de l'interprétation du récit mythique," *Communications,* 8, Paris, Seuil, 28–59.

Grimaldi, N., 1991, *Ontologie du temps. L'attente et la rupture*, Paris, PUF.

Grimaldi, N., 1983, *L'art ou la feinte passion. Essai sur l'expérience esthétique*, Paris, PUF.

Gršning, K., 1997, *Decorated Skin. A world survey of body art*, Trans. from the German by Dale, L., London, Thames and Hudson.

Guichard, C., 2009, *Les amateurs d'art à Paris au XVIIème siècle*, Seyssel, Champ-Vallon.

Gummesson, E., 1987, "The new marketing – developing long-term interactive relationship," *Long Range Planning*, 20, 4, 10–20.

Gutman, J., 1982, "A Means–Ends Chain Model Based on Consumer Categorization Processes," *Journal of Marketing*, 46 (Summer), 60–72.

Gutting, G., 1989, *Michel Foucault's Archeology of Scientific Reason*, Cambridge, Cambridge University Press.

Guyer, P., 1979, *Kant and the Claims of Taste*, Cambridge, MA: Harvard University Press.

Hartman, R., 1967, *The Structures of Values: Foundations of Scientific Axiology*, Carbondale: Southern Illinois Press.

Haskell, F., 1993, La Norme et le caprice; Redécouverte en arts. Aspects du goût, de la mode et des collections en France et en Angleterre, 1789–1814, Paris, Flammarion.

Haus, H.R., *Pour une esthétique de la réception*, Paris, Gallimard.

Hausse, T., 1998, *Design. A Concise History*, London, Laurence King.

Hazan, C. and Shaver, P., 1987, "Romantic love conceptualised as an attachment process," *Journal of Personality and Social Psychology*, 52, 511–24.

Heelas, P., 1997, *The New Age Movement. The Celebration of the Self and the Sacralization of Modernity*, Oxford, Blackwell.

Hennig, J.-L., 1994, *Dictionnaire littéraire et érotique des fruits et légumes*, Paris, Albin Michel.

Hirschman, E.C. and Holbrook, M., 1992, *Postmodern Consumer Research. The Study of Consumption as a Text*, Newbury Park, CA: Sage.

Hirschman, E.C. and Holbrook, M.B., 1982, "Hedonic Consumption: Emerging Concepts, Methods and Propositions," *Journal of Marketing*, 46 (Summer), 92–101.

Holbrook, M.B. and Hirschman, E.C., 1982, "The experiential aspects of consumption: consumer fantasies, feeling and fun," *Journal of Consumer Research*, 9 (September), 132–40.

Holbrook, M., 1987, "What is Consumer Research?," *Journal of Consumer Research*, 14 (June), 128–31.

Holt, D., 1995, "How Consumers Consume: A Typology of Consumption Practices," *Journal of Consumer Research*, 22 (June), 1–16.

Hottois, G., 1997, *De la Renaissance à la Postmodernité. Une histoire de la philosophie moderne et contemporaine*, Brussels, De Boeck Université.

Illouz, E., 1997, *Consuming the Romantic Utopia*, Berkeley, University of California Press.

Jauss, H.R., 1978, *Pour une esthétique de la réception*, Paris, Gallimard.

Jhaly, S., 1990, *The Codes of Advertising. Fetishism and the Political Economy of Meaning in the Consumer Society*, London, Routledge.

Jimenez, M., 1997, *Qu'est-ce que l'esthétique?* Paris, Gallimard.

Johannesson, K., 2011, "Le portrait du prince comme genre rhétorique," in Ellenius, A., (sous la direction de) *Iconographie, propagande et légitimation*, Paris, PUF.

Jullien, F., 1991, *Eloge de la fadeur*, A partir de la pensée et de l'esthétique chinoises, Paris, Philippe Picquier. Translation: *In Praise of Blandness. Proceeding From Chinese Thought and Aesthetic*, MIT Press, 2007.

Jullien, F., 1992, *La propension des choses. Pour une histoire de l'efficacité en Chine*, Paris, Seuil.

Jullien, F., 1995, *Le détour et l'Accès, stratégies du sens en Chine, en Grèce*, Paris, Seuil.

Jullien, F., 1996, *Traité de l'efficacité*, Paris, Grasset. Trans: *A Treatise on Efficacy: Between Western and Chinese Thinking*, University of Hawai'i Press, 2004.

Jullien, F., 1998, *Un sage est sans idée ou l'autre de la philosophie*, Paris, Seuil.

Jullien, F., 2003, *La grande image n'a pas de forme*, Paris, Le Seuil. Trans.: *The Great Image Has No Form or On the Nonobject Through Painting*, Chicago, The University of Chicago Press, 2009.

Kantorowicz, E., 1957, *The King's Two Bodies*, Princeton University Press.

Kearney, R., 1994, *Modern Movements in European Philosophy*, second edition, Manchester, Manchester University Press.

Kehret-Ward, T., 1987, "Combining products in use: How the syntax of products use affects product design and promotion," in Jean Umiker-Sebeok (ed.), *Marketing and Semiotics. New directions in the study of signs for sale*, Berlin, Mouton de Gruyter, 219–38.

Kehret-Ward, T., 1988, "Using a semiotic approach to study the consumption of functionally related products," *International Journal of Research in Marketing*, 4, 187–200.

Kirkham, P. (ed.), 1996, *The Gendered Object*, Manchester, Manchester University Press.

Kleiber, M., 1980, "Eschatologie," in *Encyclopedia Universalis*, vol. 6, Paris.

Klein, N., 2001, *No logo*, Arles, Actes Sud.

Kleine, S. et al., 1995, "How Is a Possession 'Me' or 'Not Me?' Characterizing Types and an Antecedent of Material Possession Attachment," *Journal of Consumer Research*, 327–43, 22 (December).

Kounikef, J.-L., 2001, "Le double," in Mohamed Seffahi (sous la direction de), *Autour de Jacques Derrida. De l'hospitalité*, Genouilleux, La Passe du vent, 55–9.

Krief, Y., 1986, "L'entreprise, l'institution, la marque – Niveaux de langage dans la communication," *Revue Française du Marketing*, no. 109, 77–96.

Kripendorf, K., 1980, *Content Analysis: An Introduction to its Methodology*, Newbury Park, Sage Publications.

Lakoff, G. and Johnson, M., 1980, *Metaphors We Live By*, Chicago, The University of Chicago Press.

Lamb, D. 1979, "The ethos of the brand," *ADMAP*, 15, January, 19–24.

Lannon, J. and Cooper, P., 1983, "Humanistic Advertising. A Holistic Cultural Perspective," *International Journal of Advertising*, 2, 195–213.

Lash, S. and Urry, J., 1994, *Economies of Signs and Space*, London, Sage.

Latouche, S., 1992, *L'occidentalisation du monde. Essai sur la signification, la portée et les limites de l'uniformisation planétaire*, Paris, La Découverte.

Latour, B., 1996, *Petite réflexion sur le culte moderne des dieux faitiches*, Le Plessis-Robinson, Synthélabo.

Laufer, R. and Paradeise, C., 1982, *Le prince bureaucrate. Machiavel au pays du marketing*, Paris, Flammarion. Trans.: *Marketing Democracy. Public Opinion and Media Formation in Democratic Societies*, Transaction Publishers, 1989.

Laufer, R., 1986, "Système de légitimité, marketing et sophistique," in B. Cassin (sous la dir. de), *Le plaisir de parler. Etudes de sophistique comparée*, Paris, Editions de Minuit, 209–35.

Laufer, R., 1989, "Marque, marketing et légitimité," in Kapferer, J.-N., and Thoenig, J.-C. (eds), *La Marque*, Paris, McGraw-Hill, 355–73.

Le Breton, D., 2006, *La saveur du monde. Une anthropologie des sens*, Paris, Métailié

Lefebvre, H., 1966, *Le langage et la société*, Paris, Gallimard.

Leigh, J.A., 1994, "The Use of Figures of Speech in Print Ad Headlines," *Journal of Advertising*, 23, 2, June, 17–33.

Lembeye, P., 2001, Nous sommes tous dépendants, Paris, Odile Jacob.

Leroi-Gourhan, A., 1945, *Milieu et technique*, Paris, Albin Michel.

Lévi-Strauss, C., (séminaire dirigé par), 1977, *L'identité*, Paris, PUF.

Lévi-Strauss, C., 1975, *La voie des masques*, Genève, Skira. Translated as *The Way of the Masks*, Seattle: University of Washington Press, 1982.

Lévi-Strauss, C., 1962, *La pensée sauvage*, Paris, Plon. Translated as *The Savage Mind*, Chicago, The University of Chicago Press, 1966

Lévi-Strauss, C., 1958, *Anthropologie Structurale*, Paris, Plon. Translated as *Structural Anthropology*, New York, Basic Books, 1963.

Levy, S., 1959, "Symbols for Sale," *Harvard Business Review*, 37 (July–August), 117–24.

Lhote, A., 1967, *Les invariants plastiques*, Paris, Hermann.

Lilti, A., 2005, *Le Monde des salons. Sociabilité et mondanité à Paris au XVIIIème siècle*, Paris, Fayard.

Liu, J., 1975, *Chinese Theories of Literature*. Chicago, The University of Chicago Press.

Lloyd Morgan, C., 1999, *Starck*, Paris, Adam Biro.

Löfgren, O., 1996, "Le retour des objets? L'étude de la culture matérielle dans la culture suédoise," *Ethnologie française*, *"Culture matérielle et modernité,"* 1 (March), 38–49.

Lovejoy, A., 1907, "The Desire of the Self-Conscious," *The Journal of Philosophy*, 4, 29–39.

Lovejoy, A., 1950, "Terminal and Adjectival Values," *The Journal of Philosophy*, 47 (21), October 12, 593–608.

Lyotard, J-F., 1973, *Des dispositifs pulsionnels*, Paris, Union Générale d'Editions.

MacInnis, D.H. and Price L.L., 1987, "The Role of Imagery in Information Processing: Review and Extensions," *Journal of Consumer Research*, 13, 473–91.

Mackay, H. (ed.), 1997, *Consumption and Everyday Life*, London, Sage.

MacIntyre, A., 1966, *A Short History of Ethics*, New York, Macmillan.

MacLaran, P. and Stevens, L., 1998, "Romancing the Utopian Marketplace. Dallying with Bakhtin in the Powerscourt Townhouse Centre," in Stephen Brown et al. (eds), *Romancing the Market*, London, Routledge, 172–86.

Manguel, A. and Guadalupi, G., 1980, *The Dictionary of Imaginary Places*, New York, Macmillan.

Manzini, E., 1995, "Prometheus of the every day life. The ecology of the artificial and the designer's responsibility," *Design Issues* 9(1), Fall, 5–20.

Marcelli, D., 2000, *La surprise. Chatouille de l'âme*, Paris, Albin Michel.

Marcuse, H., 1955, *Eros and Civilization. A Philosophical Inquiry into Freud*, Boston, Beacon Press.

Margolin, V. (ed.), 1989, *Design Discourse. History, theory, criticism*, Chicago, The University of Chicago Press.

Margolin, V. and Buchanan, R. (eds), 1995, *The Idea of Design. A design issues reader*, The MIT Press.

Marin, L., 1973, *Utopiques: jeux d'espaces*, Paris, Editions de Minuit; English trans.: *Utopics: The Semiological Play of Textual Spaces*, Atlantic Highlands, NJ, Humanities Press, 1984.

Marin, L., 1977, "Disneyland: a degenerate utopia," *Glyph*, 1, 1, 50–66.

Marin, L., 1981, *Le Portrait du roi*, Paris, Éditions de Minuit.

Marin, L., 1992, "Grammaire royale du visage," in Georges Didi-Huberman (sous la direction de), *A Visage découvert*, Fondation Cartier-Flammarion.

Maslow, A., 1943, "A Theory of Human Motivation," *Psychological Review*, 50, 370–96.

Maslow, A., 1954, *Motivation and Personality*, New York, Harper.

Mauss, M., 1923–4, "Essai sur le don: Forme et raison de l'échange dans les sociétés archaïques," *L'Année Sociologique*, I (1923–24), 30–186.

Mauss, M., 1967, *The Gift: Forms and Functions of Exchange in Archaic Societies*, New York, Norton. Translated from: "Essai sur le don: Forme et raison de l'échange dans les sociétés archaïques," *L'Année Sociologique*, I (1923–24), 30–186.

McCracken, G., 1993, "The Value of the Brand: An Anthropological Perspective," in Aaker, D. and Biel, A. (eds), *Brand Equity and Advertising*, Lawrence Erlbaum Associates Publishers, 125–39.

McCracken, G., 1988, *Culture and Consumption*, Bloomington, Indiana University Press.

McCracken, G., 1981, "Culture and Consumption," *Journal of Consumer Research*, 13, June, 71–84.

McQueen, J., Foley, C. and Deighton, J., 1993, "Decomposing a Brand's Franchise into Buyer Types," in Aaker, D. and Biel, A. (eds), *Brand Equity and Advertising. Advertising's Role in Building Strong Brands*, Lawrence Erlbaum Associates Publishers,235–45.

Mélétinski, E., 1970, "L'étude structurale et typologique du conte," in Propp, V., *Morphologie du conte*, 1973, Paris, Seuil, 202–54.

Michéa, J.-C, *L'empire du moindre mal. Essai sur la civilisation libérale*, Climats, 2008.

Miller, D., 1998, *A Theory of Shopping*, Ithaca, NY, Cornell University Press.

Miller, D., 1995, "Consumption as the Vanguard of History," in D. Miller (ed.), *Acknowledging Consumption. A Review of New Studies*, London, Routledge, 1–57.

Moles, A., 1972, *Théorie des objets*, Paris, Editions universitaires.

Moles, A., 1987, "Vivre avec les choses: contre une culture immatérielle," *Art Press*, Hors Série no. 7: "A l'heure du design," 16.

Morace, F., 1990, *Controtendenze: una nuova cultura del consumo*, Milan, Domus Academy.

Morris, C., 1946, *Signs, Language and Behavior*, New York, Prentice-Hall.

Morris, W., 2011, *L'art et l'artisanat*, Rivages.

Muniz, A. and O'Guinn, T.H., 2001, "Brand community," *Journal of Consumer Research*, vol. 27, 412–32, March.

Nietzsche, F., 1968, *The Will to Power*, trans. Kaufmann, W. and Hollingdale, R. J., New York, Vintage (originally published in 1883–8).

Nietzsche, F., 1974, *The Gay Science*, trans. Kaufmann, W., New York, Vintage (originally published in 1882).

de Noblet, J., 1988, *Design. Le geste et le compas*, Paris, Somogy.

de Noblet, J., 1993, *Design, miroir du siècle*, Paris, Flammarion.

Normand, J.-M., 1999–2004, *Les nouveaux imaginaires de la consommation. Chroniques du Monde*, Paris, PUF.

Nöth, W., 1988, "The language of commodities: ground work for a semiotics of consumer goods," *International Journal of Research in Marketing*, 4, 173–186.

Nöth, W., 1990, *Handbook of semiotics*, Bloomington, Indiana University Press.

Nöth, W., 1994, "The Sign Nature of Commodities," document non publié, Universität Kassel.

Olson, J.C. and Reynolds, T.J., 1983, "Understanding Consumers' Cognitive Structures: Implications for Advertising Strategy," in Percy, L. and Woodside, A. (eds), *Advertising and Consumer Psychology*, vol. 1, Lexington, MA, Lexington Books, 77–90.

Paquot, T., 1994, *L'utopie ou l'idéal piégé*, Paris, Hatier.

Paquot, T., 2000, "De l'accueillance. Essai pour une architecture et un urbanisme de l'hospitalité," in Chris Younès et Thierry Paquot (sous la direction de), *Ethique, architecture, urbain*, Paris, La Découverte, 68–83.

Parizeau, M.-H., 1996, "Ethique appliquée," in Canto-Sperber, 534–40.

Pascal Quignard le solitaire, Rencontre avec Chantal Lapeyre-Desmaison, Paris, Le Flohic éditeurs, 2001.

Pasquer, M., 1999, *Marketing et sémiotique. Une approche interdisciplinaire*, Fribourg, Editions Universitaires de Fribourg.

Passeron, J-C., 1979 "La femme-objet," in "Pour l'objet," *Revue d'Esthétique*, 3/4, 267–94.

Péninou, G., 1972, *Intelligence de la publicité*, Paris, Robert Laffont.

Pieter, R., Baumgartner, H. and Allen, D., 1995, "A Means–End Chain Approach to Consumer Goal Structures," *International Journal of Research in Marketing*, 12(3), 227–44.

Pinson, C., 1986, "An implicit product theory approach to consumer's inferential judgements about products," *International Journal of Research in Marketing*, vol. 3, no. 1, 19–38.

Pinson, C., 1988, "Editorial: Introduction to the double Special Issue on Semiotics and Marketing Communications Research," *International Journal of Research in Marketing*, 4, 167–72.

Poirier, J., 1990, "L'homme, l'objet et la chose," in J. Poirier (ed .), *Histoire des Mœurs*, I, Bibliothèque de la Pléïade, Paris, Gallimard, 901–60.

Pouilloux, J.-Y., 1990, article "Métaphore," *Encyclopédie Universalis*, Paris.

Poulet, G., 1952, *Etudes sur le temps humain*, Paris, Plon, . Translated as *Studies in Human Time*, Johns Hopkins University Press, 1959

Poulot, D., 1997, Musée, nation, patrimoine 1789–1815, Paris, Gallimard.

The Project on Disney, 1995, *Inside the Mouse: Work and Play at Disneyworld*, Duke University Press.

Propp, V., 1928, *Morfologija skazkii*, coll. Voprosy poetiki, no. 12, Gosudarstvennyj institut istorii iskusstava, Leningrad; English trans.: *Morphology of the Folktale*, 1973, University Of Texas Press; French trans.: *Morphologie du conte*, 1973, Paris, Seuil.

Proust, F., 1994, *L'histoire à contretemps. Le temps historique chez Walter Benjamin*, Paris, Le Cerf.

Quessada, D., 2000, *La société de consommation de soi*, Paris, éditions Verticales.

Quessada, D., 2002, *L'esclavemaître*, Paris, éditions Verticales.

Remaury, B., 2003, "Filiation vs rupture: stratégie de marque et changements de direction artistique," in *Repères Mode 2003. Visages d'un secteur,* Paris, Institut Français de la Mode Editions du Regard, 283–97.

Rethans, A.J. and Taylor J.L., 1982, "A Script Theoretic Analysis of Consumer Decision Making," in Walker B.J. (ed.), *Proceedings of the AMA Educator's Conference,* Series No. 48, 71–4.

Reynolds, T., and Gutman, J., 1988, "Laddering Theory, Method, Analysis, and Interpretation," *Journal of Advertising Research*, 28, February/March, 11–34.

Ricardou, J., 1967 *Problèmes du nouveau roman*, Paris, Seuil.

Richins, M.L., 1994, "Valuing Things: The Public and Private Meanings of Possessions," *Journal of Consumer Research*, 504–21, December 21.

Richins, M.L., 1994, "Special Possessions and the Expression of Material Values," *Journal of Consumer Research*, 522–33, December 21.

Ricoeur, P., 1990, *Soi-même comme un autre*, Paris, Seuil. Trans.: *Oneself as Another*, Chicago, University of Chicago Press, 1995.

Ricoeur, P., 1988, "L'identité narrative," *Esprit*, no. 140–41, juillet–août, 295–304.

Ricoeur, P., 1986, *Lectures on Ideology and Utopia*, New York, Columbia University Press.

Ricoeur, P., 1983–1984, *Time and Narrative,* Chicago, University of Chicago Press, 2 vols.

Ries, A. and Trout, J., 1980, *Positioning. The Battle for Your Mind.* NewYork: McGraw-Hill.

Riggins, S., 1985, "The semiotics of things: toward a sociology of human–object interaction," *Semiotica*, 5, 1, 69–77.

Riggins, S., 1990, "The power of things: the role of domestic objects in the presentation of self," in Riggins, S. (ed.), *Beyond Goffman. Studies on Communication, Institution, and Social Interaction,* Berlin, Mouton de Gruyter, 341–67.

Riggins, S.H. (ed.), 1994, *The Socialness of Things. Essays on Socio-Semiotics of Objects*, Berlin: Mouton de Gruyter.

Rijkens, R., 1992, *European Advertising Strategies,* London, Cassel.

Ritzer, G., 1996, *The McDonaldization of Society. An investigation into the changing character of contemporary social life*, revised edition, Thousand Oaks, Pine Forge Press.

Ritzer, G., 1998, *The McDonaldization Thesis*, London, Sage.

Ritzer, G., 1999, *Enchanting a disenchanted world. Revolutionizing the means of consumption*, Pine Forge Press.

Rook, D.W., 1985, "The Ritual Dimension of Consumer Behavior," *Journal of Consumer Research,* 12, December, 251–64.

Rokeach, M., 1960, *The Open and Closed Mind: Investigations into the Nature of Beliefs Systems and Personality Systems*, New York, Basic Books.

Rokeach, M., 1969, *Beliefs, Attitudes and Values; a Theory of Organization and Change*, San Francisco, Jossey Bass.

Rokeach, M., 1973, *The Nature of Human Values and Value Systems*, New York, Free Press.

Rosset, C., 1979, *L'objet singulier*, Paris, Editions de Minuit.

Rotchlitz, R., 1992, *Le désenchantement de l'art. La philosophie de Walter Benjamin*, Paris, Gallimard.

Russel, B., 1994, *History of Western Philosophy*, London, Routledge (first published in 1946).

Saillard, O., 2012, *Petit Lexique des gestes d'Hermès*, Arles, Actes-Sud.

Sanchez, S., 2005, « Pizzas, crêpes et autres galettes », in Communications n°77, « Faire sien », 2005, Paris, Seuil.

Sartre, J.-P., 1943, *Being and Nothingness: A Phenomenological Essay on Ontology*, New York, Philosophical Library.

Sartre, J.-P. 1965, *Esquisse d'une théorie des émotions*. Paris, Hermann.

Saussure, F. De, 1969, *Courses in General Linguistics*, New York, McGraw-Hill; originally published in French in 1915.

Schefer, J.-L., 1995, *La lumière et la table. Dispositifs de la peinture hollandaise*, Maeght éditeur.

Schleifer, R., 1987, *A.J. Greimas and the Nature of Meaning: Linguistics, Semiotics and Discourse Theory*, Lincoln, University of Nebraska Press.

Schmitt, J.-C., 1994, *Les revenants. Les vivants et les morts dans la société médiévale*, Paris, Gallimard.

Schmitt, J.-C., 1992, *La raison des gestes dans l'occident médiéval*, Paris, Gallimard.

Schmitt, J.-C., 1982, "Les revenants dans la société féodale," in *Le temps de la réflexion*, no. III, Paris, Gallimard, 285–306

Schultz, S. et al., 1989, "'These Are a Few of My Favorite Things': Towards an Explication of Attachment as a Consumer Behavior Construct," in *Advances in Consumer Research*, vol. 16, Srull, T. (ed.), Provo, UT, ACR, 359–66.

Sebeok, T.A. (ed.), 1986, *Encyclopedic Dictionary of Semiotics*, Berlin, Mouton de Gruyter, 3 vols.

Semprini, A., 1992a, "The Brand Audit," in *The Challenge of Branding Today and in the Future*, ESOMAR, Brussels, 28th–30th October, 163–74.

Semprini, A., 1992b, *Le Marketing de la marque. Approche sémiotique*, Paris, Editions Liaisons.

Senghor, L. 1977 *Liberté 3: Négritude et civilisation de l'universel*. Paris, Seuil.

Serres, M., 1993, *Le contrat naturel*, Paris, Flammarion.

Servier, J., 1967, *Histoire de l'utopie*, Paris, Gallimard.

Sherry, J., 1986, "Cereal Monogamy: Brand Loyalty as a Secular Ritual in Consumer Culture," paper presented at the Association for Consumer Research Annual Conference, Toronto, October.

Sheth, J.N. et al., 1991a, *Consumption Values and Market Choices. Theory and applications*, Cincinnati, South-Western Publishing Co.

Sheth, J.N., 1991b, "Why We Buy What We Buy: A Theory of Consumption Values," *Journal of Business Research*, 22, 159–70.

Shields, R. (ed.), 1992, *Lifestyle Shopping. The Subject of Consumption*, London, Routledge.

Shouten, J. and McAlexander, J., 1995, "Subcultures of Consumption: An Ethnography of the New Bikers," *Journal of Consumer Research*, vol. 22, 43–61, March.

Simon, H., 1969, *The Sciences of the Artificial*. Cambridge, Massachussets, MIT Press.

Smothers, N., 1993, "Can Products and Brands Have Charisma?," in Aaker, D. and Biel, A. (eds), *Brand Equity and Advertising*, Hillsdale: Lawrence Erlbaum Associates Publishers, 97–112.

Solomon, M. and Assael, H., 1987, "The Forest or the Trees: A Gestalt Approach to Symbolic Consumption," in Jean Umiker-Sebeok (ed.), *Marketing and Semiotics. New directions in the study of signs for sale,* Berlin, Mouton de Gruyter, 189–217.

Stiegler, B., 2008, *Prendre soin de la jeunesse et des générations,* Paris, Flammarion.

Stiegler, B., 2005, *De la misère symbolique,* 2, Paris, Galilée.

Stiegler, B., 2004, *De la misère symbolique,* 1, Paris, Galilée.

Tafuri, M., 1976, *Architecture and Utopia. Design and Capitalist Development,* Cambridge, MA, MIT Press.

Tazi, N. (sous la direction de), 2004, *Les mots du monde/L'expérience,* Paris, La Découverte.

Thompson, J.B, 1990, *Ideology and Modern Culture,* Stanford, Stanford University Press.

Tisseron, S., 1999, *Comment l'esprit vient aux objets,* Paris, Aubier.

Tisseron, S., 2000, *Petites mythologies d'aujourd'hui,* Paris, Aubier.

Umiker-Sebeok, J. (ed.), *Marketing and Semiotics. New directions in the study of signs for sale,* Berlin, Mouton de Gruyter.

Valette-Florence, P., 1986, "Introduction à l'analyse des chaînage cognitifs," *Recherche et Applications en Marketing,* 9, 1, 93–117.

Van Parijs, P., 1996, "Economie," in M.Canto-Sperber ed.), *Dictionnaire d'éthique et de philosophie morale,* Paris, PUF, 1996, 459–65.

Veblen, T., 1899, *The Theory of the Leisure Class,* New York, McGraw-Hill.

Velescu, C.R., 2002, "Le portrait ou l'anti-mimétisme chez Brancusi" in Les carnets de l'Atelier Brancusi, *Le portrait?,* éditions du Centre Pompidou, 55–64.

Verdier, Y., 1979, *Façons de dire, façons de faire,* Paris, Gallimard.

Vernant, J-P., 1990, *Figures, idoles et masques,* Paris, Julliard.

Vigarello, G., 1992, "Mécanique, corps, incorporel," in Luce Giard (ed.), *Michel Foucault. Lire l'œuvre,* Grenoble, Jérôme Millon, 195–200.

Vinson, D., Scott, J. and Lamont, L., 1977, "The Role of Personal Values in Marketing and Consumer Behavior," *Journal of Marketing,* April, 44–50.

Virilio, P., 1975, *Bunker Archéologie,* Paris, Centre Georges Pompidou.

Wallendorf, M. and Arnould E.J., 1988, "'My Favorite Things': A Cross-Cultural Inquiry into Object Attachment, Possessiveness, and Social Linkage," *Journal of Consumer Research,* 531–47, 14 (March).

Warnier, J.-P., 1999, *Construire la culture matérielle. L'homme qui pensait avec ses doigts,* Paris, PUF.

Weber, M., 1971, *Economie et société,* Paris, Plon.

Weblowsky, R., 1987, "Eschatology: An Overview," in Eliade, M. (ed.), *The Encyclopedia of Religion,* New York, Macmillan and Free Press, vol. 5, 148–51.

White, I.S., 1966, "The Perception of Value in Products," in Newman, J.W., *On Knowing the Consumer,* New York: Wiley, 90–106.

Younès, C. and Paquot, T. (sous la direction de), 2000, *Ethique, architecture, urbain,* Paris, La Découverte.

Young, S. and Feigin, B., 1975, "Using the Benefit Chain for Improved Strategy Formulation," *Journal of Marketing,* July, 72–4.

Zeithaml, V., 1988, "Consumer Perceptions of Price, Quality and Value: A Means-End Model and Synthesis of Evidence," *Journal of Marketing,* 52 (July), 2–22.

Name Index

Subject Index

CPSIA information can be obtained at www.ICGtesting.com
Printed in the USA
LVOW03*1129030615

440990LV00002B/3/P